Ride the Serpent

by

Jerry De Pinto

Chapter 1
The Fall of the Summer of Love

The warm, humid Midwest sky was being sucked into the Cowl Ram air induction unit to make the magical explosions between gas and oxygen. The 1968 Pontiac GTO needed a lot of explosions and chemical magic to fuel its V-8 Ram Air 360 horsepower engine. The Old Kid and Punkwillie were driving fast and hard down a wet street in the Chicago suburban town of Broadview. This was the first day of school of September 1967 and the boys were running late, as usual. The standard drill of flying down a side road was now being employed. The Old Kid loved his gleaming orange "Goat" with its rubber bumper and big block engine. This car could reach the subsonic street speed of 120 mph with little effort.

Punkwillie was the brat of the lot called "The Brothers." He always had an eye out for a prank or a good crack wise. The Punk liked to make dull day happenings into an event. "Makes life livable," he claimed. Punkwillie spotted such an event and pointed at two girls standing close to a puddle... a Cheshire smile ran across the Old Kid's face. Slaaam! The tires hit the puddle with such force that all the contents of the small pond went airborne. The two girls let out a synchronized scream as they suddenly found their new school clothes covered with mud, leaves and greasy street water.

"15 points... easy," yelled The Old Kid.

"Christ," chimed Punk. "Possibly 20."

"Really," shouted The Old Kid.

"It's posssseeble!" answered Punk.

This elevated The Old Kid into a hormonal high that made him turn up the 8 track tape player so that Canned Heat was bouncing off the car top and adding to the euphoric excitement. Suddenly, The Old Kid slammed the clutch and dropped the Goat into 4th gear, not a speed for side streets, but when late for school and a possible 20-point mud caking of two prom queens, 4th gear was a natural selection. The car's jolt sent Punkwillie back deeply into his seat and he glanced at the tachometer head'n red!

"We're off and running now, baby!" yiped Punk.

"Dis kid is fly'n," exclaimed The Old Kid.

Broadview, a town that has a race ratio of 70% white/30% black, has a police ratio that borders Orwell's 1984! The GTO rocketed passed Officer Moody's white '68 Chevy Biscayne with its police suspension and gas-whoring 454 cubic block. Moody sat up and quickly shot out into the street for a hot pursuit.

The Old Kid did not notice the white roller because his rear view mirror was permanently facing down. He liked to watch a girl give him head, he said, and if you adjust the mirror while she's doing it... well, a mood killer for sure.

When the Biscayne's siren filled the air, Punkwillie turned around and murmured, "A bogie at 6 o'clock."

The Old Kid glanced at his side mirror and said, "Looks like Moody... the bastard." The Kid then declared, "He has to catch us, 'cause I ain't stop'n."

Roosevelt Road lay perpendicular-- a major busy street. Cars, trucks, buses, and motorcycles all ran rhythmically passed the boys' distance view. Moody wasn't gaining ground because of the cruiser's weight, but he knew the GTO would have to slow down at Roosevelt. The once narrow view of passing traffic was rapidly becoming wider.

"Well Punk, what say yee?" asked The Kid. "Do we fly across or get busted?"

Punkwillie just looked straight ahead and grabbed the dash for a brace. The Old Kid stiffened his back as Roosevelt Road and all its cargo came rushing up! This gamble was about to be realized! Down to the floor went the gas pedal, up went the speedometer, and all the air that could be rammed was going down the Goat's throat. The GTO heaved passed the stop sign and, as if in slow motion, the accelerated Pontiac lifted through a God giving break in the traffic and in less than a second the boys were bounding on the other side. The loud cheer inside The Old Kid's sleigh was matched by the scream of Moody's Biscayne Michelins, burning a rubber tattoo into the wayward side of Roosevelt. Officer Moody infuriatingly crushed his half lit cigarette into a butt-filled ashtray and glared at an orange figure of a car diminishing into the warm, humid Midwest sky.

Proviso East is a high school located in the tough, middle class town of Maywood, Illinois. The demographics mainly comprise blue collar, hard working people, deeply patriotic and family oriented. Proviso was an old school built in the 1920's with its elegant clock tower sitting above the two-story structure dominating the campus. Some of its graduates included NFL linebackers Ed O'Bradovich and Ray Nitschke, Eugene Cernan, an astronaut who walked on the moon, actor

Dennis Franz, singers John Prine and Carol Lawrence. Proviso is a big school with a student body average of 5,000 students. The school has a race mix of primarily 50/50 white and black. Proviso's rich history of academics and sports produced NBA stars Jim Brewer, Doc Rivers and Michael Finley. The school was also known by historians for the number of graduates involved in the torturous Battaan Death March during World War II. Deep in tradition and a dignified past, the school had a special pride all its own, but Proviso's biggest challenge was about to take place.

The fall of '67 came fast off the summer of love's brief glint of happiness and hope. There was an air of transformation settling in like a morning fog... obscured and muddled. The politics of the hippies was starting to plant seeds of doubt into America's youth. No U.S. generation really ever questioned its leaders or government. We even thanked them in every film we could. How gracious of the Department of the Navy to let us film the sea and the Air Force for use of the sky. America was always red, white and blue... no questions asked. The mood was shifting as the civil rights movement was beginning to move. The students at universities were beginning to examine the real motives of world leaders. The Viet Nam War was beginning to separate Americans with questions about the draft and whether there was a battle plan at all. Drugs were appearing at social and unsocial events. Even sexual roles were beginning to be redefined with the women libbers and free love lovers.

All this mattered little to The Old Kid and Punkwillie who were now squealing their way into the school's weather-aged asphalt parking lot. Like the "Knights of the Round Table," the band of boys known as

"The Brothers" had their muscle cars in line on the row and shining-wax bright. Sweet Daddy's 427 Chevelle SS with its blood red paint and midnight black trim sat next to the Musclehead's navy blue Plymouth GTX, a deluxe design of a car. Cuno's Mo-Par Road Runner with its 440 hemi just rattled the ground and sent shock waves when revved up. The Chief's new 350 royal blue '68 Camaro and Punkwillie's silver 396 Chevy Nova with its shaved heads and cherry bombs exhaust just looked regal together, but the car that drew the looks and awes was Wilbur's 4 speed Ford Shelby GT-500 with its snow white body and black racing stripe. This was the Hercules of muscle cars, and the sea seemed to part when the Cobra arrived on the scene.

Like Roman gladiators perched on their chariots, The Brothers were at the zenith of teen supreme gods. They were an uncommon group of lads that had their own way of life and tribal language. Words like "treeemendous" and "it's possseeeble" were standard issue. When a question that required a negative response was asked, three or more of the boys would yell, "NOOOOOOOOO," as loud and long as possible. They didn't act like other bands of testosterone driven males. The Brothers never called each other "asshole" or anything that would "totally inflame" someone. They argued, but never fought. There was a bond that went without explanations. They were, at the core, a fun lovin' group that no one crossed based on their numbers and nature. They were always together in some form or another.

The alarm rang out declaring yet another year of education, athletics, and all the social discord that goes along with it. The boys went their respective ways to class. The Old Kid and Sweet Daddy had the same history class 1st period and got in just as the bell went off. Mr. McNeil, the history teacher, was a tall cut of a man. He was one of the few black faculty members in a school that desperately needed a racial balance at every level. He commanded the respect of all the students and was a man that exuded character.

"Good morning, class," he bellowed. "Welcome to World History. My friends call me Thomas. You may call me Mr. McNeil."

Suddenly a loud bang came from the doorway as the door flew open and in tripped Mister Mike, one of the MIA Brothers from the morning's parking lot council. Mister Mike was the offset brother of the gang. He drove a '66 AMC six cylinder Rambler affectionately called "Rudy" in honor of his Aunt Ruth who gave him the car. She couldn't drive anymore and both she and the car were falling apart.

"Sorry I'm late," said Mike.

"I'm sorry, too," answered Mr. McNeil. "Sit down and tell me how sorry you are in a 100 word essay!"

"Hey, Mike, what happened?" whispered The Old Kid.

"Me and The Hams stopped for coffee and smokes. Thought we'd make it, but..." claimed Mister Mike.

Mr. McNeil began his lesson plan on the importance of history and its meaning as the students did their best to pretend to be interested and awake. Thus began the first day with little hint of the tumultuous days that lay ahead for a clique know as The Brothers and the rest of the world.

The adolescent ritual of checking out the fresh meat had begun in earnest for the boys. The Old Kid was quite taken with a new group of freshmen he called "The Lil Foxes." Michele, in particular, caught his eye with her long, shining, coal black hair, eyes like piercing diamonds, and a nature-blessed, vixen allure.

"Hmmm," exclaimed The Kid. "I can lose my desert gut with her for sure."

The Brothers had their own barometer for social activities. "4th degree" meant you had too much to drink and were about to puke. A 3rd degree burn was serious, but 4th degree meant get back and out of the way. All hell is about to break loose! "Totally inflamed" meant you were at your anger limits and "duking" (fighting) was the antidote. "Solemn" meant that your words of a story were true and you would raise your right hand and "solemn" its truth. All "solemns" had to take place in front of two or more Brothers to be vocally "witnessed." "Triple crown" meant a Brother had "4th degree, duking and nookie" all in the same night, an accomplishment they all strived for each and every weekend. "Desert gut" was the least desired syndrome. When a Brother went without sex for more than a month he was in a desert, crawling on his belly, thirsting for love! The longer you went, the bigger the desert. If you were "Saharaed" (the biggest desert of all), a trip into Chicago's Olde Town was procured. Olde Town was a happening area on the near north side of Chicago. Hippies, tourists, and the Queen of the Sahara, Lady Madonna, resided there. Claims of conquering "desert gut" had to be "solemned." The oath of the "solemn" was never compromised. It meant your word and character as a human being. The Brothers had a strong sense of bonding based on character. As fun loving as they were, a Viking's sense of trust had to be present.

The hallways of Proviso East were an ethnic melting pot that neared the boiling point. The mix ranged from predominately Italian, Melrose Park tuffs, Forest Park's hard German kids, Broadview's wide range of nationalities (that comprised The Brothers' kingdom), and Maywood's substantial black contingence. The black community in Maywood found itself on an island surrounded by some uncompromising white forces. Martin Luther King brought his crusade to nearby Miller Meadow for a rally and march. After being physically assaulted, Dr. King said he felt more racial hatred there than anywhere in the south. The civil rights movement was under full swing in the nation, but was hitting a wall of white tradition in the blue-collar neighborhoods of Chicago's western suburbs. Proviso East housed the youths of this social crossroad, but the subject was largely ignored by the school's administration. New voices were being heard from both sides of the fence, however. The black community had worked its way into middle class, and Fred Hampton, a young, articulate black youth and graduate from Proviso, was becoming a new spokesman for Maywood's black neighborhoods. Fred was aware of the newly formed Black Panthers in Oakland and wanted to establish a Chicago branch. This way he could coordinate his ideals of a new Black America. The media gave Mr. Hampton its attention as well as the FBI. Proviso East had become the ideal proving ground and possible battleground for race relations in middle America. All these racial and nationality cultures were a perfect recipe for constant and unyielding social pressure. The question was just how was a combination of nationalities going to stay under control. That question would be answered.

The fall semester moved slowly along and the traditional events such as Homecoming were just ahead.

"Whoa," said The Old Kid standing in front of his school locker. "Dis kid is going to ask lil fox Michele out to the Homecoming dance."

"Good luck," retorted Sweet Daddy. "She's on the Court and running for Homecoming Queen. You have as much chance landing her as the Cubs winning the pennant. Besides, she's a Climber."

There was a distinct social order at Proviso- the "Climbers," with their white jeans and madras shirts, primarily the jock crowd, and the "Greasers" with wide khaki work pants, Dago t-shirts and black leather coats. The Brothers were definitely Greasers with the exception of Punkwillie who wore white jeans and a black leather coat, a social misfit among social misfits.

"I will apply the Rays... she can't resist," claimed The Kid.

"Careful with the love rays," remarked Sweet Daddy. "You might misfire and hit Handjob Rita. How sweet that would be."

The Old Kid was looking down the hall in the direction of the lil foxes. Michele was a babe and a half, with her friend and fellow vixen, Candy Miller, right behind in the lust ratings. The Old Kid put it in smooth as he approached the girls.

"Hey."

As the girls twirled around to see who was "heying" them, there stood The Old Kid who was an imposing 6' 3", 210 pounds with the skinny Sweet Daddy in tow.

"Hey what?" said the petite Michele.

"Did you hear the one about the poor little deaf girl?"

The girls knew this was pick up time and tried hard to hide their puzzlement over this guy's technique, without waiting for a response that didn't seem to be coming.

"Neither did she... haa," joked The Kid. The awkward pause of silence that every male must endure at these occasions was now for-taking.

"Swing and a miss," whispered the Sweetman.

Nature has instilled in the female the automatic reaction of removing proceeding signals to the male. The Old Kid now stood on the plank of rejection that every man must face. Michele did give him her eye to eye salute since it was obvious to her she was the target of this conquest. The two couples now did the dance of the "what's next tango." Candy was looking at Sweet Daddy like a side dish she didn't order. The Old Kid was transfixed, however, on this cute, little senorita that was in his crosshairs. He pulled the trigger again, knowing that the big game hunter shoots 'til the game drops or runs away.

"Look, this isn't easy... ok?" trying the 'honesty is the best policy' approach. "I just wanted to get to know you and I have the world's worst lines... ok?"

This was scoring up the big points as Michele's face seemed to lighten with a smile that transcended the message of "move on to door number two, Romeo." Nature has a way of conducting these moments of gestures and gazes that sends all conscious messages to the brain. The heart reads these signals and interrupts and misinterprets all incoming messages. The rough road was crossed as The Kid relaxed and smiled back at his lovely new flame.

The rays were firing hard and true because Michele was a girl that the more you stared at her, the better looking she got, and the better looking she got, the more you stared at her.

"Well, I'll see you later, ok?" was all The Kid could muster.

"Ok," replied Michele in a manner and pretense of "you're allowed in the secret garden." Sweet Daddy, however, was firing his look of "scram" at Candy and she was firing right back. These two were water and oil and the twain shall never meet.

The bell sounded for first lunch and most of The Brothers had structured their schedules for it. Like a band of Cherokee warriors they sat with games and challenges of the fool hardy. The sport of "chomps" was the most popular. Its rules were simple: how many chomps does it take for one to devour a piece of food! This event was a real crowd pleaser to the surrounding tables of students that were highly entertained by The Brothers' antics. Musclehead relished his role as modern day Neanderthal. Physically he resembled Elvis with his jet black, wavy hair and boyish good looks. Mentally, however, he had the manners of a Cossack. He could easily "chomp" a cafeteria burger with one Tyrannosaurus swipe. The ketchup dripping from his mouth added to the savagery. Opening his mouth for all to see the carnage was a real "ewwww" getter and appetite loser, but it was his barbaric laugh that gave his "chomps" the ghastly reputation he so cherished. Cuno just loved the action and would make book with anyone within earshot, to out "chomp" the Muss. There were not many takers, but Cuno would find a sucker or two. "Firing homelies" was another favorite pastime of the crew. To fire a proper homely, one must muster the ugliest look on their face they possibly or impossibly can. The Hams and Punkwillie with his John Lennon glasses were capable of some of the most repulsive, hideous, facial contortions ever seen by man. Some truly believed these two were devil possessed as to fire such world-class homelies. Everyone in the area would look in amazement at a group of fairly attractive lads doing their best to demonstrate just how ugly a human being can look! The other big amusement was to give a "friendly Mel." Melvin Bergstein was the school's champion chess player. He was also the school's biggest geek, a real poster boy for geekdom. His super sleeked down hair complete with the badge of honor, his pocket protector, made Mel a stand out. The Brothers tried hard not to be bullies, but Mel made the miscalculation of sitting right next to their table. The Brothers found out rather quickly that if you waved at Mel, he would wave back with a signature salute of his own. His hand would shoot in the air like an SS officer meeting the Fuehrer, and then Mel would bow his head down about 90 degrees almost looking straight down. This pose stayed struck for nearly a full ten seconds. Mel was just too good of a target to be completely ignored. The Brothers couldn't resist a few laughs at poor Mel's expense. The only really bad thing they ever did was to place a dish of mash potatoes from time to time under Mel's butt just as he was about to sit. Mel could have moved, but he seemed to like the attention as well. In fact, sometimes he just sat in the potatoes... this added to his weirdness. When the bell sounded for lunch to end, the boys all gave each other a "friendly Mel" and went on their merry ways. The deserted table always looked like Gettysburg and D-Day all rolled into one. Chomped out burgers and witches brews of coleslaw and whatever abandoned nutriment was around is not a pleasant sight. The cafeteria lady complained bitterly, but Proviso had bigger troubles to deal with than temporary teenage insanity.

"Punk, I need your help. I'm in a bad sitch (situation)," cried The Old Kid.

"Wha you need Bo-Sham (my brother)?" replied Punkwillie.

"I've got to hunt down the lil foxes after school and get Michele alone. I need you to keep her friends busy with your wisecracks."

"Let's just invite them all to Gino's this Friday night, Kid."

"Yeah! Ok, good idea, but I still need you to help me peel her away from her friends even at the party. They are, like, joined at the ass."

"No prob, Bo. I know that most of the lil babes live near Lindop not far from Gino's house."

"Cool beans... dis kid is gonna score solid nookie," said The Kid.

Lindop was an elementary school in Broadview that was a favorite haunt of The Brothers. It had a nice, big parking lot that sloped downhill and hid the boys from view. The police knew they were there, but the boys really didn't do much wrong or commit any vandalism. They just sat around and drank their beloved Schlitz Malt Liquor by the gallon. Schlitz Malt came in small, 8-oz cans so litter became a problem. The Broadview police were thankful that the boys didn't trash the school lot with empties. This is why they were left alone. That and they were white and not really causing any trouble, so they got their little corner of the world. Some of the peripheral friends of The Brothers were cops' sons and what better way to keep tabs on the kids instead of chasing them out to another town? The police always did wonder just what happened to those empties. That was answered two years later when the parks department removed one of the sewer covers in the school's lot and found the sewer full to the brim with over a thousand empty malt liquor cans. The other three manholes were in the same state.

Most of The Brothers were in their junior year, except for Punkwillie who was Mister Mike's first cousin. The Punk was a senior and bragged about his older wisdom to the younger dukes. Dating anyone outside of your grade is usually looked down upon at most schools, but The Brothers had no such restrictions. The lil foxes were all freshmen but looked much older. They knew how to apply the make up. They also lived in Broadview, but went under the radar until now. Being tribal like most teen girls and their numbers could swell up to seven or eight with Emma, aka Maya, was the only bow-wow in the lot. Michele, Candy, and Cindy were the stars of the show with poor Maya (the elephant) getting all the abuse.

"She must be their protection," teased the boys. "It's possseeeble."

Chapter 2
The Lil' Foxes

Gino was a Brother that had a nice, empty house because his single mom was either working or partying. She was cool with The Brothers until they would leave their ritual mess in her living room. Parties there were legendary. Gino liked to throw lit strings of firecrackers indoors to get things jumping. At Gino's, you could meet anyone from anywhere and hear anything at anytime! The new sound of stereo music was the big buzz. The Beatles were the staple diet and "Sgt. Pepper" in stereo was just astonishing to the ear. When Gino announced that his pad was what would be rock'n Friday night, this gave The Old Kid a great way to close in on Michele and, even better, no date, no freight. He was stepping up to the line for a free throw.

Most of all The Brothers' moola was tied up in their muscle cars. Times were very prosperous in America during the late 60's. In fact, some say it was America's peak. Everyone seemed to have a new or cool car, except perhaps for Mister Mike and his four door, 6 cylinder Rambler, Rudy.

Friday night had finally rolled around. The usual rite of the night was to meet and gather in the Lindop parking lot and plan the high level strategy there. The Old Kid was psyched because Michele said she would come to Gino's bash. The boys all roared into Lindop with their powerful, killer machines. They were careful not to rev up their engines or burn too much spin out rubber, wanting to draw as little attention to their actions and vices. Sweet Daddy and Cuno decided to go wheel'n around before hitting the party at Gino's. They were in the Sweetman's Chevelle SS cruisin' to Miller Meadow. The meadow was an old airfield that Charles Lindberg flew from moons ago. Now it was a huge public park and hangout for the car crowd. Boppin' around in a ritual circle of hot rods and cool motorcycles, Cuno noticed a pink Pony-66 Mustang he never saw before and, to make it even more unusual, a girl driver.

"Get next to her, Sweetman. I gotta see this better."

The Mustang had a 350 V-8 emblem with sweet Craigar deep-dish wheels, but what made this ride supreme was its custom, shocking pink paint job. The boys got closer and noticed a painted slogan behind the right front wheel well. "If you can beat me, you can eat me" it boldly advertised, and the kicker was the driver was a hot, hot hunny from planet bunny. Her long, blonde hair seemed electrified and stated a strong sexual contrast with her curled, ash lashes, ocean blue eyes, and gloss pink lipstick. The mad rush of hormones and testosterone was too much for the two teens, who rolled down their window and in a puberty cracking voice asked the kitten if she "wanted to run." Her response was a blistering wail of pistons and torque as she headed for the strip. The strip ran down 1st Avenue about one mile in length. Since it bordered two towns, it wasn't well patrolled... hence the perfect drag strip! The street heading east was empty. Sweet Daddy pulled alongside the Pink Pony and sounded one beep... then two beeps... on the third both cars screamed the most God fearing technology western man had to offer. Both cars simultaneously lifted into the air as if to take flight. The pink Mustang was much lighter and took a slight lead as Miller Meadows' fence posts went blurring by. Sweet Daddy slammed his Hurst clutch into third and, like all good drivers, waited for the rhythmic engine whines to signal pop it to 4th. The SS was a great white shark of a machine. Like all muscles cars, it had no cornering ability, but in a straight line it was unmerciful. Cuno was jumping in his seat clapping his hands frantically as if it helped. The foxy, little lady was holding her own. In fact, she had a half car lead with a quarter mile left to run.

Cuno then yelled, "Roll up your window! Roll it up!"

Without question the Sweetman obliged. Suddenly the car lurched with even more speed due to the now improved aerodynamics. The SS and all its 360 horses were galloping to a victory and booty of unimaginable conquest. Zooming past the white strip on the street, the Chevelle downshifted to a safe squeal. Surprisingly, the Mustang did the same. Was she going to honor her creed? Were the lads going to realize a teenage fantasy?

"Nice job, boys," shouted the sultry driver.

"Hey, we won," yelled back Cuno rolling down his window. "Do we get our reward?"

"Why, dial it down, sailor. Don't rush things, ok? I'm Sadie and I honor my word. I will show you both a great time, I promise you that," said the sexy girl with a sexy smile.

"We are going to a party in Broadview. You want to come to it?" replied the wide eyed aroused bucks.

"Sure, but first I have to pick up my best friend, Linda, ok?" quoth Sexy Sadie.

"Is she as hot as you?"

"Hotter and great in bed. Believe me, I know."

The boys' mouths dropped and froze. She wrote her number on a card and gave it to the juveniles.

"Here is my number. Just give me the address of your party and I will be there in about an hour, ok?"

They exchanged their info and the boys smiled with their teeth showing, a sign that psychologists claim means male sexual visions are dominating their thoughts. The hot pink mustang then squealed out and the boys headed to Gino's with teethie grins.

The crowd was starting to arrive at Gino's. Wilbur pulled up with his Shelby and proudly announced he had "major stinko material." He stole a bottle of Jack Daniel's from his parents' stash. He knew they wouldn't notice or care. They bought and gave him lots of things out of guilt. Hell, they even bought him his exquisite Cobra. The street in front of the house quickly became filled with cars and young minors who wanted a major good time. Gino had a great, nice basement to hold all the kids and their noise. Finding a drunk outside a bar and paying him a $5.00 service to buy cases of malt liquor and Old Style beer usually bought the booze. Sometimes, if they were low on moola, they would require the services of Handjob Rita, the town sleaze. She would flash the old winos for their help in bootlegging. Rita was party girl extraordinaire. She always had a bottle of Ripple in one hand and a lipstick-ringed cigarette in the other. She sure loved the boys. In fact, she loved lots of boys, literally. Handjob Rita was 18 going on 40 and claimed she couldn't cum and that's why she banged any guy that needed banging like some kind of conquest. Everyone in Broadview had a nickname for one reason or another.

Cueball was because of his skinhead hair cuts, Lunchmeat was a kid who ate nothing but, Biz Bag was a guy whose clothes looked like a garbage sack, and Handjob Rita was bestowed for giving guys rubs on the school bus since the 6th grade. The Brothers all had nicknames save for Wilbur. Everyone thought that name was funny enough.

The Old Kid, whose real name was Danny, was quietly pacing around Gino's living room with a can of malt liquor in his hand and an eye on the street. He was on look out for the lil foxes to come prancing up. Instead, Sweet Daddy and Cuno came flying on the avenue as if their balls were on fire, climbing out of the SS waving a paper like Neville Chamberlain himself proclaiming "Peace (of ass) in our time."

"Whoa, Kid," yelped Cuno. "We just beat a hot fuckette with a treeemendous Mustang in a drag race. She's on her way over. She even gave us her phone number."

The Old Kid gave the mandatory reply, "Solemn dis."

Both dragsters raised their right hands and yelled, "SOLEMN!"

The Old Kid spun quickly around to see The Hams sitting on a speaker, realizing his civic duty. "Witnessed," testified The Hams.

"Look, she wrote a message," said Sweetman. "For the time of your life call 255-421-9999... Sexy Sadie!"

"Well, then call her!"

"Not now. She's probably on her way. She said she's a woman of her word."

"No such thing," joked The Hams. "Chicks will say anything to lose losers and you two are World Class."

"Suck a wet fart, Hams," quipped Cuno. "You're ornery 'cause of your deep DG (desert gut)."

"She ain't showin', Bozo," fired The Hams. "The only action you're getting tonight is from Rosie Palm and her five sisters!"

Just then, there was a soft knock at the door, which triggered a neck-breaking whirl from all participants. Boys know what girls sound like even from the other side of the door. Sweetman tripped over Cuno's feet in a hunter's plunge to claim his quarry. The door flew widely open and there stood six sensual minxes known as the "lil foxes" on the porch.

"Is this Gino's house?" timidly asked Candy.

"Bingo, you win... come on in," said Sweet Daddy looking over their heads with coast-to-coast scanning eyes for a hot pink Mustang. The girls walked in quickly filling the room with all the fragrance common perfume could muster. Every guy was eyeball'n every chick as they paraded in. Maya, of course, was in the back, greeted with "I don't think I can get that drunk" looks, except from The Hams who was in a deeper desert then anyone realized. The Old Kid was trying hard to hide his suddenly rapid pulse as he walked up to Michele.

"Oh, so you made it? Thought you might have something better to do." Michele said nothing, but had the look of play it right and all this could be yours. She liked The Kid, but was going to play it by the rules. To win her affection you must show your respect. You have to charm a classy girl with class. If you spin your wheels too long with self-absorbed tales of your grandness, you forfeit the game. "Well, come on down to the Casbah and meet the heathens."

The girls all followed The Kid to the basement and with each descending step on the stairs the music became louder and louder. The lil foxes were trying their best to act cool, but the truth be told this was the first real teen party they had ever been to and they felt like a page was turning in their lives. The usual crowd was there. Musclehead was talk'n to his babe, Long Tall Sally, and Ace, the kid who could fart on request, was sitting next to Punkwillie. Punk had his radar set on one of the lil foxes they called Wham Bam Pam. Her boobs bounced like luscious bags of Jello with every stair step she took. Pam was the tallest of the girls and with her dishwater blonde hair and almond eyes, she left a scent that the Punk just had to sniff. The girls all stood huddled and a little nervous as they could feel the visual inspection taking place.

"Hey, welcome," shouted Gino. "This is my girlfriend, Paulette. I don't know who the rest of these people are." Everyone laughed. "You girls want a coke or something stronger?"

The girls collectivity looked at each other and Pam said, "Do you have any beer?"

Punk took his cue and jumped to the frig and showed its contents... wall to wall gusto and stinko material. "Help yourselves, ladies. We have the finest selection of cheap booze in town."

The Old Kid walked over and grabbed a tall, cool Old Style beer and gave it to Michele. "Here ya go. Do you like beer?"

"Oh, sure, I love it." She cracked it open and took a big sip as her face told her true feelings about the suds.

"Hey," said Gino. "I bought this album. Some new group called The Doors. I like them."

1967 was an amazing year for music. The standard groups of The Stones, Beatles, Jefferson Airplane and The Animals were cranking out the hits left and right, but the new counter culture was beginning to get into the mainstream. Jimi Hendrix, Janis Joplin, Otis Redding and The Moody Blues were taking rock into a true renaissance. This was a great time to be a teenager. The furor and sense of adventure seemed to be everywhere. The energy that President Kennedy tried to instill in America seemed to be taking place. People were exploring space, art, music and new alternative lifestyles. Drugs, too, were being explored and abused by many, including adolescents. The Brothers were not into the medicated scene. They preferred their stinko to any other high. "Break on through to the other side" chanted The Door's album and the mood became festive as the lil foxes could see these guys meant no harm. The lil foxes were aware of the clan's reputation with girls like Grant going through Georgia, but they seemed pretty harmless. Meanwhile, upstairs Sweet Daddy and Cuno were still keeping a vigil for Sexy Sadie to come rolling up. Sweetman pulled out the tattered card she gave them with the message "for the time of your life call 255-421-9999... Sexy Sadie!"

"Fuck it, I'm calling."

"Go ahead," said Cuno. "It's a Chicago prefix so what the hell."

Sweet Daddy picked up the phone and dialed. He held the phone close to his ear. It started ringing, then a woman's voice answered, "At the tone it will be 11:32 and ten seconds... beep!"

"Cunt," yiped Sweetman. "She played us like a Jew's harp."

There was a brief moment of defeated, dejected, discouraged silence, broken by the hyena-like pitching laugh of The Hams. "Yeeeeee, you guys got axed to your knees. Yeeeeeeeee." Cuno and Sweetman just looked at each other like two sailors whose boat just took a torpedo. "Yeeeeeeee, with one mighty swing she chopped you both to your ankles. Yeeeeeeee. 'The time of your life is 11: 46 beeeeeeep!' Yeeeeeeee haw."

"Blow it out your ass, Hams. I don't see you with any nookie cookies on your lap!"

All three of the boys shrugged their shoulders and went down to join the bash at the Casbah. The place was filling up with the usual suspects and whoever's... Sachamo, Billy Q's, some floozies from Melrose Park that cracked gum with every breath.

"Nice place," Candy said to the host, Gino.

"Thanks."

"Thought all you guys had nick names?"

"We do... my real name is John."

"Why do they call you Gino?"

"Don't know, but it fits."

The Old Kid was making his move towards Michele who now was up to three whole sips of beer. "Slow down, what are you a booze hound?" joked The Kid.

"Ahh, I'm just being careful. Don't want to go home all drunk and pass out on my parents' bed."

"Nah! You won't. I'll watch you."

"What a relief... the fox watching the hens," rejoined Michele.

"Nope. More like the sheep watching the foxes."

"Huh?" responded Michele.

"Never mind."

Michele just looked stunning. At fifteen a girl looks perky and perfect. Everything was in its place. The cottage cheese had not yet set in. The Old Kid was becoming tunnel visioned with this girl, a sure sign of amour stroking the heartstrings. She seemed to like the boy's handsome looks and honest smile.

"If anyone gives you a hard time here, let me know, ok?" said The Kid.

"But what if it's you?" asked Michele. The smile on his face was a salute to her quick wit.

"Hey, Punk, King B is on, King B is on... call him, man... you got to call him, man," Chief yelled.

Chief was a guy who either started or ended every conversation with "man." When he was asked why, his answer was, "What ya talkin' about, man?" Not until someone once called his house was the puzzle revealed. His mom answered the phone with a "Hey, man."

"Come on, Punk, call him, man," requested Chief.

Ron Britain was a popular DJ on Chicago's WCFL radio. He commanded the airwaves with his jokes and cool humor. Chicago was a town of clever comebacks and wisecracks. Many great comics such as Steve Allen, Bill Murray and John Belushi were from Chi town. Being streetwise called for a quick command of one's senses and a sense of humor seemed to be a by-product and defense mechanism for living in crowded, tough neighborhoods. Punkwillie would from time to time call

Ron Britain and became something of a favorite on air son of King B. The Punk had a lot of jokes in his repertoire and King B would let all of Chicago hear the gags while playing a perfect straight man. Punkwillie was becoming something of a minor celebrity as WCFL reached a radio signal of 15 million listeners.

"Ok, give me the phone," said Punk.

As he dialed, the stereo went down and the radio up. King B was blabbing on about some new band called Led Zeppelin playing in the Chicago blues bars. He picked up the phone and when he recognized the Punk's voice, he went on air with it.

"Hey, King B! Punkwillie here."

"Hey, Punk, what's new?"

"Oh, King, I'm going on a blind date tonight."

"Oh really, Punk? Sounds interesting."

"Yeah, she's deaf, too."

"Now, Punk... " All of King B's replies had an undertone of laughter. "Be nice."

"It's ok, King, because I had to let my last girl go."

"Oh, really?"

"Yeah, she kept telling me how much she liked music and art. Then last night I caught her with Art."

"Oh, Punk, how awful."

"Yes, that was an awful joke. Speaking of awful jokes, King... did I ever tell you about the one big, big girl I dated once?"

"I don't think so."

"Well, she was so big that when I took her to Mc Donald's, she got stuck in the arches. She liked to show me her world class collection of food stamps, and there's even a Richter scale in her bathroom."

Punk was machine gunning his crack wises and King B let him fly.

"Now come on, Punk, you're getting carried away."

"No, King. I asked what does it take to have sex with her and she said flowers, dinner, and a building permit."

"Wow," went King.

"She has a great job, too. She's a model... for a ship building firm."

"Oh please, Punk, please."

"King, one last thing. I finally got her in bed and she said I had a small organ, so I told her, 'Well, I didn't know I was going to play it in a CATHEDRAL!!!.'"

"Now, that's enough, Punk. I'm going to have to call the authorities," joked King B.

"Yeah, but what ya gonna call em! AAAH! Punkwillie over and out."

The party went into applause mode for the Punk's theatrics.

"Hey, man, that was good, man... that was good, man," shouted the Chief.

The Old Kid got a nice jolt of surprise as Michele sat next to him on the couch. He gave all the calling cards necessary and the ball was in her court. The two sat there trying to get to know each other better. They chatted for about an hour when The Kid asked if he could give her a ride home.

"Ok, but we can't stop anywhere else. I'm late already."

The party was winding down and the beer had run out. Mister Mike for some odd reason was guzzling salad dressing. "It's the only bottle left with anything in it," he belched out.

Everyone was pairing off and heading somewhere else. Punkwillie laid claims to Wham Bam Pam and was hoping she lived up to her hype. Gino and Paulette were upstairs trying to hide the evidence of a party, but someone hit 4th degree and the carpet smelled awful. The guilty party was not hard to find as Sweet Daddy laid with his head inside a small garbage can filled with puke. Obviously, he couldn't make it to the toilet. He and Cuno were burying their sorrows about receiving the golden axe from Sexy Sadie. Cuno was nowhere to be found until someone looked under Gino's mom's bed. He was out cold, and snoring like an aged pig.

The Old Kid drove Michele home as he pulled up in front of her house and parked.

"Well, you're fun to be with, Michele."

"Thanks. You're nice to be around, too."

He leaned forward for the big move to find out just how nice he was to be around. She surprised him with a kiss that started out school girl and rapidly became French whore. This girl knew a thing or two about the art of smooching. All hands on deck... All hands on deck... went The Kid's brain as he quickly wanted to pursue the boundaries. His hand ran up her side and, losing control, he was in the danger zone faster than he realized. No elbow... no elbow... thought The Kid. She left the door open to libidinous bliss. A fifteen-year-old girl will sometimes leave the door open a little too long thinking it's a sign of maturity she desperately desires to display. Michele wanted The Kid to think of her as an older girl, but was losing control of the situation fast. He amazedly got to her breast and he thought even a quick feel is a trophy for the great white hunter, but he'd gone into full gear. The Old Kid was now peeking out of his supposedly closed eyes at Michele's taut, firm boobs. His head was swimming in a hormonal sea without a life vest and he was drowning. They kissed even deeper, as if this was possible, and teenage lust was beginning to steam up the windows. They both could feel each other's heart beat and had to break to just take a long endearing look. This is a ritual guided by the hand of nature. Cupid was firing away and hitting its target. Michele gave a quick look at her house and saw no waiting silhouette. The Old Kid was breathing hard and trying to regroup for round two, and as he leaned in for another passionate sojourn, a blinding, blazing, white light shined into the GTO. He quickly jerked back to see if a UFO had landed behind him, but it was a cop car. Officer Moody's car to be precise.

"Well... well... well... If it isn't Fireball Robert's himself," asked Moody walking toward the GTO. "What the hell are you two doing?" he said leaning inside the window.

"You probably do need an explanation," laughed The Kid.

"Look, punk, I got you for evasive and reckless driving of a motor vehicle and now it also looks likes statutory rape of a minor."

"Moody, we are just sitting here and I don't know what you're talking about with the driving thing."

Moody leaned in even further as Michele's parents came out to the car to see what was going on. "You two have been drinking, haven't you?" scowled Moody.

"No," said The Kid, thinking how things went from heaven to hell in a flash.

"Is this your daughter, folks?" asked Moody.

"Yes, officer. What's the trouble?" inquired Michele's dad as he closed up a flapping robe.

"Well, it seems your daughter likes hoodlums I'm afraid. She's been drinking with this renegade and when I walked up they were engaging in sexual intercourse."

"That's a lie!" cried out Michele.

Her dad leaned into the other side of the car window and gave The Old Kid a look of deathful hatred. He then sniffed near Michele's trembling mouth.

"Tell you what, folks. Take your daughter in. I'm sure you can punish her better than any judge. I'm booking this degenerate, however."

Moody made his crowning capture as he cuffed The Kid and escorted him to the back of the squad car and drove off to the police station. The Broadview holding cell is a small 10 x 10 no frills cage. Officer Moody gave The Old Kid a hard shove into its vapid entrance, and slammed its tempered steel door shut.

"We're calling your parents. They should be thrilled." The Kid said nothing as he sat on a torture rack of a bed. Moody pulled a police baton off the wall and glared at The Kid with a menacing look. "I should knock some sense into you, you lousy bastard," Moody gnarled.

The Kid stood up and looked the cop squarely in the eyes. "Come in here with that and just see what happens."

The Old Kid may have been young, but he was imposing, and Moody's sense of police judgment told the officer he was dealing with a real warrior. The cop turned and walked out mumbling something about "today's youth and lack of... "

Chapter 3
Peace to Pieces

Monday finally rolled around and the daily routine of Proviso was in full swing. The Brothers were gathering in the parking lot reliving the triumphs and tragedies of the weekend. They were pawing over the latest Motor Trend magazine and talking about the new AMC's AMX, a cool looking roadster with two doors and full hatchback. The Old Kid pulled up in his Goat and everyone wanted to know the sitch with his parents.

"They're inflamed, but I can still drive until my court date," reported The Kid. "I don't think I'm gonna have to answer for the drinking char... " Just then The Kid spotted Michele across the street and walking into school. He made a mid sentence bolt for her. "Hey, Michele... Michele... hold up."

She looked at him with an ambivalent smile. She had experienced quite a lot for her coming out weekend. "Danny, how are you? Are you ok?"

"Yeah, yeah, I'm fine," he said. "Just a li'l action. Did you catch hell from your folks?"

"Yeah. They act like I'm a whore now and need counseling. Haa! They did say I have to stay away from you and you are not allowed to come around my house!"

"Damn, not cool," The Kid remarked. "Maybe I can talk to them?"

"No, not right now, Danny. You better let things settle. How long were you in jail?"

"Just a few hours. I dug my way out and escaped." Michele gave him a look of "nothing is funny about this buster!!"

"Well, Old Kid, don't worry. We will still see each other. You're not at fault for what happened. What was that reckless driving thing the cop was talking about?"

"Nothing. Moody got me mixed up with my brother."

"I thought your brother was in Viet Nam?" asked Michele.

"He is. He just came home for a couple of days or something. Hey (shifting gears), today's the voting for Homecoming Queen, huh?"

"Yeah. I'm so nervous. I know I'm not going to win."

"Well, you're the only freshmen with a chance to be on the Court. That's an honor and The Brothers all voted for you."

"Even Wilbur?" asked Michele, as The Kid's face went quickly to four shades of red.

"What! Why do you care who he voted for?" fired back The Kid.

She played the jealous card to perfection.

"Oh, nothing, just curious."

"Well, I voted for you five times."

He bit the bait a little too hard and was just spouting words now. The bell rang and the student body, warts and all, headed to first period. The Old Kid and his new lil hunny said good-bye and both disappeared into the flowing river of juveniles.

The day was rather warm for a Midwestern autumn day. Chicagoland does not have a lot of fair weather days, but this was surely one of them. The clean, crisp air filled the classrooms and even the boys' gym locker room was almost tolerable... almost! Third period had just ended and The Kid was outside of the gym near the football field. He was heading to machine shop when a dull roar of a noise coming from the school was grabbing his attention. He turned and looked at the school and could see nothing initially, but the roar was becoming louder and filling up with screams of female students. The Kid took a few steps towards the school when the doors nearest him flew open and students were running out, some yelling, and all with a look of terror on their faces.

"Is the school on fire?" he thought, but there was no alarm. He walked briskly at first, then into a jog. As he drew nearer the building, he could tell not all the students were leaving and some from the parking lot were going back inside. When he reached the doorway, the roar was full and had a scary viciousness to it. He looked down the hall in amazement. Somehow the corridor had become a war zone. Students were fighting everywhere with each other, but at a closer look The Kid quickly deduced it was white against black.

"What the hell is going on? What the hell?" The Kid stood there trying to sort out the confusing scene that was before him. He searched the crowd for a recognizable face and came across Jimmy D from his homeroom. "Hey, Jimmy, what the hell is going on?"

The intense fighting seemed to move down the hall as Jimmy came over. "The fuck'n coons are rioting," he said gasping a little. "They announced the results for Homecoming Queen and all five of the Court were white." He went on, "The black broads got all pissed about it and went wild. They are tracking down those five white girls and beating the shit out of them. They caught Donna Banarzie and pulled her hair out, and threw her down the stairs."

The Kid's face became ashen and the thought of Michele came racing across his mind. He looked in all directions and started flying down the hall. This was serious duking... battle mode!

Michele was with Candy Miller deep in the corridors of Proviso. "Here, put this on." Candy was handing Michele a scarf to hide her face some. The girls were desperately seeking protection and ducked into an empty classroom. The teachers were out in the halls trying to break up fights and all the classrooms were pretty much vacated. The noise of a riot was banging on the halls and doors throughout Proviso. It was terrifying the girls severely. "We'll be safe here," said Candy as Michele was beginning to shake and tears were clouding her eyes.

Screams outside the door were mainly from black girls yelling about "this is enough shit... this is enough." There were twelve girls up for the five positions on Homecoming Court, seven white and five black, and when the voting was announced, all five positions were awarded to the white girls. This was an unkindly cut to black students who were still deeply immersed in the racial history of American prejudice. America was about to enter its time of reckoning with just how tired the black race was of being treated like sub humans and poor Michele was in the crosshairs.

The Old Kid was fanatically running and shoving his way through the halls. He still couldn't digest the scene that surrounded him. The riot had taken on a life of its own. Most of the fighting was taking place in a front line that seemed to move throughout the school like a raging serpent. Classmate against classmate, most of these kids had grown up together and got along just fine. The blacks were really striking out at the world of suppression. It was not so much a personal assault against the white students of Proviso East. The black society as a whole talked openly about this at church functions. They live in a world no white person knows or has any real idea of what that world is like. How many whites even know what Juneteenth is, or its significance? The winds of social change were blowing strong and blew the lid right off the powder keg called Proviso East.

"Hey, Old Kid," yelled Wilbur. "Where you going?" Wilbur was standing outside the library with his shirt torn and lip swollen. "I've had major duking with the titsoons!" (Italian slang for blacks.) The sound of police sirens were adding to the charged atmosphere as the fighting seemed to be heading on outside.

"Will, what happened?"

"I don't know, Bo," said Wilbur. "I just know some of the Homecoming girls got the shit kicked out of them by some black girls."

"Lookout, Will!" barked The Kid as a book flew out of the library apparently thrown aimlessly by a white kid. "Have you seen or heard anything about Michele?" The Kid asked excitedly.

"No, but I saw a black chick with clumps of long black hair in both hands."

"Christ," exclaimed The Kid. "I've got to find her."

The boys started to head up the now ravaged hall when little cloud balls came rolling in through the doorway. "Tear gas, Will, cover your mouth." The situation was now getting worse by the second as the cool, crisp, fall air was being replaced with toxic, eye burning, throat gagging tear gas. The boys covered their faces and disappeared into a gloomy haze of venomous vapor.

"Candy, my eyes burn," said a shaken Michele. The fumes of the tear gas were gradually filling the entire school. Candy looked at Michele as both girls were hiding under desks and noticed both their noses were running with a clear, mucus material. The noise of broken glass and chair tossing was quickly subsiding, but the whining sirens outside were ever mounting as if the whole state militia was forming ranks. The two girls knew they had to get out of this newly formed gas chamber and started to get up to walk when suddenly the door jolted open with such force the glass pane exploded.

"We got one! We got one!" yelled two black girls as another three behind them bolted into the room.

"No!" Candy yelled, and pushed Michele down to jump and cover her, but the white girls were no match. The room filled with horrifying screams from both parties as Candy was pulled off and thrown against the blackboard. One of the black girls ran up and whacked Candy hard across her face with an umbrella and the fifteen year old dropped half unconscious to the floor. The other girls were focusing their hated attention to Michele, who recognized one of the black girls as one of the Homecoming contestants.

"We gots you now you white motherfuckin' bitch," said one of the attackers. "You ain't gonna be so pretty anymore."

They all started kicking at Michele, but were actually hitting each others' legs because they were so bunched together. They were all so much on an adrenaline high, the tear gas clouds had very little effect. The biggest girl in the group reached down and started pulling on Michele's long, flowing hair. "I'm gonna yank this white, straight shit out of your head, girl."

Michele became quiet and was now in a shocked state that mugging victims fall into where the body closes down and starts to pass out.

"Rip her clothes off," cried another girl.

The biggest one reached down to Michele's unraveled blouse and buttons started popping off like popcorn as she violently tore at the material. The girl with the umbrella was winding her weapon up behind her head for a killer blow to Michele's face when BAM... she got wildly blind-sided by a furious raging bull. The Old Kid had mercifully rushed in and tackled the umbrella assailant. Wilbur charged into the room with fists flying at anyone standing. It went way beyond the boys' morals to hit a female, but morals are nowhere to be found in warfare. The black girls fought back and gave the boys all they could handle. The one with the umbrella got free and was wielding her busted garment like a battle axe. She caught Wilbur upside the head with a huge smack and his ear started bleeding. The battle ended suddenly when the girls realized no back up existed in the halls. Their boyfriends had left the building long ago.

"Fuck this shit. Let's bolt," cried out the biggest one, and like quicksilver the girls left into the gaseous mist.

"Michele... Michele... " said The Kid as he rushed over and picked her up in his arms. She faintly looked at him, but was in shock and an ashen color filled her face as she laid her head back. She had a bloody nose and a half, her clothes were shredded, but she was going to be fine. Wilbur went over to Candy and she was out cold. Her nose looked broken and lips swollen, but nothing more than a bad trimming was her prognosis. The boys carried the battered girls out of the tattered classroom and outside though the school's grand arch doorway that had a painted sign that read "Homecoming this weekend... be part of the fun!!!"

Police were everywhere and paramedics came up and took command of the girls. The Old Kid looked to his left at the parking lot where his precious GTO slept and saw flames of fire dancing upward. Apparently, two motorcycles were turned upside down and the leaking fuel was ignited. The Maywood fire department was on the scene and TV crews were jumping out of vans like cattle prods were up their asses. The police from other surrounding towns and the Illinois State Police were called to help squelch the rioting. Fathers and big brothers were driving up to rescue their daughters and sons. This was adding to the confusion as now even more blacks and whites were meeting in the streets. Things could go from bad to worse fast. Screaming was still in the air and The Old Kid glanced over his shoulder as his precious Michele was being lifted into an ambulance. He knew she would be ok, but wondered what was next for the students of Proviso. The street directly in front of the school became a dividing line, angry whites on one side, angry blacks on the other, both sides yelling and swearing at each other. Amazingly, no gunshots had sounded and most of the fighting was hand to hand combat. The police were gathering between the two charged groups ordering both sides to disperse. Riot gear was now being issued to the officers and long battling batons were being dispensed. The TV news crews with their walkie talkies were precariously around the scene and The Kid noticed they were telling small pockets of youths where other opposing forces lie. This was a deliberate attempt to agitate the situation for more violence and greater news footage. The old journal adage of "if it bleeds, it leads" was being played out in front of The Kid.

"Hey, Old Kid," yelled Mister Mike. "Get your dead ass over here." The Brothers had all grouped around their cherished chariots and were trading glories of battle. "I'm totally inflamed," barked Mike. "What the fuck are the titsoons doing? Why are they so fuck'n mad?"

"Hey, man, cause none of the black babes got voted on the Homecoming Court, man," answered Chief.

"Well, tough that shit, the black boys should have voted for them, but the lazy bastards probably blew it off."

"Fuck'n du' A," said Wilbur.

"Hey, I got Darnell Coals good. He was running up the hall swing'n at some chump and BAM... I caught his ass with a haymaker," boasted Mike. "I swear I saw Friendly Mel waylaying some coon near the office."

"Probably his bitch," joked Punkwillie.

Just then a squad of riot police walked up with the long, smacking sticks in hand and started yelling for everyone to clear the lot. The fighting had ceased and both sides were surveying each other as the realization was setting in that Proviso East would never be the same and just what was going to happen tomorrow? The Brothers all headed back to Lindop parking lot listening to the news reports of riot on the radio. Beloved DJ Dick Biondi was reporting that some of the students were in critical condition and for everyone to remain calm. This could easily turn city wide as Chicago has the right ingredients for a full scale street riot. The gang's muscle cars all roared up to their usual hitch'n post at the school. The streets were very alive with much scurrying traffic as news spread throughout the region. There was a nervousness in the air as paranoid parents were collecting their thoughts and children.

The boys sat around talking and smoking their Marlboros like great Indian warriors reflecting on the day's events. The Old Kid wanted to go to Michele's house to find out how she was doing, but he knew he was not welcomed by her folks. Wilbur was showing his umbrella wounds to his head and arms. All the boys were comparing notes on just which of the blacks that they knew were most involved. The consensus seemed to be that the black dudes were fighting at the insistence of the black chicks. The white boys were fighting once the white girls got attacked.

"Why don't we just let the girls duke it out on the football field," asked Cuno. "I would make heavy odds."

"Well, tomorrow is going to be interesting for sure," said Sweet Daddy.

The young battlers went to their homes for supper and watched as Proviso's burning parking lot played on television with Walter Cronkite and the other stiff white guys of the national media. Proviso had suddenly become national news, and parents of the near western suburbs of Chicago, Illinois had to come to grips with the tough decision of sending their children to school in the morning and mornings thereafter.

The sun rose the next day but no one could see it. A heavy layer of putrid, gray clouds hid the star, and a chill-filled wind was blowing through from the north like a frosted freight train. The Old Kid called Mister Mike for a ride to school. He didn't want to have his glorious GTO Goat in harms way. Mike laughed because four other brothers called, too. No one wanted to chance their dream machines to the tar pit of a parking lot. The fire from the motorcycles melted away at the asphalt and left an eerie impression on the ground. It looked like a Picasso painting of the end of the world. Wilbur, Punkwillie, Cuno, The Old Kid and Mister Mike all crammed into Rudy, "the four door eye sore," as it was affectionately known.

"You's all like the Rude now how" cited Mike. "Rudy to the rescue. Save us all, Rudy."

This was the era of the muscle car, hot rods, choppers, and raked up trucks abounding on every street, but this and all fashions of the day went sailing by Mister Mike. He still religiously clung to his Elvis 8 track, while the rest of the world was immersed in Beatle mania and the emerging underground sounds. Mister Mike was the pit bull of the lot. While everyone had the deep look of concern on their faces about the rioting, Mike was profoundly admiring the imprint of Darnell Coals' teeth on his fist. His beat up AMC Rambler just fit him perfectly-- tough nut of a car, no frills or thrills. The back seat floorboard was more of an historical collection of beverages, brews, motor oils, chips and UFO's (Unidentified Food Orgy). One had to be careful and not slip into the Black Hole of Rudy. It was a terrible way to go. The biggest question of all about the unwashed, unwaxed Rambler was on the dashboard. AMC, the makers of the Jeep and other ingenious inventions, installed something called the "Weather Eye." No one knew what the Weather Eye did, exactly, as it sat just above the radio with no button or lever, but surely it was something important and futuristic.

"Say what you want about Rudy," claimed Mike, "but none of you have the mighty Weather Eye and deep down I know you's allll want it more than life itself."

It's possseeeble, Mister Mike," was the response.

The Rambler rambled into Proviso's parking lot and the usual sight of students going about their usual paths to school had completely changed. There in front of the boys was a scene straight out of "Dragnet 67." Proviso had transformed into a police state. There were more cops and men in suits walking around the school grounds than students.

"Whoa, we have guests today," said Cuno as all the boys surmised the sitch. "Who are those guys in the suits?"

"I dunno," answered Wilbur as he lighted a smoke.

"I know who those guys are," exclaimed Punkwillie. "They're nice guys with ties."

"Yeah," laughed The Kid. "They eat pies, fries, spoons, balloons and soon, titsoons."

The boys gave a war call laugh they knew so well. The prime reason this pack all bonded so much was the clever wit and humor that demonstrated their profound wisdom no matter what the report cards reported. The boys loved to laugh and they gave each other a lot to laugh at. This day, however, was no laughing matter as their high school had now become a police state. The media was nowhere in sight. They were ordered to stay one mile away since it was discovered how they contributed to the discord. The Brothers were all gathering in their usual parking spaces and they all drove different cars, except of course for Mister Mike.

"Hey, there goes Fast Eddie," shouted the Hams.

Fast Eddie was a black student that The Brothers all knew and liked, but he was now the enemy and both parties just pretended not to noticed each other. He was walking with Fred Hampton who seemed to be trying to organize the coloreds. He was shouting something about "now is the hour" and "unite for the cause." This got the quick attention of the "Nice Guys in Ties" who The Brothers could tell were actually FBI agents by the gold badges inside their dark suits. The Chief of Police for Cook County, Joe Woods, was on a megaphone calling out for all students to carry their school ID's in front of them as they entered the school. The Brothers crossed 1st avenue and walked towards the school and there, standing on both sides of the sidewalk entering the school, were helmeted police.

"Wow," said Wilbur. "The Gestapo is out in force."

Just then some Italian students from Melrose Park walked up and started relaying what the buss was. Frank Caleno, the school's best wrestler, was the leader of these tuffs and he knew The Brothers well.

"Hey, man, how you like our welcome wagon?"

"Yeah, a lil over kill, huh?" said The Old Kid.

"Nah, the American Nazi and KKK are here. Some of them got busted in the halls already for trespassing."

"Really?" replied The Kid.

"Yeah, 30 year old dudes kinda stick out a little... haaaa."

"Yeah, some shine gang from the south side called the Peace-stone Rangers are here, too," said one of the other Dagos.

"This looks like major dukin' will be on the menu today," said The Kid.

"It's possseeeble," replied Cuno.

"There haven't been this many rumors fly'n since Hotel Hello blew up," quoth Punkwillie as the joke went nowhere.

Everyone sensed safety in numbers and the groups joined up and walked to the walkway flanked by Cook County's finest. The first observation of the schoolyard was the absence of the white girls. Parents were not about to let their treasured daughters enter the battlefield again. The second discernment was that all the white kids were entering the main doors and black students were disappearing to the back of the school.

"Pull out your ID cards and hold them in front of you," barked a cop that was dressed for the Apocalypse. The scene seemed surreal as students proceeded down a walkway displaying their photo school ID to the lined up policemen. The boys stayed bunched up and when they reached the middle of the procession, Punkwillie started "firing homelies." The guarded look of the patrolmen became even more guarded as they quizzically glared backed at the lad. Through their face masks the officers seemed to be unintentionally firing their own homelies right back. The Hams then gave the guardsmen a "friendly Mel" and the other boys chimed in.

"Good morning, friendly officers," said Musclehead as he held his right hand high in the air. The police were not even close to being amused and a few started tapping the ground with their long batons to give warning. Once inside the school the surrealism continued as the halls were teeming with police from every town, county and parts beyond the local area. The boys stopped their joking ways when they saw coppers with automatic weapons at the ready. The seriousness of the sitch was quickly being realized as The Brothers found themselves literally looking down the barrel of the long arm of the law. The halls had an eerie quiet to them as they were full of people, but devoid of sound.

"You can taste the tension," remarked Mister Mike.

The usual tradition in the morning was to go to the cafeteria and shoot the bull. The boys all followed the habitual routine as Sweet Daddy was waiting at the door outside to "the slopbox."

"Hey, Old Kid," he said. "My sister talked to Michele on the phone this morning." This got 101 percent attention from The Kid.

"How is she?"

"She was a little swollen, but alright. She wants you to call her today."

The Old Kid was about to respond, but when he entered the cafeteria all his attention changed lanes. Historians talk about the calm before the storm at great battlefields-- Gettysburg, The Little Big Horn, Normandy Beach-- and now the lunchroom of Proviso East High School sat in a morose silence of impending conflict. The two sides were divided virtually right down the middle of the room with a line of police between them. The school's administration was nowhere in sight and it probably was best. The Brothers gathered around their favorite table and watched the nervous cafeteria ladies doling out oatmeal. The women had one eye on the soupy, grey mix and the other on the two swelling mobs facing each other.

"Hey," shouted The Old Kid. "There's Moody." Broadview's officer Moody had joined the thin line of police between the groups. He was wrapping a bicycle chain around his fist.

"He's preparing for battle," said Cuno.

Moody and the rest of the hastened together patrolmen had an anxious look in their eyes. The bell for class was still four minutes away and the growing anxiety was mounting like ejaculated lava from a volcano. Noticeably missing from the two throngs were girls. The whole reason this was all going down was because of the people who were nowhere in sight. It really didn't matter because a teenage male needs very little reason or rationale to go off. This was all dangerous, exciting, and unpredictable. What more could a juvenile ask?

Suddenly, some music started playing over the school's PA system. It was Smokey Robinson and the Miracles. The administration was finally trying to intervene to calm the beast with music. Both sides liked Smokey Robinson, but this wasn't about to quell a thing. The Brothers were all sitting around the table when an opened carton of white milk came flying out from the black students' area. The container spurted a white milky trail... it looked in slow motion as it fell into the whites. No sooner had it landed, and a chocolate milk carton came whizzing out of the white kids' section aimed at the black students. The mind can compute much information in a very short time as the opening salvos fired. The slam of counters from fleeing cafeteria women, yells of commands from agitated police, frenzied screams from students on both sides all filled the air simultaneously. The world had violently changed and all hell was breaking loose as both groups charged each other... all this in mere seconds.

The thin line of police was rapidly buried by an avalanche of frenzied teenagers. The officers could barely get off some tear gas grenades and started spraying the new chemical, mace, into the nearest face. Punches were flying fast and hard and the two wild eyed groups furiously merged. The Old Kid and most of The Brothers were in the first wave that slammed into the battling blacks. Suddenly, loud thumping sounds were echoing off the walls as the lunchroom chairs started to fly through the air. The boys were all swinging like spinning cyclones as they were hitting and being hit all at the same time. There was no time to even swear at one's opponent for hand-to-hand combat is incredibly fast and vicious. Ripping clothes, grabbing throats, kicking groins, poking eyes, biting ears, spitting teeth, stepping, punching, and gouging at anything and everything. No one wins at barbaric forms of fighting. Everyone just tries to survive. The Old Kid saw Punkwillie and The Hams go down in a heap and now he was trying to save his friends. The noise from the chairs wildly hitting the walls and students was deafening as it added to the hysteria. Swarms of back up police were storming in as best as they could, but the human sea of bodies was impenetrable. The air stung with mace and tear gas, but when a human has their adrenaline flowing like ejaculated lava, chemicals have little effect. Riots create a mass euphoria that starts to control the people involved. They become high with the power they possess and begin to lose a sense of control. Glass starts breaking and vandalism comes into play as a release of raging energy. Everything that was not bolted down in the cafeteria became a victim. The historical lead pane glass windows were shattering apart as chairs, books, table trays, and even a cash register came crashing through. The fire alarm was set off and blended wildly with the screaming. The Old Kid caught a glance of Mister Mike charging headlong into the fracas carrying a long pole used to open ceiling windows. He looked like a knight in a jousting match as he disappeared into the battle. Just then The Kid tripped over something, and it was Johnny The Hams' head.

"Kid, get me up... get me up," pleaded The Hams.

The Old Kid reached down and tried pulling his friend up, but it was harder than he was ready for. Getting trampled to death was another realization in this mess. He pulled even harder this time and shoved people out of the way to make some room, but nothing doing. He looked down and saw The Hams' face get stepped on. At the same time a fist came out of nowhere and crashed into The Kid's jaw. He wouldn't let go of his amigo for it could mean death for a kid named after the only meal he cooked. Footing was becoming a growing problem as a slimy mixture of milk, water and blood sheathed the floor. A violent push came into The Kid as police were wildly swinging their riot batons. This push sent The Kid backwards and gave him the force needed to rescue The Hams.

"Oh my God, Kid, thanks," yelled The Hams who now looked like he was spit out of a tornado. His shirt was more off then on, blood ran from his lip and nose, and he had a slicing cut above the eye.

The black kids were no longer fighting as the mostly white police were head bashing them good. There was a mass rush to all doors by the combatants. Heavy coughing was the only sound as gaseous vapors still hung in the air like a following ghost. The Old Kid was searching the floor for Punkwillie who he saw fall earlier, but the Punk was nowhere in sight. The Kid and Hams joined the crowd for a way out. They had to step over many of the injured students who lay damaged on the wet, battle scarred floor.

"This way, Hams," called The Kid. The Hams' eyes were nearly closed shut from the pounding he took on the floor and tear gas he had ingested. The Old Kid grabbed his comrade by the shirt collar and dragged him though the human river. The fighting had ceased and somehow the two races separated to different areas of the school. No one was giving commands, yet both sides seemed to know where to go and regroup.

The PA system started to crackle with an announcement for all concerned students to go the assembly hall for a meeting and discussion of the events. The students that needed medical attention went outside where paramedics waited with a make shift triage. Most of the injuries were superficial and only required a saline cleaning of the eyes. The Kid guided Hams to one of the attendants who administered the required first aid to the wounded gladiator.

"I'm going to that meeting," said The Kid.

"Go ahead. I'm going home," replied the weary Johnny Hams.

The Old Kid started for the huge assembly hall as civil servants scurried in and out of the school attending to casualties of the insurrection. The number of students seriously hurt wasn't as bad as The Kid thought. Youth can take a lot of punishment, as many of the students who were on their backs unconscious, now milled about with the other students. The Kid spotted some of the other Brothers head into the meeting.

"Hey, Musclehead," yelled The Kid.

"Yo, Kid, how's your dead ass? Did you get major duking?"

"Hell yes. Me and The Hams were in the middle of it. I saw Punk go down, but haven't seem him since."

"Mike got busted by Moody. I saw him dragging him into a squad car," cited Musclehead. "He told me he charged into a group of titsoons with a window pole and ended up ramming Moody in the back."

The boys entered the assembly hall and imminently policemen were in their face shouting orders where to sit. The upper balcony was closed and two lines of riot-geared police ran down the center aisle acting as a human barrier separating the two factions. Black students were sent to the left and white to the right with surprising little banter between the two groups. The administrators of the school were on the stage sitting behind a microphone and a table with a tape recorder on it. Students who 30 minutes ago were fighting each other with reckless abandonment, were now gathered under one roof. There was a feeling that both sides had something to say, but a strong wind of unpredictability was fanning flames of conflict. Students filled the auditorium seats with the center section remaining empty. The police stood nervously twitching and scanning for any peace disturbers.

Principal Pitman walked to the mic... "Students, we ha... " he started to say, but the booing and other audible words drowned him out. Principal Pitman was a distinguished looking man, molded right out of straightforward disciplined days of old. He had no concept or experience in handling anything like the explosion his school was encountering. He let the interruption ride its course.

"Ok... ok. Students, the time has come for us to discuss our problems and try to resolve them. You all will get your chance to come up to the microphone and tell us how you see things." The administration was making an awkward attempt for students to talk rather than fight. "We want to record this meeting so that other community leaders can hear what you have to say."

The auditorium was full on both sides with the majority of white students being Greasers. The Climbers were more interested in graduating with a good GPA then any social issues the school faced. "Proviso East is a family, and like all families we will have our differences and must work them out," said the principal. This was met with silences interestingly enough. Students of both races had many relationships with each other and some were even good friends, but battle lines had been drawn.

However, there was a certain ambivalent feeling of remorse that the situation escalated to this level so fast. The white students had no idea just how much prejudicial treatment was on the minds of black students. After all, the old saying of, you must be in someone's shoes to actually know how they feel, seemed quite true. Blacks were acutely aware of how white America was. "Leave it to Beaver," "The Beverly Hillbillies," "Gunsmoke," "Bonanza," were all the huge hit TV shows of the time. Yet, black people were nowhere to be found on these programs. It was like they didn't even exist or were not invented yet.

The great American forefathers were great noble men, but they were also great bigots. When American history is taught, prejudicial treatment of blacks is looked upon as a thing of the past, but the harsh truth was, it still was alive and well. The white students never thought about these issues and really weren't aware of them.

"This is just how things are in the world," they were taught. White kids were raised on "Ozzie and Harriet," "Father Knows Best," milk toast America, even the beloved Mouseketeers were truly snow white. Blacks were good for a step'nfecthit, "Yes, sur, masta," zippy do da laugh or a black faced Al Jolson sing'n "Mammy" on his knee. White America always enjoyed the many talents of the Negro race, but from a safe distance. The New York Yankees could have had Willie Mays, Ernie Banks, and Frank Robinson in their line up, but passed them off to the lowly National League. Jim Brown was running rings around the beer gut white linemen of the NFL, and the clumsy, lanky, alabaster NBA was about to be reborn. All this just blew passed the white kids of America, but now in front of the eyes of Proviso East's Caucasian contingent of students, the bitter resentment of racial mistreatment had festered.

"I would ask now that a student from this group please come up to the mic and express any questions or comments you may have," said the principal as he pointed to the black side of the room. Gary Washington, a student with dark skin and green eyes, jumped up and quickly walked to the microphone stand. He was well known in the school as a class clown. "Please state your name," asked Principal Pitman.

"Never mind my name, man," barked Gary.

"Ok, never mind your name," Pitman said as he yielded the podium.

The heckling was starting to get louder each moment, so Washington barked into the mic. "Why do the cops hit the black kids in the heads with their sticks and not the whites?"

"Cuz your head is hard as a coconut," shouted back one of the white students. This remark caused a huge uproar from the white kids and the police were going to show how off the cuff remarks would be treated. Officer Callieno from Broadview's finest bolted over to the student that shouted the quip and grabbed him by his back collar. The officer was small in stature, but soon showed how powerful he was when he yanked the teen right out of his seat and bounced him over three rows backwards. The student was taking a solid pounding as he slammed into each row. The officer then crashed him into the aisle as surrounding officers pounced on the defenseless student like sharks during a feeding frenzy. The police were sending two messages with one swing... no one will heckle, and whites will get a racial equality ass kicking. Everyone's attention was on the student getting carried out like last week's garbage when a familiar voice broke the ramblings.

"I was just out in the hall and there is a lot of blood on the floor." It was Mr. McNeil, a man everyone at the school looked up to, and his presence brought on a sense of embarrassment by both sides. He was a black man that had great attributes; he carried himself as a leader, educated, well groomed and articulate. Boys at Proviso all secretly wanted to become what he was... a man that commands respect regardless of his color. "The blood is red... not black, not white," he continued. "I'm not sure whose blood it is, but I know one thing," he stated as his eyes stared out at the now silent crowd. "It came from a person who believes they are fighting a hated enemy, but the truth is, they are fighting a fellow human being whose only difference is the color of their skin." Mr. McNeil glared across the audience that now seemed to be hanging their heads lower with each powerful word. "Yes, we are black, white, red, yellow or whatever pigment God gave us, but we are human beings first with a common bond, and that bond now lies in red pools in our hallways. Whose blood is it? It's all of ours... the people of this planet that must live together... in peace. Hopefully, we can become educated enough to understand our world better and I pray that you are the first generation to have the wisdom and courage to accomplish this ancient vision."

The passion in his voice drew everyone into a calm drift. A chief was addressing the warriors and his words ran with truth. "We live in a world that has many differences. We must be more sensitive of each other. The better we cultivate knowledge, the better we will communicate and unite. You students and this school must make a stand for all mankind that the days of old are over. War solves nothing. We must move beyond immoral traditions that imprison us and ascend our society to the dream that is within our grasp. I'm reaching out... will you join me... I can't do this alone... I need you... I need all of you... will you join me... " McNeil stood for a moment and the expression on his face gave an affectionate pathos conclusion that no words could convey.

The children of the "New Frontier" sat stunned as they knew they just heard not just a speech, but a prayer, and its answer fell onto their laps. The entire auditorium became suspended in silence as Mr. McNeil turned and walked off the stage. A faint sound of clapping came from the back and like a flowing wave of energy, the entire hall burst into a full ovation. Students from both sides of the aisle stood and applauded the emotional lesson they had just received.

"Good talk, good talk," said The Kid.

"Fuck'n A," remarked Musclehead.

Mr. McNeil's eloquent soliloquy had definitely changed the mood of the teenagers, but no way was one speech going to end the conflict. The microphone stand stood like a solitary soldier awaiting orders. Out of the shadow from the back came a student, Dino Chicanilli, a greaseball and a half from the Little Italy section of Melrose Park. He stood looking out over the masses who were eagerly awaiting his thoughts.

"Ah, what we got here... is a failure to communicate." The hall erupted with immense laughter and yelling. This was a bull's eye of a remark. The line came from the summer's big movie "Cool Hand Luke" and Dino helped ease the situation even more with a good dose of humor. He also made a strong point, for there was very little communication among students, staff, police or the administration. Things just seemed to unfold. There was no plan, no talk about race relations at the school. Everyone had their head in the sand and when your head is buried, it's easy to get your ass kicked.

The Old Kid jumped out of his seat and started pointing his finger at the group of administrators seated on stage. "This is all because of you," he yelled, aiming his finger. "All you people know is how to lay the law down and make rules."

The police had the good sense not to intervene as The Kid walked down the row towards them. Suddenly black students started yelling and pointing in concert with The Old Kid. Words were no longer distinguishable, but the message was loud and clear. Faster than a Koufax fastball, the high and mighty school governing body had now become the scapegoat. Whether the administrators were true geniuses or just dumbfounded, they sat motionless in their chairs. This gave the two opposing forces a new common enemy and a cause to unite together as one with a new focus for their anger.

Principal Pitman walked up to the microphone and announced, "School is called off for today and tomorrow." He was on a roll, as unintentional as it was. The wild cheering declared the students' feelings.

"This is Treeemendous," shouted The Old Kid as he slapped five with every hand in reach.

Somehow this unplanned sequence of events worked perfectly. The bitter contempt eroded away in minutes as students of both colors stood shoulder to shoulder, fist to fist, shouting at their new founded opponent. The administrators gathered the tape recorder and left the stage. The students all took off to the exits to celebrate their mini vacation. The Kid was with Wilbur and Musclehead as they shot out the door into the daylight. This was their first whiff of mace free air in hours.

"Let's go to Lindop and party," said Musclehead.

"We can't," explained Wilbur. "They still have school. AHHHH."

"Miller Meadow then."

"Yeaaahhh!"

The boys walked to the parking lot as police walked about still on the edge. They all saw Mister Mike's Rudy and surprisingly Mike next to it. "Hey, thought you got busted by Moody."

"Nah, the asshole let me go when we got outside. He was so scared he just pushed me away and went in his squad. Let's get some stinko and go to the Meadow."

All the boys were climbing into Rudy when The Kid said, "I will catch up with you later. I'm going back home."

Mike teased in a very high pitched voice, "No, you're not. You're gonna see your best girl... and act like the big... kids." The Kid just smiled and turned for the bus stop.

"Oh, Kid, don't forget tab A into slot B, if she's got her friend, the backdoor it will be... ahhhhhhh!!" yelled Wilbur. The Kid didn't even respond, but walked faster to escape the hecklers. "Shut her down... she's pumping mud... aaaaahhhhh" was the last thing he could hear, as he looked down and saw a crumpled newspaper.

He picked it up and read its unusual font. "The American Nazi" was the banner of the paper with a ripped headline about "The King Coon" and a picture of Martin Luther King next to it. There was a column to the right in bold print. "Jews in the News" had a list of Jewish celebrities and political leaders with a brief description of why they were in the news. "Wow, what hatred some people have," thought The Kid. "They even have a grudge against the Marx Brothers. How crazy is that?" He crumpled the paper and threw it down, realizing that the only people who walked in the parking lot were students and the police. He was now getting a better idea on why the blacks have such issues with the cops. The world, he was finding out, was a big place with skeletons in its closet.

The Kid got home to his gorgeous, orange Goat and slammed all four barrels down the quiet streets of Broadview. He drove towards Michele's house, and for the first time in many hours he started to relax, and pain from the thumping he took began to flash in. He leaned into the mirror to check his look and was shocked at the reflection. His face looked like a 50 cent steak that had been tenderized with a rubber hammer. Scratches raked both cheeks, an imprint of fingers stained his neck, and the hairdo was another story. "This kid needs some grooming," he thought as he pulled his comb through the minefield on top of his head. "My God, I don't wanna scare her to death." He cleaned up the best he could and the GTO peeled out towards his lovely lil fox flame.

The Kid slid his sleigh right up to Michele's two story, Georgian style home. He walked up to the door feeling the mounting pressure of teenage anxiety with each step. My hair is a mess, my face is too blushed, too many zits in too many places, all the usual school boy quaking. The Old Kid knew that the great white hunter must meet and beat his fears or they will beat him. He rapped on the door and it flung open as soon as he stopped. Michele stood in the shadow of the doorway.

"Hey, Michele I wanted to see how you were doing. How you feeling?"

She stayed hidden in the dark, obviously not wanting to be viewed. "Danny, I want to thank you for saving me from those girls. I was in big trouble if you didn't come in."

"Ah, Michele, I was glad I got there in time."

She started to step back to even darker regions of the hallway. "Right now I really don't want you to see me, ok?"

"Why not?" asked The Kid.

"Because I'm marked up and I look awful," she answered.

The Kid peered in the doorway. "You look awful? Look at me! I look like the floor of a taxicab."

"Danny, what happened? Did you get those marks from rescuing me?"

"No, we had another rumble today in the cafeteria. It was wild, but worth it. We got today and tomorrow off."

"I know," she replied. "Proviso is all over the news again. I was watching a press conference 'til a real loud car pulled up."

The Kid smiled. "Where're your parents?" he asked.

"They're at work."

"Well, come on. Go wheel'n with me then."

She stepped even further back into the house. "No way. Not right now. I'm glad you came over. I really wanted to see you, but now you must go."

She started to close the door slowly and The Kid stepped back respecting her wishes. The door was gradually closing when it smacked with a thud. The Kid stuck his work boot in the path.

"Danny, please don't, ok?"

"Michele, I have something to give you... first let me in."

"What? What do you have?"

He pushed the door back at her with steady force and she conceded. How could she deny a guy who probably saved her from a terrible beating, if not her life? The Kid was now inside the doorway, but could only see a silhouette of a girl. He reached out into the shadow and found her chin and lifted it. She remained reluctantly silent. The Kid stepped into the shadow and a glint of soft sunlight sprayed onto Michele's petite face. He told himself not to react and expect anything. She was now in full view and the marks of her brutal beating were clearly apparent. Her eyes were violently puffed with a hue of dark blue circling them like menacing storm clouds. The once perfectly pointed nose now looked unfairly swollen with a reddish band across the bridge. Scratches and cuts raked her angelic face, neck and arms affirming the fierce hatred the attackers felt. The most alarming sight was a disconcerting bald patch on the left side of the scalp, the result of being tossed across the room by her long, satin mane.

"You don't look so bad," exclaimed The Kid in the manner he quietly rehearsed.

"Danny, you're just being sweet as usual, but I look like a nightmare, but it could have been much worse if you and Will didn't barge in. I owe you both."

"Ehh... you just owe me," half joked The Kid. He had had his fill of wonderful Will. Jealousy always lies in wait deep inside a romantic heart and The Kid had a big heart filled with teenage emotions.

"Let's go wheel'n over to Miller Meadow," said The Kid.

"No. I don't wanna go out."

"Michele, you need to go out. Some fresh air will do you good."

The Old Kid knew why she didn't want to go. Her wounds were not something she wanted anyone to see. He tenderly reached her chin up and slowly leaned in to kiss her lips and she closed her sore eyes and met his smoocher.

"Ouch," they both yelped in unison. Their lips were swollen and sore, much more than they realized.

The young lovers both stepped back and laughed. This was the first laugh in a long time for either. Michele's spirits seemed to pick up and she grabbed her jacket and walked out the door.

"Come on, Old Kid, let's blow this pop stand."

The bitterness of the last few days was not enough to erase the power of nature and its courting rituals. These two kids had endured more than their share of the world's problems the past few days, and it was time to celebrate the fact that they were young, alive and full of adolescent energy. These are the days that should fill one's memory museum with adventure and excitement with a dash of danger. The GTO roared its supercharged announcement that The Old Kid was back on the streets with his honeybee at his side.

"Let's go to the Meadow," said The Kid, but his real intention was the remote area of Miller Meadow called "the Love Den." Michele just seemed to be happy to be out and about, reaching over and cranking up the Animals' "We Gotta Get Out of This Place." She knew her appearance was almost scary looking, but she had the character to overcome obstacles, knowing that in life you handle your fears or they handle you.

The Old Kid blasted into the Meadow's extensive parking lot and beelined to the out of sight love den. The air was cool and crisp, but the sun was beaming and trees were on their brilliant, fall color parade. The Kid peered as he noticed Punkwillie's shining silver 396 Nova with its floor waxed BF Goodrich Rally wheels. He hadn't seen the Punk since he went down in a crowd during the Battle of the Cafeteria. He drove up closer and noticed that the Punk was sitting alone, but seemed not to notice The Kid's powerful dual exhaust bellowing.

"Look, it's your friend, Punkwillie," exclaimed Michele. The orange Goat pulled along side the Nova. Just then a head popped up from the Punk's lap.

"Look, it's your friend, Pam." Wham Bam Pam had a surprised look on her face that was quickly replaced with embarrassment, as she wiped her hand across her mouth.

"Hey, Punk, what happened to you? I saw you go down and you got swallowed up."

"Oh, I got carried out by some cops as soon as I hit the floor and they threw me outside." Punk was zipping up as he told his tale. "Some cop told me to wait right there and when he left, so did I."

"I see you're getting a little ahead in life," laughed The Kid as Michele forcefully rammed her elbow into his rib cage. Michele and Pam were communicating telepathically, a gift females have. They knew everything that was going on and about to go on, all this information transmitted in seconds.

"Kid, you look like you've been in a hell of a spar." Michele was hiding from view best she could. She did not want any critiques of her appearance from the Punk. "Hey, we are off four days man... 'til Monday!!!" shouted Punk. Pam was remaining silent and looking in the visor mirror for any missed evidence of love lotion on her face. Punkwillie stuck his head out of the window and hooted, "Hey, let's go downtown to the Kinetic Playground. Otis Redding is playing. Man, it will be hot."

Michele looked at The Old Kid. "I can't go anywhere for awhile. In fact, I'm not even supposed to be here. My parents are way paranoid about what has happened and I'm on a short leash."

The Kid asked, "Are they still pissed at me?"

"Yeah, kind of. They said since you've been around, nothing but bad has happened."

"Well, do they know I saved their daughter from getting waylaid?"

"Yeah, they know, and they are grateful, but my dad is hardcore Dago and he is always pissed about something."

The low rumble of engines was fast approaching the Love Den as all of The Brothers were out in force and a supreme line of American auto muscle was now on display. All chances of any nookie for The Old Kid evaporated like exhaust from a diesel. The only lucky one today was going to be Punkwillie, a guy who The Kid had given up for dead, but instead had two of the three steps for a "Triple Crown." All he needed now was to puke his guts out, and the day was still young.

The little gathering slowly broke up as time ticked by and the supper bell was about to sound. The Old Kid brought his Michele home and dropped her off a block down from her house. They both knew some time had to pass to let her dad, dubbed "The Bambino" (he looked like Babe Ruth, gut and all) to cool off. The lovers kissed and parted with Michele giving The Kid a "you better behave tonight" stare.

Chapter 4
New to Olde Town

The early fall darkness was fast approaching as Lindop Elementary parking lot began to come alive with the growl and rumble of a stampede of horsepower. The past few days had been a pressure filled span of chaos and violence that summon confrontational instincts of pubescent youth. The Brothers were thrusted into a world of social unrest that Huntley and Brinkley even debated. The talk around all of Chicagoland was about the rioting at Proviso. The best thing to do was leave this area where so much attention was focused. How could anyone guzzle down a malt liquor with so many nice guys with ties prying about? The boys piled into Musclehead's stunning, robin eggshell blue GTX and Cuno's raked up 440 Road Runner. Both cars fishtailed out of the lot leaving a rubberized cloud of troubled youth for all the world to see. King B Ron Britain was blasting out of the radio with a perfectly timed "roll up... roll up... to the magical mystery tour... step right this way." The boys were heading to the near north side of Chicago where the new counterculture was taking root. The area of North Wells Street was fast becoming a happening place. The long haired hippies were taking the Beatles' message of self creativities to new heights with new highs. The word was spreading fast that unfamiliar drugs with crazy names were now becoming a fashionable way to get stoned. LSD, angel dust, crystal, kanebinol, reds, Quaaludes, downers, uppers, speed were now appearing in the pockets of fresh faced, Midwestern teens. The Brothers, like all inquisitive kids, wanted to know what the buzz was all about, but were not about to give up their beloved malt stinko. The blacks at Proviso knew all about reefer and the traditional drugs that came out of the Chicago ghettos, but now it seemed like this newly, highly educated generation wanted even more thrills.

The two cars went slowly by the Playboy mansion just north of downtown and all eyes beseechingly stared out at the hopes a bunny might come hopping by. When they got near Wells, they parked and piled out ready to explore this strange, new land. Wells was very busy with people that had a different look about them. The first thing noticed were the bright colors that flashed around the terrain. The lighted store signs, the clothing in the windows and on people in the streets were a brilliant mesh of radiant hues. The air was alive with foreign sounding music from alien instruments. The scent of flavored smoke filled the streets that transformed the quaint neighborhood into a carnival atmosphere. The boys knew they had stumbled into something that was not traditional or even cliché. This was their first glimpse of real hippies and the counterculture they had heard so much about.

"Whoa, take me to your leader," shouted Punkwillie to a beaded freak wearing a purple bandana and a vest covered with flowers. Like explorers in a new world, the boys gathered into a tight gang formation letting the locals know this group had the numbers. There was a complete absence of hostility or danger on the street, something that was quite foreign to the visiting Brothers. Chicago is comprised of a tapestry of ethnic neighborhoods that are tightly bound. All outsiders are quickly noticed and given warning glares of trespassing.

"I'm picking up my first hippie vibe," said Musclehead staring at a poster that simply read PEACE. "I want peace. I want piece of ass from a hippie babe."

The group of adventurers all laughed and started yelling at a group of long haired girls across the street. "Piece... we want piece... give us a piece." The long haired girls all turned around to reveal it was a group of three guys and one babe.

"Yikes! Forget it," shouted Mister Mike.

The boys noticed that they quickly drew more attention than needed. Nice guys with ties starting appearing out of doorways, peering at the noisy boys. There was a strong presence of either narcs or G-men dressed in the wrong undercover clothes.

The boys made their way to a store called "Stick it in your Ear." The bizarre music they had heard was coming from there and curiosity sent them in. The walls of the establishment were collections of paintings and posters with a wide variety of subjects. Flowers, people, monsters, planets, slogans like "Make Love Not War" all decorated the store. The boys found the source of the strange music- a small group of musicians playing sitar and other exotic drums. None of The Brothers said much as they were taken by a world and culture that was hard to realize. This was the American Midwest and traditional values are the doctrine. All this colorful nonsense was hard to digest. The Old Kid bent over a glass display case that featured a huge assortment of little handcrafted pipes and cigarette papers. The clerk was lighting a stick of incense that gave the messy store a scent of perfumed smoke.

"What are all these pipes for?"

The long haired, hippie babe behind the counter just smiled and sang, "Go ask Alice, when she's ten feet tall." The Kid's look told of his confusion and the long fleeced honey pointed to a black light poster that had a message: THE ONLY THING I SMOKE ARE MY TIRES AND THE ONLY THING I POP IS MY CLUTCH. "This you man?" asked the hippie babe. The Kid just looked at her. He knew he didn't speak the lingo of this new world order.

Punkwillie and Wilbur walked into the back alleyway that seemed to connect all the stores and music clubs. There was a huge jukebox with a freaky looking man leaning on it. "Welcome lads... I'm the Pope of the Serengeti... anything you want I have... if I don't have it... I can get it... if I can't get it... you don't need it!" Wilbur looked at the huge glowing jukebox and noticed it only had one song on it: A-7 "The Hurdy Gurdy Man" by Donovan.

"Hi, Pope. I'm the Punk of Chicago and the only thing I need is a good time."

"Punk, my boy, the Pope can provide your ride to the stars and back."

"Sign me up, Pope."

The Pope started scouting the area for nice guys with ties. "Do you want a nickel bag or a lid of Panama Red? For the first time Punkwillie finally understood what the conversation was about. Now came the big decision. The Brothers were very leery of drugs and anything that seemed too un-American, and this hippie scene was a real 180 from their salt of the earth world. "The Pope gives hope and has the dope for a real magic carpet ride," said the weirdo dressed all in white sheets and an Arabian sheik scarf headdress.

"Ok, we are buying a ticket," exclaimed the Punk as he looked at Wilbur for approval. Wilbur not only approved, but started digging deep into his pockets for five Washingtons. The exchange was made and as the two youths headed back to join their mates, Punkwillie glanced back over his shoulder to get one more look at the Pope, but he had disappeared into the night.

"Hey, my Bo Shams, take a look at what we got," Wilbur said waving a clear plastic bag of wackie tabaccie.

The Old Kid grabbed it and quickly stashed it in his pocket. "Why not shoot off some flares, too, so all the cops know."

The hippie honey behind the counter clacked down a smoking pipe. "You'll need one of these, boys, unless you can roll a dovetail joint." The Kid whipped around and threw out the required coin for the little pipe with a bowl cut out of dice. How fast things can change in the big city. The boys all grouped together and went back into their awaiting wheels.

"Let's go see Otis Redding now," shouted Cuno "and smoke this stuff there."

The lads had nervous smiles as they hastily drove up farther north on Wells turning for North Clark Street, home of the Kinetic Playground. This is just what The Brothers needed- some more, good old, law breaking fun to help relieve the bitter tension of the rioting.

The Kinetic Playground was a medium size music club that was situated about three blocks north of the infamous St. Valentine's Day Massacre, one of Chicago's historic gangland sites from the prohibition days where Al Capone let Bugs Moran know who was boss. The north side of Chicago had a little more stability in its neighborhoods than the south side. There was still plenty of danger lurking about, but white kids were not open targets. The south and west sides of Chicago had become no mans land for any Caucasian. The north with its Wrigley field and Lincoln Park Zoo still held hope for Chicago to stay diversified. Not all the white families had run to the suburbs. The Kinetic Playground was fast becoming the "in" place to be.

The underground music scene was quickly emerging with bands that had an edge. Songs that lasted 17 minutes like Iron Butterfly's "Inagoddadivita" or the fast tempo, acid rock of Blue Cheer were played. AM radio was not ready to handle this artistic revolution and FM belonged to the rich with their classical music stations. The only exposure the new music was getting in Chicago came from Punkwillie's DJ hero, King B. Ron Britain hosted a show called "Subterrain Circus" on Sunday nights playing acts like whiskey-voiced Janis Joplin or psychedelic god, Jimi Hendrix. The Kinetic Playground gave these new acts a venue that mirrored New York's Electric Circus and San Francisco's Fillmore.

The Brothers had parked in the back of the club and tried to pile into Musclehead's GTX. The Old Kid pulled out the newly purchased reefer and filled the cool little dice pipe. The boys all knew about weed and how your supposed to smoke it, but they soon realized it took a little practice as each one took too strong of a hit and coughed it out. This was breaking into a new experience for the gang of thrill seekers. They took a hit and passed the pipe through and around the car. Everyone took his turn except for Mister Mike whose redneck manners and attitude kept him from smoking the piece pipe.

"You're all going to be long haired, hippie communists now, aren't you?" he asked. "This shit will shrink your balls and make you love men."

"Whoa, Mike," injected Punkwillie. "Back it up, bro. We just wanna see what the buzz is all about. Besides, I don't think we could love a man unless you sprout a nice set of cones. Then your mine, brother!" This made everyone laugh and cough out loud.

"Hey, man, let's go inside, man," said Chief. The boys got in line in front of the club. Their mood changed as they paid the five bucks to get in. The reefer was working its magic and a new sensation was now clouding the young fertile minds, except for Mike who chugged a malt liquor in seven seconds.

"Whew I'm hearing some tunes like never before," stated The Old Kid.

"Yeah," chimed Cuno. "It's like I got headphones on."

The boys walked through the lobby and ducked under a screen that led into the main section of the Playground. Once again the boys' senses were bombarded with a new experience. The shock of an assemblage of multi media the likes of which they'd never seen before stood in front of the now stoned and beautiful boys. The screen they had to duck under was one of a full circle that completely surrounded the main club floor. The screens all displayed huge images of movies or slides. Film of two naked people hugging was on one, while slides of soldiers fighting in Viet Nam filled the other screen. There was a gel that was pulsated and pressed between panes of glass shown on a giant overhead projector that gave a rainbow of colors and designs. Music by The Quicksilver Messenger Band was being resoundingly pumped in through speakers that seemed to cover the entire roof. Strobe lights that measured nearly six feet long hung lengthwise just below the speakers and blasted radiant illuminations of light that made everything flicker. To make the atmosphere even more abstract, small weights were placed inside beach balls to make them spin out of balance. When the strobes kicked in and a lopsided beach ball was coming at you, it was impossible to catch.

The crowd was a wide range of young people from filthy rich brats to homeless hippies all dancing and walking around with pharmaceutical smiles.

"This kid is sky high," exclaimed The Old Kid.

"These hippies sure know how to party," said Cuno. "I want this in my basement."

The boys stood there taking in the brave new world they had come across. The new aura of reefer and the playground just banged the gang hard in the senses. They all started to split up and explore the dwelling even more. The Old Kid and Mister Mike ducked back out under the movie screen to get a break from the bombardment. They noticed little structures throughout the club on the floor. The purpose of these little igloos was just what the two lads were seeking- a time out from the festive commotion. They walked up to one of the little white oases and stuck their heads in, just as a skinny, morbid looking man began sticking a needle and squeezing an immoral looking brown swill into his bulging arm vein. Mister Mike just squinted his eyes and looked at The Kid with disgust on his face. Two girls were laying folded over one wearing no pants, obviously wiped out of their minds.

A guy in the corner was doing a handstand and said, "Welcome my friends, come ride the serpent."

"Fuck you, hippie" yelled Mike who then beer belched his way out of the door.

The Kid followed as they cautiously peeked into a neighboring igloo. There was a poker game going on with six people. In the corner of this tent, a girl was wildly balling a guy and passionately kissing another girl.

"Free love... free love," yelled Mister Mike.

"Come in, boys, the water is fine," said the dude pounding away. Harmony will do you both."

"Really?" asked The Kid. Harmony was way too busy to respond or even care what the hell was going on.

"Let's go for it, Kid," yiped Mike. "I'm bad desert gut."

"Go ahead," said The Kid. "I'm not watching your naked dead ass humping. Besides, she's probably got every disease known to man."

"Kid, you can really kill a buzz," replied Mister Mike knowing The Kid was full right. Just then the balling dude flipped his hippie honey on her tummy and began to slide the salami up her dirt road. "Whoa man... buck that bronco... hi-ho-silver," cheerleaded Mister Mike.

Punkwillie came up to join his friends and stuck his head in the tiny room and witnessed the rear-ending. "God damn! Shut her down, she's pump'n mud, she's pumping mud!

Cuno and Musclehead came crashing in and now the oasis became hell with too many bodies. "Let me see! Let me see!" yelled Musclehead and, like the young bull he was, he unintentionally pushed all his pals onto the high hippies. The stoned dude just fell over as the three lovers screamed protest. The dude doing a headstand fell onto the pile like a human Jenga piece.

"Hey, is this an orgy, man?" yelled Mister Mike.

"Stop squeezing my boob, dude," yelled Harmony trying to push her way out of the mess. "You're a rude dude," she snapped at Musclehead who was grabbing at her breast like an enraged rhino.

Suddenly, a loud cheer came from the main room as the record stopped. "Damn," said The Kid. "It's Otis Redding I bet." Now the human bowl of spaghetti was scrambling to get out the door of the igloo and back onto the dance floor.

The boys regrouped on the fly and ducked their heads back under the movie screens just as the stage lights came beaming down. The loud cadence of a steady back beat in 4/4 time came booming, as the small crowd rushed to the stage. Then, like a cosmic blast, a figure of a large man came flying out into the bright glare of the lights. The roar of the crowd sent a shock wave that bounced off the ceiling of the Kinetic Playground. Otis Redding, a magnificent looking man wearing a fire-truck red jacket with dark chartreuse pants came bounding across the stage pumping a microphone and pumping up the crowd. If James Brown was the Godfather of soul, Otis Redding was its King. The man oozed charisma and showmanship. His voice and songs he wrote blended into a perfect illustration of the new, modern style of rhythm and blues. He had the crowd in his palm before the band hit their fifth measure.

The Brothers all had beaming smiles as Otis hit the first verse of "Respect." They wanted a night of fun and excitement and in this newly discovered world they were getting more than hoped. The terrible events that transpired only 12 hours earlier at Proviso had quickly evaporated. The stage was only two feet off the ground. You could feel the sweat of Otis Redding as he gaited across, working the crowd into their own sweat.

"This guy is treeemendous," shouted The Old Kid as he slapped five with Chief.

"Hey, man, this guy is working it, man."

The Hams, who is never really satisfied or happy, started complaining how hungry he was. "What's the matter, Hams? You got the munchies, you hippie?" yelled Mister Mike.

Otis was hitting on all cylinders. His name was spreading fast since the Monterey Pop Festival three months earlier as one hell of an artist. The band segued into the next three songs with no breaks. The King of Soul was singing his heart out with each song that might have changed tempo, but not mood. After an energetic set, Cream came out to join for an encore with Eric Clapton's version of "Killing Floor Blues." The sense that this crowd was truly lucky seemed to prevail. Anyone with any intelligence could see that this new music was not going to be contained by a little club like the Playground for long. The playbill for tonight and the following weeks was posted above the stage with its Peter Max artwork, heralding the coming of the new culture like Roman tribunes: "Tonite only-- Otis Redding with blues legend Muddy Waters and Cream! Next weekend Big Brother and the Holding Company with Janis Joplin, Led Zeppelin, The Byrds. Special guest-- The Doors... $5.00. The night went merrily on as the boys unknowingly witnessed music history before their eyes.

The lads had seen enough of the underground thing, and when the fresh fall night air hit their faces two thoughts came forward.

"Let's grab some grub," shouted The Hams.

"Let's grab some nookie," retorted Cuno.

After some huddling up, a game plan was in order. If you're hungry, go with Musclehead's GTX. If you're horny, get with Cuno's Road Runner. Punkwillie grabbed a half empty bottle of Ripple from the GTX and guzzled it. He still needed a 4th degree to claim a Triple Crown and by God he was going to do it.

The two rides split up with Cuno's group head'n back to the Olde Town area. "I know this hooker my brother told me about called Lady Madonna," said Cuno. "She's supposed to hang around some joint called 'The Bird Cage' off Wells."

Chicago is a city that has many neighborhoods that are actually their own worlds. When you go to an area like Rush Street or Olde Town that are popular, you are relatively safe, but you venture even one block in the wrong direction and you quickly find out just how dangerous a big city can be. The boys in the Road Runner felt secure and ready to handle any trouble that came their way, even though they knew they were unarmed and most people in these neighborhoods were packing. Nature has a cruel way of mass injecting young juveniles with hormones that dominate their minds. Teenage boys will follow any path that leads them to a possible release of this controlling behavior. Risking one's life is a small price to pay to find a female that will answer their musk. The Road Runner rumbled around the Olde Town district that still had plenty of life in the midnight hour.

"Whoa, check out the talent over there," stated The Old Kid as he pointed to a black woman dressed in a higher-than-high cut skirt with spiked heels that were engineering marvels.

"I think that's her," shouted an excited Cuno. There were other obvious hookers in sight, but this girl stood out like a diamond in a coal bucket. Hookers have a built in radar and know when tricks are sizing them up. Cuno pulled up to the sultry vixen who looked into the car and pointed around the corner. "That's her for sure my bo shams."

Mister Mike rolled his window down as the car parked in a dark section of street. "Are you Lady Madonna?" he immaturely asked.

"Sugar, you can call me anything you like," she said waving them to a rundown apartment that had absolutely no light coming from it. When a teenage boy's testosterone kicks in, all bets are off. The boys piled out of the car like they were going to a Sunday picnic. No matter they were in a high crime area where homicides and other assorted felonies were daily occurrences. No matter they were completely out gunned and out numbered. No matter they were about to enter a decrepit building with rats the size of dogs that scurried about in its cracks and crevices. A voluptuous Pied Piper was leading them to a land of enchantment filled with sexual wonders and that's all that really mattered.

Lady Madonna went up the front stoop and opened the door to the Land of Oz. The boys hotly pursued the whore's trail. Once inside, the group of teens had yet another world of exploration before them. This world was far more different then anything they had ever imagined. The staircase leading up to the upper floors was occupied with black hookers and their drunk johns.

Lady Madonna was signaling the boys to follow her up the stairs and the suddenly apprehensive males started to snake their way up. The Old Kid looked around as an infused odor of dirt, cheap perfume, and booze blended with the cigarette-choked air. There was amazingly very little sound coming from the couples strewn on the stairwell; grunts and groans from the stinkoed white businessmen who all seemed to have wedding bands, and sexual murmuring from the prostitutes. The hallway had big red lights glaring down that mixed with the dingy air making it all look like a scene from hell itself.

The Kid watched as a hooker spread her legs and instead of taking off her panty hose, she burned a slit down her crotch with a lit cigarette. "For twenty more dollars I's can make it better, honey," she told the chump client of hers. Another hooker further up the stairs was gargling rubbing alcohol in preparation for a blowjob to a sailor slamming down the last of his Rock and Rye.

"This is the second time tonight I've seen somebody having sex and it's not me. A disturbing trend," noted Mike.

Lady Madonna must have been someone of distinction as she had a room of her own on the second floor. Her dwellings looked like a surreal Salvador Dali painting-- purple lights in the lamps, with clothes and underwear of all shapes and sizes lying about.

"Hey, man, smells like the ocean," cited Chief. "All the salt air."

"That ain't the ocean you're smelling, Chief. It's spooey," answered The Kid. The look on the Chief's face said more than the Bible.

Lady Madonna lit a cigarette and gave the boys an eyeballing. "Ok, boys, fifteen dollars each for some head cuz I don't fuck and I don't care what you say bout it." This was the first real look the lads got at this mysterious women and she was surprisingly quite pretty.

"Damn, you look like Dianna Ross," said Mike. "I'm first... I'm first," as he pulled out a crumpled pile of moola and flipped out fifteen legal tenders.

"Let's go in the bedroom, sugar, and make some magic." Madonna grabbed Mister Mike by the hand as the bedroom door closed like a lid on a casket.

"Damn, this place smells like an upside down outhouse. Phewww," complain The Kid.

The boys in waiting had all noticed at the same time that the bedroom door had creaked open a hair. They all gave each other a mischievous glance and crept a little closer. The voyeuristic power of a teenage male could fuel the world for an eternity, and this magical power had the boys in its spell. What vision lay just through the tiny door slit? Per chance a view of oral pleasure with its gratuitous depravity and ingested contortions. The boys all peered in the narrow crack and scanned the room's dark, foreboding features. They could barely make out an outline of two figures silhouetted against a dimly lit nightlight. Their night vision was coming into focus as the layers of darkness melted away. The sight of Lady Madonna on her knees and Mister Mike sprawled on a bed like an open umbrella, quenched the thirst of curious eyes. Neither the busy Madonna nor the moaning Mister Mike noticed the intrusive onlookers and their squelching giggles.

BAM... BAM... two loud bursts blasted from the outside hallway shattering the exotic mood into a quick rash of panic. Intense screaming then filled the whorehouse. "You crazy mother fuck'n bitch," yelled an angry black man's voice. The bedroom door flew open and Lady Madonna bolted out towards the hallway and looked down the steamy stairwell.

"Stop that crazy shit," she yelled down the stairs.

"Shut up, bitch, and mind your own business," came the wild reply.

Mister Mike came limping out pulling his pants up as best he could. "Shit, I think some idiot is shooting the place up." Screams came whaling up as if from the depths of hell. The hooker that was with the sailor was getting a pistol whipping from her pimp, and he just started shooting aimlessly into the air.

"Let's get the fuck out of here!" yelled The Kid. The boys ran for a backdoor that had more locks on it than Fort Knox.

"Hey, you boys, don't go. Get back... get your asses back here!" Madonna shouted.

Mister Mike finally got the door unlocked and the lads took a collective glance over their shoulders at the shrieking slut. Not long ago the boys were doing everything in their power to get with this woman, and now they were doing everything in their power to get away from her! They jumped down the stairs as the screams and ruckus from the beating resonated from the two-story dump.

The teens reached the safety of the ground when a loud and growing growl came rushing up. The shadow of a dark beast lunged out, lashing at The Chief. "Hey, man, it's a dog, man." Chief threw a defending arm in the path of a mouthful of vexed fangs. The dog was huge and knocked down its victim with little effort, then started to shake its head violently to shred the meat of the quarry. The Old Kid with his engineer boots kicked the attacking animal in the side with a blow that made a loud cracking sound. The beast squealed with a shriek that only a broken rib cage can produce. The animal rolled over and gave out high-pitched yips as the boys picked up their fallen comrade. Once again they found themselves dealing with another army of locks with the backyard gate. "Hey, man, that thing took a chunk out of me, man." The Chief held his arm out.

"Nah... your leather protected you. Your coat is ripped, but I don't see blood."

Finally, the rusted fence way opened and the intrepid lads made their way back to the car for a fast drive to beautiful Broadview. The hemi-powered Road Runner roared down Roosevelt Road and fishtailed into the Lindop school lot. The rest of the gang was all there outside and all cheering. Cuno's crowd piled out of the Chrysler to see what was up. "Go-go-go-go" was the chant as The Old Kid broke through the gathered circle. Punkwillie was bent over with a bottle of Boone's Farm strawberry wine in his hand.

"He's trying to hit 4th degree so he can have a triple crown!" cried out Johnny Hams.

Punk raised the bottle and guzzled down the gut rot as he stumbled and staggered around in a small circle. The young Vikings shouted their encouragement with advocating cheers as the fully-stinkoed brother gave a glassy-eyed smile. "Kid... kid..." mumbled Punk trying to look in The Old Kids direction. "I remember telling you to slow down... slooow dooown," rambled the plastered Punk.

This statement caused a huge uproar from the rest of the tuffs. "Punks drunk," said Musclehead. "Come on, hit 4th! Hit it!"

Suddenly, three squad cars came squealing around the corner and flying into the parking lot. The patrol cars all trained their airplane landing floodlights on the rowdy teens. "It's the Moody patrol, man," yelled Chief. The boys formed a human wall to shield the stooped over Punkwillie. Moody got out of his roller as did the Chief of Police, Donn George.

"What the hell are you boys doing?" inquired Officer Moody as he peered at The Old Kid. "Don't you know every cop is out tonight on riot patrol?"

Donn George knew all these boys since they ditched kindergarten. He was a tall man that had the respect of the community, a community that was now scared of what the future could bring. Captain George had to not only keep the peace, but keep paranoia from taking over the town. He walked up to the line of boys now fully illuminated from the searchlights. He could hear the obtuse sounds of an unstable being.

"What the hell is this?" he roared as he plowed through the boys. "What the hell is he doing?" he demanded pointing at a kneeling Punkwillie.

"Ah, he's trying to hit 4th degree," wisecracked Mister Mike as the boys all howled with laughter.

Chief Donn George was not remotely amused as he walked over to the slumped over boy. "Have you been drinking, son?" asked the peeved cop.

There was little movement from the Punk, only a quiet murmuring of "slooow dooown, slooow dooown." Punk thought he was still in a car and wanted the driver to slow down, because the excess speed was making him sick.

The top cop pulled the punk's head up by the hair and then noticed the almost empty wine bottle between his legs. "Ok, my little friend, you're going in."

This seemed to have given Punkwillie a sober slap as he looked at Chief Donn George and said, "I'm not drunk... I swear... George Donn."

Broadview's Captain of Patrol let go of the boy's hair and the teen lapsed into a heap of wasted youth. Officer Moody started to walk over to assist and gave a shove into the shoulder of The Old Kid. Just then another plain, unmarked car came zooming into the lot with a dash mounted, red light twirling. The door flew opened and out came four "nice guys with ties."

"Chief, we have three car loads of Black Panthers cruising around Walgreens," said one of the necktied gentlemen.

Donn George whirled around and ordered the boys to "Get your asses and that drunken li'l bastard home." The Chief of Police then got back in his car and, faster than a fairy fart, they were gone.

The boys stood there in the silence of the night, when an inhuman sound started to emanate from the heap of wasted youth. "ERRRRRRR...... AHHHHHH." Punkwillie had hit 4th degree with a vengeance reserved only for cataclysmic volcano eruptions and earthquakes of Biblical proportions. The lot spun around and a loud cheer filled the chilled air with each and every gut-spasmic blast the young punk internally offered. The glorious goal of nookie, duking and puking had been achieved by the Punk for his honor of a "Triple Crown." All glories were his! His friends shared in his accomplishment with a boisterous rendition of the Italian opera song "Santa Lucia." The police weren't coming back, they had bigger fish to fry, so the boys all merrily belted out like the puerile tenors they were.

"Santa... Lucia... Santa... Lucia... " standing in a circle paying homage to the pile of drunken debris know as Punkwillie.

"One last cheer," shouted Cuno. They all chimed in with "Silly Willy... thought shit was chili... so he order himself a bowl... YEAHHHHH!!!" Surely the gods smiled down on this crazy club known as The Brothers. After delivering the four sheets to the wind Punk to his parents' tepee, the long, turbulent day and adventurous night finally ended for the warriors.

Chapter 5
Death in the Classroom

The next few days at Proviso went surprisingly well and no real trouble came to focus. The boys were back to the wacky world of "friendly Mel's," "firing homelies" and celebrating "chomps" from their grub. The one major difference was the considerable absence of white girls. Parents were not about to gamble with their snow-white princesses, so off to the private schools they went. The lil foxes held their ground and stayed at Proviso, including brave Michele whose battle scars mended better than hoped. Her angelic glow was returning and she received no threats or intimidation from black girls. There weren't exactly waves of amicableness extended her way, but she had paid her dues. The fact she returned to Proviso seemed to gain her creditability among all students. The school seemed as resilient as the tough teens that attended the hallowed halls.

The only incident of any real prominence came when the mischievous Punkwillie had his geology teacher, Mr. Bolt, drop dead in class. Seems the punk brat came in fashionably late as usual and the 65 year old teacher had all the pranks he was going to take. There was a big test he was handing out and would not give Punkwillie one. "You do not deserve to take this test. You're not part of this class. You're either tardy or not here," he shouted disparagingly at the black leathered, white jeaned teen. Mr. Bolt hurriedly passed out the test booklet to the other students and walked up to the front of the room and gave an icy stare in the general direction of the uncaring Punk.

While the students quietly took their exam, the room's peaceful ambience was intermittently interrupted by the flicking of the Chicago Tribune's sports pages. The Chicago Bears had beaten the Green Bay Packers and Proviso's alumni Ed O' Bradovich had a key interception. Punkwillie was reading every word of every article about the solid thumping his beloved Monsters of the Midway dished out. He came out of his frenzied state when he peered over the top of the paper and noticed Mr. Bolt had become beet red. "Wow," he thought "the old timer is still steaming at me. Hope he gets over it soon."

Suddenly, Mr. Bolt bolted for the door as a strange gurgling sound emanated from the teacher. He then seemed to stumble, and slammed hard into the antique wood and windowpane door. The elderly man then slowly slid down the door as blood began to flow out of his mouth and nose. He had punctured a lung and now was drowning in his own blood.

When Mr. Bolt hit the tiled floor, a female student stood up and started to scream so hard and violently she threw up. Punkwillie jumped to his feet and ran over to the slumped teacher who was now blocking the doorway. The Punk sprung a leap over the unconscious man and galloped into the hallway at full speed heading for the nurse's office. The hall monitors quickly noticed the running kid zipping through the hall and began to chase him. The geology class was at the opposite end of the school from the nurse's office and the corridor was nearly one block long. The longer the Punk ran, the more hall monitors joined in the chase. There was now an elongated string of students of all shapes and sizes trailing and yelling "halt" commands to the speedy Punkwillie.

Teachers from the lounge who heard the commotion also mixed in, as well as two security cops. Neither group had any idea why they were after a student.

Punk possessed a good set of wheels and no one had gained on him as he made a 90 degree turn for the nurse's door. He shot in like a greasy bullet and rammed into the nurse's desk and with an out of breath statement he yelled, "Mr. Bolt has collapsed to the floor and blood is pouring out of his face."

The nurse stood up and barely got out, "What room?" when the door flew open again and a long collection of pupils, police and preceptors came crashing in like the Keystone Cops. They finally caught up with the track star only to find he was on a mercy mission and no apprehension was warranted. The nurse calmly collected equipment into a bag and told everyone but Punkwillie to leave. She then called for an ambulance and told Punk to watch her office and quickly disappeared with the escorting police. The nurse's station became empty just as fast as it had become full.

Punkwillie sat behind the desk and did what every red blooded, nosey teen would do-- go through the drawers. He found a pamphlet on "Health issues of the menstrual cycle." He flicked the pages and checked out the illustrations of a young girl's vagina and thought, "Wow, all the energy guys put in to get to one of those and look at it. It looks like a venus fly trap... ready to trap my fly, ha!" He turned the page to a photo of "extreme bleeding scenario" and all sexual excitement came to a screeching halt. The pamphlet was slung back into the drawer like a used tampon.

The events of the morning were now being realized by the lad and remorse started to set in as the Punk knew that he played a role in getting the old teacher to vapor lock. The siren of an ambulance was heard rushing towards the school as the phone rang. The Punk answered the phone to find out it was an overbearing mom asking why her daughter wasn't allowed to take her medicine. She thought the boy was the school doctor and Punk thought to himself, "Gee, Dr. Punkwillie, M.D." "Can you hold, please?" asked Dr. Willie, M.D. Then he hung up the phone. He had this medical profession down. The phone rang again and the doctor turned the ringing volume down to zero. "This is easy stuff," he thought as he now began to search into a gray, standing filing cabinet and, as luck would have it, he came across students' health folders. There were just too many to actually take any real time to explore, so he thumbed his way through for names of students he might recognize. "Hmmm, Jose Garcia is a hemophiliac. Wow," thought the Punk, "Jose likes guys!"

He was about to pull out a huge file on Wam Bam Pam when he heard footsteps coming fast. The door flung open just as he closed the cabinet and it was the school nurse, Miss Stinger, aka Miss Stinger... Miss Stinger... with such cold, cold fingers. "Well, son, I'm sorry, but poor Mr. Bolt did not make it I'm afraid." Punk's first thought was if he was going to be charged with murder or being the reason his teacher blew a gasket, if there was such a crime. The compassion in the nurse's eyes told him he was not in trouble with the law and he quickly transformed his face into the mourning student who maybe should be sent home. The nurse walked over to him for what he thought was going to be a comforting hand, but instead she handed him some paper towels.

"Could you clean up the mess in the doorway? The janitor is too afraid and upset to do it."

Punk robotically took the towels while thinking, "Maybe this is my punishment for my deed" and started back to the classroom. He made it about halfway down the hall where there are doors and a driveway and when he got to the driveway the paramedics had just arrived. They were just about to load a big collapsible stretcher that had a body covered in a white sheet. Punkwillie stood there and looked at what a short time ago was his first period teacher and now a ghostly corpse. The men raised the carriage up and a strong gust of fall wind shot by and lifted the white sheet just enough for the punk kid to see his dead instructor. "Wow, look how blue his face is... yuck! Maybe he should have let me take the test after all." He started walking again and reached the doorway of his classroom. The kids and teachers from adjoining rooms sat there watching in an eerie silence. Punk noticed that none of his classmates were anywhere in sight. He looked down at the door's threshold and a disgusting puddle of blood and chalk laid there like demonic soup. The Punk bent down and used the paper towels to clean up the vile pile of unsightly evidence.

He threw the soaked, ragged paper in the trash just as a security cop came up. "Where are the rest of students?" asked Punk.

"We sent them home," answered the cop in his usual 'screw you' voice.

"I want to go home, too" said the unconvincing, mourning student.

"No, we may want to question you later. All the students said you're the last one he spoke to."

The Punkyboy just stood there with thoughts of doing hard time yet! The bell clanged sounding the end of the first and last period of a man's life. Punkwillie turned and went upstairs to his second period math class. The halls were abuzz with the sad news about Mr. Bolt and rumors started immediately that Punkwillie had dark powers from hell-- that Mr. Bolt scolded him and dropped dead on the spot.

When the Punk walked into his math class, the stories had already preceded him. His math teacher was a meek, geek of a man and walked up to the supposedly distraught student. "What happened to Mr. Bolt," asked the teacher.

Punkwillie looked at him in the eye and stated with a Bogart smirk, "My first period teacher died in class, and I'm trying for a perfect day!" The bewildered look on the math teacher's face gave a summation of 'all hope is lost for this young soul.' Teenagers use a different part of their brain than adults for basic thinking. Clearly Punkwillie had found a dark corner in his and that is where he dealt with these tragic events.

Chapter 6
Chumps, Suckers and Thieves

After such a troublesome beginning to the school year, the climate in Proviso had calmed down and the placidity of the daily routine settled in. Something is to be said for the rut! The football team had a good year beating archrival Oak Park, only to get trounced by New Trier in the playoffs. The Brothers also had become acclimated to the daily grind of higher education. Cuno was convinced he was a high rolling gambler and started to play some action on parlay cards. The cards, though illegal, were quite easy to obtain. Mister Mike's older brother, Bill, worked as a mutual man at the local horse race tracks and had all the connections needed to make sport bets.

When dealing with anything even slightly illicit in the Chicagoland area, you are playing with fire because the capital of organized crime in America is the windy city on the lake. In Chicago if you have the money, you can beat any rap or trouble you get into. Vinnie Calabrese, a student at Proviso, had a fender bender in his hometown of Melrose Park. Vinnie got out of his car and started yelling at the middle-aged man who accidentally swiped his Vette. The middle-aged driver wasn't about to take crap from no 17 year old greaseball and got out of his car. Vinnie pulled out a 38 snub nose gun and shot the poor guy dead. Turns out, Vinnie's dad was well connected with the mob and beat the charge of first degree manslaughter with a defense of self defense.

The middle-aged man and father of two had no weapon and, according to witnesses, didn't seem remotely hostile to the teen. He just wanted to get things settled down and file his insurance claim for a lousy fender bender.

The city of Chicago is often referred to as "the City that Works" and it can work wonders if you're connected. The mob, whose roots in Chicago were well entrenched before Al Capone came on the scene, has one basic rule of control... Terror! You can rule the roost if you use force and excessive intimidation. The mob in Chicago was ruled by terrifying men like Sam DeStefano who liked to use blowtorches on his enemies. The Brothers had seen an old Capone hit man, Tony (Big Tuna) Accardo. He ate a late night Sunday dinner at a pancake house near Miller Meadow. The Brothers would go in for a bite to eat and were warned by the waitress to watch their manners because that slightly built, elderly gentlemen peacefully sitting with his family is responsible for over 500 deaths and convicted of none. The boys were on their best behavior, but couldn't help but notice how many tables had "nice guys with ties" eating their pancakes and watching the mob boss. Cuno's little gambling venture had tipped his toe into a sea filled with menacing sharks and there is no life guard on duty... ever!

No city in America loves it sports teams like Chicagoans. The Cubs and Sox have combined for over 150 years and no World Championships. Yet fans sit on the roof across the street of Wrigley Field and Sox fans venture into some of the most dangerous ghettos just to watch their beloved losers. The Bears are a charter member of the NFL and it was their owner, George Halas, who organized it and gave it a business plan that is still in affect today. The Blackhawks sellout most of their hockey dates, and the new kids on the block, the Bulls, have a strong following as well. Listed in "Ripley's Believe or Not" is a story that Chicago has two horse tracks that sit side by side. Amazing, as it seems, the story is true. Hawthorne and Sportsmen Park are literally neighbors. One track operates in the day, the other at night. Chicago offers little in the way of scenic nature beauty, but is a horn-o-plenty for sport fans and bookies.

Cuno, a kid that is always on the excitable side of life, is sometimes called "Mr. Excitement." He likes his action and gambling fuels his flame. While the boys are out drinking and fox hunting, Cuno prefers a room full of smoke, stale pizza, cheap whiskey, even cheaper girls, and a poker table decorated with assorted chumps, suckers and thieves. This is what Mr. Excitement found exciting!

Cuno and Mike sat in the front yard of Mike's three flat filling out their football parlay cards. The minimum bet was a five dollar, three team wager. "I like the Colts getting three against the Rams. Johnny U is back healthy. They're a lock," Cuno proclaimed as he scanned his 3 x 4 card.

"I dunno, I think the Browns are the lock. Jim Brown is going to tear up the Steelers as usual and I only have to lay six points," retorted Mister Mike.

Both boys filled out the rest of their gambling guess work as a Ford 1/2 ton pick up pulled up and hurriedly parked. Mike's sister, Maureen, a blonde beauty, got out with her boyfriend, Ike. "Hey guys how goes it?" said Ike who was very tall and thin, and was the picture of health.

"Gonna bust the bank with my picks," said Cuno as he handed Mike his card and a small wad of greenbacks.

"Whoa, Cun, how much you giving me?" asked Mike as he flipped through the dollar bills.

"$75. Make sure you tell your brother so he remembers." Mike's older brother, Bill, supplied the cards and turned in all the bets (supposedly) to his bookmaking friends, but he would bankroll a player if he felt the card was a for-sure loser.

Ike turned around and grabbed his baseball mitt from the back of his pick up. "Hey, who wants to fire me some heat?"

"I will," said Mike who ran in and ran just as fast back out with a mitt that looked like a glove Daniel Boone threw away. Ike was a great pitcher in his high school days, but like most great high school hurlers he blew his arm out throwing the curve-ball. WHAM! The ball smacked into Mike's worn glove so fast you could hear the seams screech in the wind.

"I could hit that easy," bragged Mr. Excitement.

"$20.00 says 'no way'," answered Ike as he smiled into Cuno's eyes.

Once again Mister Mike ran back in and out of his house in mere seconds, this time waving a bat. "This is the bat Billy Williams gave me after a Cub game."

Cuno looked it over. "This is all I need, baby."

Ike walked a few paces and faced the brown brick three flat. "Three strikes and you're out."

Cuno backed up to the front of the wall. "Mike, you ump. What if I crush it and it goes through a house window?" asked Cuno as he took his mighty warm up swings.

"That's not happening, baby," fired back an arm twirling 19 year old.

Cuno stepped in and Ike immediately started his long arm reaching wind up. WHOOSH. The ball shot by Cuno so fast he was still looking straight ahead and hadn't moved a muscle.

"Strike One," barked Mike. "Right over the knees."

Cuno now realized he had bit off much more than he could ever chew, but refused to show any emotion on his face. Ike picked the ball back up and started another spiderman type wind up and again fired a thermo, heat seeking missile. This time Cuno lifted his foot and shifted all his weight forward with a mighty swing and heard a loud BAM. Unfortunately, the loud blast was from the ball striking the wall so hard it cracked a brick.

"Hey, what the hell are you guys doing?" yelled Maureen who came out of the house arm waving like she was landing a plane.

"Strike twooooo," cried Mister Mike.

"Maureen, relax, honey. This kid is going to pay for our dinner tonight."

Cuno dug in and choked the bat up and once more Ike uncoiled a fastball that seemed to look like an aspirin as Cuno let out a war cry. The ball hit the same exact spot on the bricks and caused a huge chunk to come flying out. Cuno in the meantime had swung so hard he corkscrewed into the ground.

"Strike three, the batter's outtttt!!!!"

"AHHHHH! I told you, baby," yiped Cy Ike Young. "Pay up, pal," he said as he walked over to the unraveling kid. Cuno begrudgingly dug into his pockets and forked over his allowance. "Thanks man. Anytime you want to try again let me know. I could build a house with you around."

Ike walked away with Maureen who looked back over her shoulder. "You better get that brick fixed before Dad comes home."

Mike looked at his sibling and spit between his teeth, "Breeze my shorts, woman."

Maureen walked her beau, Ike, to his cool looking, blueprinted 1/2 ton and kissed him adieu. She walked back towards her brother and Cuno as Ike pulled away and informed them that Ike had joined the Marines and would soon be on his way. She went back into the three flat with a chipped out brick as Cuno and Mister Mike returned to the wonderful world of football fortune telling. The Bears plus three, how good can it be!

Chapter 7
Audience with the Pop

The days and weeks smoothly transitioned from autumn to the frosty crispness of a Midwestern winter as life for the band of boys continued on like a power down shift in a hemi driven machine. The Old Kid and Michele had become quite an item as time moved on. Michele even wore The Kid's class ring as a sign of "going steady," a ritual rite that is one notch below the final anchor-- marriage. His ring was much too big for her petite ring finger so the difference was made up with angora angel hair wrapped around the bottom. They had been dating and getting seriously into sex which sometimes got out of control. Michele had to slow The Kid down as well as herself with the command that females possess and males seem to be without. Things were going pretty smoothly for The Kid as he told his mates "that he could drive his car with one hand and drive Michele crazy with the other." That was about all he would say as the boys had a strong bond of not talking about girls that made the grade.

Things were going a little too smoothly for him, but as life would have it, all roads must have their bumps! They were driving down picturesque Lake Shore Drive in Chicago. The GTO was humming. The Mamas and the Papas were singing. The sun was beaming. The Kid was smiling away. Then Michele turned to him and said, "I think it would be great if you came over and met my folks." The Goat lost some control as it hit a pothole the size of a large pepperoni pizza. This made the 8 track jump and stop playing as storm clouds suddenly appeared on the horizon obscuring the daylight.

"What?" muttered the off-his-game Kid. Michele leaned in with her pretty, angelic face and eyes that hypnotized, galvanized, and even specialized in the complete control of the twitterpated Bambi.

"It's time you met my parents. They have asked me many times to have you over."

"Michele, your dad hates me. Remember he was there when Moody busted me. He was totally inflamed."

"No, Danny, he thinks differently about you since you saved me at Proviso." The debate went on for sometime but as any guy knows, if you want a steady stream of top shelf nookie, you must pay the price or be shown the door. Males are at a complete disadvantage by nature. The Kid was getting schooled in matters that girls practice their whole life. When little girls play house, it's actually spring training for the big game. They manipulate little dolls around in a series of relationship situations. They are well trained in the art of boxing in their prey. Courtship to a male means to demonstrate an ability to be to be a romantic, flower bearing, door opening Sir Galahad. Sex in return is his justly earned reward, but the snare is pulled by the female to test his level of commitment. The tried and true verification of "time to meet the parents" is a toll many men have had to pay to stay on Lust Island. The Old Kid finally gave in and agreed to one of the most intimidating adventures a young man must face: a pow-wow with the big chief and clan. Since he agreed, he wanted his chip count doubled, so he pulled into the Alder Planetarium parking lot for the breathtaking, romantic view of the Chicago skyline. Many Chicagoans were conceived on this little peninsula that jets pristinely out into Lake Michigan for a truly scenic view that melts girls' hearts and grants safe passage into the Tunnel of Love. Michele was elated that her beau was becoming domesticated and soon to be house broken.

She would now reward her good little boy and pulled out a French tickler and showed it to The Kid. "I want protected sex and I want to see how this feels." The two lovers once again caused the GTO windows to steam up from all the intense heat, but no laughter could be heard from Michele even though she was getting a good French tickling.

The weekend rolled around and Sunday was the big day for The Old Kid to meet the elders. He showed up at the door surprisingly on time, as Michele was all thrilled at her chance to play house with real live dolls. He walked through the door wondering if this is how a guy feels when he goes to the electric chair. He wore his Sunday best and looked quite handsome. The Kid even brought Michele's mom some flowers, which racked huge points. He knew he would need every ally he could muster in his council with the Papa Bear. The Old Kid walked shyly into the foyer and was quickly greeted by the entire household sans the Grand Potentate himself. That honor was just around the corner in the room with the Bear game blaring like thunder. The traditional ritual of dad meeting the boy who is jumping his daughter's bones is done with subtle gestures and motions. Michele escorted her old kid doll into the TV den and graciously introduced the young buck to the head of the herd. Her dad gave The Kid a solid once over look with no visible signal of welcome to the flock.

The Old Kid, even though quite nervous, demonstrated his courage with a polite "Hello Mr. Gambini. I'm Dan Cuccioni," as he extended his hand.

The elder got out of his overstuffed Lazyboy and shook the lad's hand with a warm smile and a cold stare. "How do you, son," he grumbled.

They both sat down and quickly turned their attention to the television as Jack Brickhouse was jumping out of his socks as the Bears' Kansas Comet, Gale Sayers, was returning a kickoff for a touchdown. "He's at the 20... the 15... the 10... the 5... TOUCHDOWN BEARS!" Jack shouted with his trusted old sidekick, columnist Irv Kupcinet whose only reply to anything Jack said was "Dats right, Jack." Gale Sayers may have not been the greatest running back the NFL has ever seen, but he definitely was the most exciting. His zig-zag running style and tremendous speed made him a magician in cleats. He holds the rookie record for touchdowns, 22 in a 14 game season, and he didn't play in the first two games. Michele's dad was clapping his hands, wildly cheering with every word as Brickhouse described the replay of the electrifying run. Jack bellowed the names of all the key blockers: guys like Mike Pile, Reibold, Rosey Taylor, Butkus, all giving their all.

"Dats right, Jack."

"You a Bears fan?" asked the dad.

"Sure am, sir. Love 'em," replied The Kid. In truth he rooted for the Cleveland Browns. The Kid wasn't about to make waves in a sea of tension. The two males chewed the fat a little, but mostly gave the football game more than its share of attention. He noticed some wildlife photos and a hunter's cap with an embroidered slogan "IF IT FLYS IT DIES" written on the front.

Michele walked into the room. "Dinner's about ready, guys. Wash up and mangia-mangia."

The Kid sat next to his treasured senorita. The rest of the family filtered to the dinner table as well. This included Michele's hot, bigger sister, Connie, (who was well known to The Brothers for her cute face and a great set of cones), her brother, the buzz cut Cue Ball, and her mom, a full blooded Mexican beauty. It was easy to see how the girls got their sexy looks coming from this stable.

Pops came roaring into the room with his usual 100% Italian pride flag, the Dago-T tee shirt, with a full complement of static hair jutting out from all the gross places a man has to offer. He sat down and looked up. "Let us say grace." They all bowed their heads in semi-complete reverence with just enough room to peek at the dinner guest to check on his compliance. The Kid had his head tilted down and hands sharply pointing to the heavens with the best, angelic face he could muster.

"Test one passed," he thought to himself as he caught Michele with an approving smile.

Pops rambled on with his Italian preghiera about some perdono and grato, while The Kid pretended to follow along. He thought to himself of the price a guy must pay for high-octane poon-tang.

"Let us now eat," exclaimed the padre as he lifted the silver cover off a silver tray to reveal the offering. The Kid's mind went off the road as he tried to stay on the path of composure.

"What the hell is that?" he thought rapidly going through his museum of recollection of similar game.

"So, son, have you ever had squirrel before?" asked the beaming dad.

The human mind is an amazing device. It can process so much information and recollection in milliseconds. The Kid thought of all the squirrels he had seen in his life... climbing trees, chased by cats, squashed on the road, looking like high class rats. All these images shot instantaneously through his mind as a bright, gleaming silver tray of brown rodent was heading his way for consumption.

"No, sir, can't say that I have," he politely replied giving Michele his what the hell is this eye.

"You ever go hunting, son?" asked the senior male.

"Yes, sir. I go to my uncle's farm near the Dells in deer season," answered the boy as he lifted his head from the table noticing that every eye around the table was trained on him.

"Well, good. This is some game I bagged last week in Indiana."

The Kid was doing his best under this intense pressure. He liked the look he was getting from Michele's sister and her mom. In fact, he could swear there were some rays being sent his way from both females! The lad had a full plate of mash potatoes, corn, and headless squirrel. He ate his food and gave a good share of compliments, even though the squirrel was tougher than the nuts he once buried.

"You know, son, I wanna thank you for sticking your neck out for my daughter at Proviso. You're a good man."

"Sir, I'm just glad I got there in time," The Kid replied as he noticed the smearing grease around the dad's mouth. He looked like a Neanderthal man in his Dago-T and smeared mouth of dripping, oily fat.

"I know you and your friends are quite a rowdy bunch, and you have nicknames for everyone. I was wondering what mine might be," said the father with a smiling wink at Michele.

"Well, I don't think you have one, sir," remarked The Kid knowing from the wink Michele had informed him.

"Well, it wouldn't be the Bambino now would it? The great slugger with the big belly?" laughed the host. The Kid wisely kept quiet and went on pretending he was having a good time. The long, laborious meal had finally ended and the males retreated into the TV den just in time to hear Jack and Kup give their weekly eulogy of how the beloved Bears got waxed again. "That damn Jack Craphouse. He's got to be the worst announcer ever. He doesn't know shit from shinola," yelled the Bambino. The Old Kid realized he didn't know what shinola was either but kept quiet.

Michele joined the group and mercifully pried her played out boyfriend from the ongoing interrogation. She suggested that they go for a drive, a suggestion that was agreed upon by The Kid in world record time. They left as a couple and The Old Kid laid out the old charm as he thanked his host for a wonderful meal. He swore he got another blast of rays from Michele's mom as he walked out. Was it real or just fantasy? Asked the song...

The lad let out a huge sigh as he got into his natural habitat of the GTO. He looked over at Michele who seemed to be replaying her successful endeavor of playing real life house. She quickly snapped out of her domestic reflections and asked, "So that wasn't so bad, was it?"

The Old Kid, who couldn't get the clutch down fast enough, answered, "What was with squirrel meat? I thought we were going to have lasagna or something Italian?"

"I'm sorry. My dad was all excited about having his catch and we are all so use to it."

The Kid looked over at her and said, "Don't you know I'm a huge fan of Rocky the Flying Squirrel? All I could see was little Rocky crying out for Bullwinkle to save him, but noooo... I was eating him and, by the way, it might look like chicken and smell like chicken but it tastes like... " he wisely ended the statement realizing his choice of words could easily undo all the work he put in with the Bambino.

The Goat drove around the familiar routes of the Broadview streets. Since it was Sunday, not many of The Brothers would be seen for a while. They had serious hangover issues to resolve. The cool, orange car headed up 18th, a street filled with great memories for The Kid. Every house seemed to have its own recollection for him. "Hmmm... there's Barbara Holt's house... my first dry hump... why is it called dry when it's anything but that... and King Crap's home where I accidentally kicked a soccer ball right through their picture window... what an explosion that made... and to make it even funnier, King Crap's mom was napping on the couch by the window when the ball sailed passed her." King Crap got his name from having the special ability to flick his wrist at a guys nuts and smack 'em while you could never reach his. That seem to be his only major functional advantage in life and so was dubbed potentate of all piddling, paltry manners-- King Crap for short!

They drove straight into Lindop's parking lot and noticed a beat up '64 VW Beetle. "Hey, there's Stevie and Evie, the together twins," noted The Kid.

"Who are they?" asked Michele.

"They're a couple that have been going out since like the sixth grade. They are always together like black on beans." The GTO slid next to the '64 war wagon. "Hey, you two, what be happening?" shouted The Kid.

Stevie held up a pint of Southern Comfort and shook it. "The South shall rise again, my friend. The South shall rise again," replied a stoopered Stevie in a fake southern drawl.

"And what? Get its ass kicked again?" laughed The Kid. "What you guys doin'?"

Stevie looked at Evie and started laughing as he stuck his tongue deep inside the bottle of booze. Michele was taken back a little by this vulgar action, but didn't show much reaction. She was busy trying to see what the girl looked like. Females check out all and any competition within their territorial domain with a vengeance of a forbidding falcon. Evie also was returning fire as she was buttoning up her blouse.

Stevie asked, "You guys wanna go out and party hardy? I know a dude with materials."

The Kid looked at Michele with a "Let's do it." She had heard about Stevie and Evie being the ones who do or try anything. They were doing drugs and having serious sex when everyone else their age was playing spin the bottle for big thrills. Michele gave the green light smile and The Kid waved the other couple to get in the Goat.

"Here, this will grow some hair on your chest," said Stevie as he handed The Kid the half empty pint. The two girls gave each other a warm smile as the boys didn't even bother with an introduction. Michele quickly noticed that Evie's blouse still had a few top buttons wide open and her cleavage was for the all world to enjoy. Evie saw the Italian princess glancing downward and gave Michele a smile with a hint of pink tongue. The Old Kid was finishing his gusto gulp and turned back to hand the bottle to Stevie when Evie's Grand Canyons caught his eye. The male species is rendered completely incapacitated when an unsolicited or even a solicited view of breast comes breathtakingly on the scene. Civil war broke out in The Kid's mind as to how long of a granted peek he would get at the world class display of Golden Bozos. He could feel the heat coming from his girlfriend who was staring at him for over staying his stare time, and he begrudgingly faced forward giving Stevie a "what a lucky guy glance." The Kid quickly turned his attention to the ignition key trying to vend off Michele's rays of jealous anger. He turned the key and a loud sound of grinding metal was heard. The car was all ready running. This gave further evidence of The Kid's loss of consciousness, that and a stream of drool running out of his mouth. Michele really couldn't blame him. She even turned her peek into a strong look. She realized Stevie and Evie were a "good times any time" couple, so she buckled her seat belt a little tighter.

"Hey, let's go downtown and check out the new Hancock tower," said Stevie. The John Hancock tower was the newest skyscraper on the Chicago skyline reaching 99 stories tall, a simple design but with a striking, lighted top.

"Yeah, cool beans," replied The Kid.

"First let's check out my friend, Chaino's. He has an apartment in Oak Park. I need to refuel there," laughed Stevie. The burnt orange GTO squealed out of the school and down I-90 towards the Chicago loop. "Get off at Harlem and his place is across the street from the hospital." The Oak Park hospital is an immense building built around the turn of the century. It is where Ernest Hemingway's father spent his entire career as a doctor until he committed suicide. In fact, Ernest himself was born there as well as Punkwillie. The hot Pontiac muscle car roared up to a four-story apartment building. "This is his crib," said Stevie as the couples all got out. The girls were still running full radar scans on each other as they engaged in small talk. They entered the musty lobby that smelled like fresh pine Lysol surrounded in a moldy, mildewed, dead man fart, and rang the bell. After waiting one long minute, they rang again figuring this dude Chaino had to land back on earth. Finally a squeaky speaker kicked in with an even squeakier voice.

"Who is it?" asked the voice.

Stevie bent down and spoke. "It's..." is all he got out before being interrupted by an earsplitting, semi-electronic BUZZZZ that sounded like the gates of hell itself opening. Stevie led the way up the creaky stairs that covered all octaves with each step.

"They must pay people to live here," laughed Michele, which got a good response from all.

Just when they reach the top floor and the stale air odor had become all-consuming, Stevie pounded hard on a chipped, wooden door that still had its turn of the century charm. No answer to the knock and all they could hear were the muttered sounds of Jimi Hendrix's "Crosstown Traffic." Once again, Stevie slammed on the door and finally a voice sounding as if it was coming from a closed casket.

"Yeah, man, yeah. Who is it?"

Stevie rolled his eyes. "It's..." That's as far as he got. The door scarcely budged as the sound of a collection of chains and locks and more chains unclicked, unbolted, and unlocked to free the old wooden door from its metal bondage. A slim slit of passage presented itself and the group forged in, met instantly by a montage of odors and scents. The Kid tried to adjust his eyes to the dimly lit room.

"Hey, bro, dig a sit," said a boney figure sitting yoga style on the floor. "I'm Chaino. Welcome to my palace." The Kid gave Chaino a Viking handshake as he surveyed the area. Chaino gave both the girls a smile and yelled, "Hey, Crystal, we got guests."

The bedroom door behind Michele opened and out came an Edgar Allen Poe vision of a girl. She was tall, lanky and even under the soft, forgiving light from the candles, pale as an Irish ghost. "Groovy, it's my lil Evie," said the girl ghost as she walked towards Evie and gave her a kiss that was more sensual then a hello peck. The boys all smiled and Michele once again fired a warning shot over The Kid's bow. He was walking the plank and one more gazing stare would send him into the soup!

The Kid look around and noticed that the walls all had writing on them-- names, slogans, symbols and other abstract bullshit. "Cool, what's with the walls?"

"Oh," responded Chaino, "we like our guests to leave their mark."

Stevie sat next to Chaino and asked, "Dude, you have anything new and exciting?"

Chaino smiled back. "Kanebinol, amigo."

Stevie sat up. "Ka what inol?"

"Kanebinol... it's to angel dust what hash is to weed."

"Strong ass, huh?"

Michele looked for a place to sit down between the stains on the sofa. This was not the freedom she had in mind when envisioning growing up. Looking at the hapless apartment with its black light posters and drugged out occupants made her realize that many people do not live in her style. How do kids get into a sewer like this? She could now appreciate her mundane home life a little more. She kept an eye on The Old Kid to see how he perceived all this. She knew he was adventurous and ready to explore the many facets of the modern world, but if he dove into this new hippie counter culture he was swimming alone. This was not for her. She didn't mind some experimenting with values and maybe bush league drugs, but taking the base of Angel Dust, whatever the hell that was, was going off the chart. She sat there watching this deal go down thinking to herself how sad it was to watch kids heading the wrong way. The flirty looks from the two bisexual chicks didn't bother her as much as the low life situation in the room, and she was watching her beau to see just how far he would go in all this. Little bags of powder and leaves were exchanged as Stevie handed over the mean green for the mellow yellow.

The Old Kid had picked up a magic marker and started writing on the wall. As he did, the skinny, junkie babe walked over and read it. "Hey, man, fuck you," she said. "What's this shit your scribbling... 'Who Cares?' My walls care, man. That's who cares." Chaino mumbled something to her to shut up. He didn't want any commotion going on and he could see that The Kid was no one to tangle with.

Chaino focused his attention back to Stevie and warned him, "Be careful with the Dust man. It's high octane. Just do a match head. It will send you into deep, deep space."

"That's cool," replied Stevie. "I've always wanted to see what God looks like." The kids all laughed and then went on their way.

On the way out Michele gave a peek into the kitchen and saw a pile of garbage, dirty dishes, and moldy food stuck on the wall. "Hell of way to live," she thought. "Who knows, I could end up this way." She suddenly found new motivation for her schoolwork. This little episode in the world of vice was very educational for her. The two talking skeletons she just met would stick in her memory as a reminder of people that chose a destiny of despair and gloom. How heartbreaking to witness kids on the threshold of life fall flat on their face before taking one single step.

The Kid and company all got in the GTO and now zoomed toward the Chicago Loop once again. The two couples talked about Chaino and his doghouse apartment. "There's a cat there, but it's eaten so much cat nip and weed it just lays under their bed. It never comes out," said Stevie.

Michele and Evie got to know each other a little better as they talked about people they each knew. Michele looked at Evie and asked, "Did you ever go to Camp Wahoes? I swear I remember you there."

Evie turned a little red in the face "Yesss. I'm afraid that was me. I was hoping you wouldn't remember.

I had braces, a pizza face, and weighed more than a Buick."

"That was you? Wow!" exclaimed Michele, "and didn't you... " Michele then quickly stopped as her words came out faster than her recollection, and when it caught up, the stop sign came out. Evie turned even redder.

"What?" asked Stevie "What did she do? This ought to be good."

Evie looked at him. "Oh, just the usual whore stuff I'm so well known for," she laughed. "I got a bad case of poison ivy on my back and ass, while two of the camp counselors had it on their knees and elbows."

"Just two?" laughed Stevie.

"Hey, I was 13. Give me a break."

"Damn, girl, you take the cake," said Stevie.

 Stevie started to roll a joint as the GTO rolled down the highway. He lit the reefer and passed it to Evie who took a long hit and jumped when the ash fell on her lap unprotected by her mini skirt.

"Shit," she cried out, and accidentally struck Michele near her eye in the panic attack.

The Old Kid reached over and plucked the doobie out of her hand and took a toke. Michele watched him closely and he felt the radar, but continued anyway. He passed it to Michele who just shook her head and said, "You better be able to drive, Cosmic Kid."

Stevie broke in. "This is Mexican grass, not all that powerful, just a friendly buzz."

Michele turned back to look at Stevie and noticed Evie's hand was rubbing between his legs. "Damn," she thought, "these two are one long party."

The Kid reached for the radio as Ron Britain announced that Punkwillie was on the phone. "It's the Punk," yelled The Kid as he cranked the stereo.

Britain spoke. "Wella... wella... there is no Waukegan... it's 29 degrees downtown at 3:35 on this wunnerful-a-wunnerul afternoon... and we have Punkwillie on the line to make it even more wunnerful. Hey, Punk."

"Hey, King B."

"Tell me, Punk, what's up?"

The couples in the car all leaned forward knowing that waves of jokes were coming.

"King, my rent is up, the stocks are up, I got stood up, so I will shut up, 'cause I give up."

"Now, Punk," replied the smooth King B, "why don't you CHEER UP?"

"Oh, King, I do believe you just... you just... PICKED ME UP!!!"

The couples all smiled knowing that all this comedy was ad libbed which made it even funnier.

"Hey, Ron, did I tell I got to fly on Hugh Hefner's jet?"

"No, Punk, tell me."

"I just did! Ahhhhh! The plane was amazing. It is slim and long with two huge engines. I mean more than a mouthful huge."

"Now, Punk, this is a family show. Keep it clean, you know, like you're talking to your grandparents."

"My grandparents!! You mean I gotta repeat everything twice?"

"So, Punk, tell me more about Hugh's jet."

"Well, my seat number was 38DD and the stewardess showed us how to unbuckle our seat belts by using just one hand."

"I still can't do that," chimed in Ron.

"The best part was that a few playmates were on board, too."

"Punk, I know you're lying, but keep going."

"Well, they were all beautiful and very nice to me, except Miss December... she was kinda cold... but Miss July was really hot and Miss February was the shortest... and, Ron, don't broadcast this, but they really, really wanted me."

"Punk, you were dreaming."

"NO, King B, I'm telling ya they all really... really... wanted me... to LEAVE! AHHHHH!"

King B gave a good laugh and added, "And so do I. Punkwillie, ladies and germs. Punk, God bless ya."

"Why? I didn't sneeze."

Click.

The loud drum hit from the Doors "Light My Fire" segued in and The Kid turned up the radio as he and Michele laughed about the routine they just heard. Michele turned around to get a reaction from Stevie and Evie, but he had rounded second and was heading home. Michele quickly looked away, but then fell prey to one more tempting look at a live sex show. "Funny," she thought, "all this passion and commotion and both couples have their eyes completely shut." She look at The Kid to see if he was catching this exhibition by the exhibitionists, but he seemed more interested in a '65 hood scooped 426 hemi V-8 Plymouth Belvedere that buzzed in the next lane. Both drivers gave each other the challenge stare of beware. Both cars seemed to be gearing up for some dueling dual exhausting. Even the normally mild mannered Michele seemed interested in the pending dare as both cars lunged forward and back as the drivers played with the clutch and gas pedal. The candy apple red Belvedere honked his horn once, then twice. Stevie and Evie sat up to witness the race. As the third and final horn called out, the young couple was blasted back into the seat as the GTO roared its high octane voice. The lanes were pretty much clear ahead for both drivers and the valiant vehicles shot down the Ike. I-90, aka the Eisenhower, runs like a picket fence through the Chicago west side ghetto. From Harlem Avenue to the downtown post office, police presence on the Ike is minimal. They have far more pressing issues on the side streets that border the expressway. The American muscle car is not known for its cornering or handling, but in a straight line... watch out. This is an awful lot of power to be in the hands of teenagers who just a few years ago were thrilled at taking off their training wheels. These cars can go from zero to 80 mph in just a few ticks on the clock. The Old Kid gripped his steering wheel tightly as the Belvedere jumped to a half car lead.

"Damn, it has no passengers. Less weight," yelled The Kid.

"Want us to jump out?" shouted Stevie.

"Just you," laughed The Kid.

He glanced at his redlining tach. His four speed was "giving it all she's got, captain," and the cars flew passed other traffic as if they were all parked. The Goat was gaining. The road was rushing past the front window and Michele was beginning to get scared. She had never been in a drag race before and the speed with all the thunderous howling was as deafening as it was terrifying. She knew they were going fast when the cars passed an "EL" train with its passengers pressing to the windows watching the contest. They were already at Racine Avenue, home of the "Taylor Street Dukes" and the tough Italian neighborhoods. Both cars were still about even as the GTO had a slightly bigger block and more torque to make up for its extra weight. The Kid glanced over at the driver of the Plymouth who glared right back. There might be honor among thieves, but in street racing it's "Go to Hell and keep on going, pal." Suddenly, the scream of a State Trooper's siren let its presence be known and the occupants of the Goat all freaked, except for The Kid. This was familiar territory for him. Downtown Chicago was just a few minutes away and the cars would pass under the post office and over a bridge. Traffic was mounting, too, and now came the time for quick thinking. The trooper's patrol car was directly behind the GTO, but The Kid knew as long as he was traveling fast, it was almost impossible to get his license plate read correctly. Both cars now had to brake harder than first realized as they shot into the dark shadows of the tunnel way through the post office. The Old Kid had to apply the trick of pumping his brakes to keep from locking up and losing control. The screech from all three cars was terrifying, but in a glint, a clear lane to the far right appeared and the GTO raced at it with the Belvedere chasing close behind. The state trooper had used much more caution entering the tunnel and was about 50 feet back. The right lane was a feeder to the underground Wacker Drive and now all the engine noise would be enhanced by the enclosed roadway.

"Whoa, dude, this is too much. Don't let the fuzzy nab us. I have beau coo drugs on me," yelled Stevie. The girls sat glued in their seats, too scared to talk. Michele noticed that her boyfriend actually seemed to be enjoying all this and she wondered whether he was incredibly cool or did criminal behavior run through his blood? The cars couldn't get any real speed going because lower Wacker has hairpin turns through its course. This had now turned into a Gran Prix event. The trouble was The Kid knew the state trooper had to call for assistance and that five minute window was about to close, so something daring to had to come about to shake the trooper.

He fixed his downward facing, rear view mirror to see that once again the cop was in his lane with lights swirling and siren singing. The Old Kid saw his chance and quickly acted on it. In moments like these there is no time for considerations or options. A true warrior acts on instinct and the time called for action. They had passed an exit to upper Wacker Drive and The Kid, in one fine motion, down shifted and spun the wheel hard left. This caused the Goat to go into the left lane and face 180 degrees in the wrong direction. He punched the Ponch's gas and bolted as the state trooper shot by in a blink with the safer option of going after the candy apple Plymouth. He once again made a semi-donut as he called out "Bat turnnn!!" and the Goat shot up the ramp to the pleasant views of downtown Chicago. No one said a word as they realized that the old son of a bitch'n kid gave them a rush and a half. "This is the stuff memories are made of," proclaimed the Houdini of dragsters.

They arrived at their destination-- the newly built John Hancock building on the city's near north side. Once inside they marveled at the size of the lobby. "Holy shit," said Stevie as his profanity profoundly echoed off the marble walls. "This is one big ass building." The couples entered the world's fastest elevators and Stevie then made an acute observation. "You know, they say our last names come from what major characteristics or trade your forefathers had. For instance, if a man was a blacksmith, his family was known as Smith, or if he worked with clothing, they would be called Taylor. I wonder what the hell John Hancock's family did to get such a name. Ha!"

"I dated a guy name Woodcock," added Evie.

"Who haven't you dated?" asked Stevie.

"My neighbor is named Allen Wrench," laughed Michele.

"I bet he's got big lug nuts," added Houdini.

The elevator came to a controlled jolt of a stop and the doors swished open. "Whoa, my ears popped," stated Michele.

The kids all stood for a second overtaken by the breathtaking view. The Illinois landscape is even interesting, as the full windows of the observatory 99 stories above the street gave a spectacular view. Lake Michigan to the east with its sky blue, white capped, fresh water looked like a surreal, glistening carpet stretched out beyond the horizon. The mesmerizing overlook north towards Wisconsin with billowing, cotton candy clouds and glorious chartreuse fields of green was overwhelmingly powerful. This was all offset with a glimpse south as a burnt orange, toxic smog covered Gary, Indiana like a sheet over a corpse.

The two couples went to the west window and The Old Kid put 25 cents into a rental telescope to see if they could find beautiful Broadview. Michele was first to use the scope as she called out the landmarks. "There's O'Hare, and I think it's Hines Hospital, but it's too far to make out. I can see our drag strip, the Eisenhower."

Michele followed their path to downtown as she stood almost straight up on the viewing stand. "I can see your car, Danny," and then she became eerily quiet for a moment. She began to tweak the focus ring and stood up on her tippy toes. "Hey, there's somebody leaning on the car."

No sooner did she get her words out and The Kid roughly bumped her over. "Wha... let me see," as he adjusted the scope. "HEY! HEY! SOMEBODY IS TRYING TO BREAK INTO MY CAR! HEY, GOD DAMN IT!" The other three pressed against the window to get a better look, but the cars looked like micro machines and people were mites. "HEY, YOU FUCK'N BASTARD!" yelled The Kid as he started to jump on the stand.

All this commotion brought the security cop over. "What's wrong here?" he asked.

"My car is getting broke into," as the group all ran for the elevators.

"I'll call down to the desk downstairs. It will take you 15 minutes at best to get to the street," said the cop.

The kids cut in line and jumped into the next elevator as the people waiting yelled their protest. One man whose family was next came up to the teens and shouted, "Hey, what the hell do you think you're doing?"

The Kid glared at him and yelled back, "Sorry, mister. My car is getting robbed. I have to get down there."

"I don't give a shit about your car, pal," replied the man.

"I don't give a shit that you don't give a shit," fired back The Kid as the chime sounded and the door started to close. The man started to put his foot in the door and

The Kid came down hard on his foot with his Red Wing lineman boots. The blow sent the man back and the elevator door slid closed as the muffled sounds of a man yelling disappeared quickly above their heads. The elevator descended as The Kid rubbed his hands together formulating his battle plan.

"I couldn't tell if he was black or white," said Michele.

"I think he had blue eyes or maybe just contacts," laughed Stevie.

The Kid gave Stevie a look that a lion gives a wildebeest before it's slaughtered. The elevator hit the lobby floor and The Old Kid hit the floor running as the doors parted. Once outside he flew around the corner of the building and saw his cherished chariot sat looking rather unharmed. No one but passing pedestrians were the only people near the car. The crook had vanished. The rest of the group came up as The Kid inspected the crime scene. "The 8 track is gone," called out The Kid, "and the tapes."

Michele noticed that there was no damage to the windows or doors. "How did he get in?" she asked.

"Looks like he used a jimmy" answered Stevie.

"A what?" said Evie.

"A jimmy. It's what all car dealers and thieves use to break into a car. It's a long, thin piece of metal that you can slide down the window and jimmy the lock until it clicks open."

They headed back home in a somber mood. It was bad enough the tape player was ripped off, but The Kid's collection of tapes was salt in the wound.

Michele was doing her best at comforting her victimized beau. She even unbuttoned her top much like Evie's to get his mind off the ripoff. This seemed to have more of an effect on Stevie and Evie as Evie told Michele she reminded her of Cleopatra. "Did you know Cleopatra was bisexual?" said Evie. With Evie there was very little reading between the lines. She was pretty much as direct as a headline. Michele had been getting Evie's flirtatious advances and just let them fall by the wayside. She did find them somewhat flattering. "Cleopatra also used a primitive form of vibrator. It was a small cone shaped box filled with bees."

Michele turned around to the back seat. "You're sure an expert on Cleopatra, Evie."

"No, I'm not. I'm a expert on vibrators. Haa!" retorted Evie. This broke everyone up including The Old Kid. Michele turned her head forward and smiled when a little buzzing sound and tickling came into her ear. She whipped her head around and found a slender pink tube near her face jiggling about. "Say hello to Pinky Lee," laughed Evie, "my home away from home."

Michele jolted back in her seat. "Eeeeewww. Is that your vibe?"

"Yes, my portable buddy. I carry it in my purse in case of emergencies."

Stevie grabbed it from her hand and said, "Please, Evie, you can be so embarrassing. I'm trying to act mature and dignified while you behave like such a sleaze."

Evie started laughing out loud and once again Michele looked to the back seat and once again she let out a "Eeeewwww." Stevie now had Pinky Lee in his mouth.

"That's a good boy. Lick the spoon for mommy," laughed Evie.

The Old Kid kept to himself during all this, but being a streetwise hoodlum, he had a feeling where Stevie and Evie were going with all this sex talk. He looked at Michele and pictured her in bed with the other couple. The thought of her and big boobed Evie together put a teethie grin on his face. Michele was glad to see him break out of his hurtful mood. She didn't realize it, but in a young teenage boy's imagination she was breaking laws against nature.

The Kid and gang cruised into Broadview and to the tar pit of Lindop school's lot. The usual routine of The Brothers was being played out. The boys were nursing hangovers and trading pumped up stories of the their conquests of the past weekend. Cuno and Mister Mike were listening to the final details of a football game between the Los Angles Rams and San Francisco 49ers. Cuno needed the Rams to hang on to their two-point lead to collect on his parlay card bet. He laid down $50 and if the wager clicked, he was going to make $350. The rest of the crew gathered around the powder blue Camaro as the broadcaster was blaring about how all the Rams had to do was make a first down and they could eat the clock for a win.

"Come on, Rams," said Cuno as he pumped his closed fist up and down.

He turned up the radio. "The ball is on the 48 and it's 3rd and 3 for the Rams... 1:32 minutes left in the game... Roman Gabriel over the ball barking out signals... Gabriel takes the snap and it's a play action pass... he pumps to the tight end... and scrambles... he's being chased by a blitzing linebacker... he throws to an open Dick Bass... it tips off Bass's fingers and it's intercepted by Rosey Taylor and Taylor takes off... but he's caught from behind at the Rams 30."

Cuno started punching the dashboard like a wild man. "AHHH, NO... NO... GOD DAMN RAMS!" He lit a cigarette, which was unusual for Mr. Excitement since he didn't smoke.

Everyone stayed quiet except for Musclehead who thought this was all kinda funny. "Ah, Cuno, you're gonna get snaked by those homos."

Cuno bent over towards the radio as the game continued. "Brodie calling an audible at the line... John David Crow shifts in the back field... it's a quick hitter to Crow and rumbles straight up and is hit and hit hard by all of the Fearsome Foursome... it's 2nd and 5 at the 25."

At this point all the boys were heavily under the influence of football until Evie leaned over the front windshield to join the crowd. All eyes shifted quicker than a fly's fart to the exquisite view of the land of milk and honey smashed against the window like tender bags of lust, desire and temptation. All hands on dick... all hands on dick... became the silent battle cry of all the hormonally overdosed lads except Mr. Excitement who was clutching his cigarette so tightly that it broke in two.

No one except Cuno even heard the second down play that gained three more precious yards. The radio blasted away the description. "The 49ers are out of time outs and are going to have to kick a field goal on 3rd down... the kicking team is ready for the 34 yard attempt... the kick is up and it's..." The signal began to fade and static filled the speaker, and then came weakly back and the first word they heard was "GOOD" and everyone let out a collective groan. "...The kick is NO good and the Rams win a thriller!" The groan had risen from the dead and the tar pit was once again alive with the sound of nonsense. Cuno was screaming and everyone was slapping him five, even The Old Kid, who had been musically castrated earlier that day, was in full smileage.

Chapter 8
Killed in Action Reaction

The night had crept in and the lads went their way, some to actually do their homework or at least make a valiant attempt. Cuno and Mister Mike drove to Mike's three flat to give his winning ticket to Mike's brother, Bill. The boys walked up to the brownstone brick building and as they got near the front lobby door, the sound of muffled crying could be heard. When they entered the apartment, all of Mike's sisters and mom were huddled around the kitchen table gently sobbing.

"What happened?" asked Mike.

His mom slowly lifted her head and looked at him. "We got terrible news today. Ike, Maureen's boyfriend, was killed in Viet Nam." That announcement escalated the weeping. Mike and Cuno both recalled in their minds how they were playing catch and trying to hit Ike's fastball just a little while ago.

"Mo, I'm so sorry. He was a great guy," consoled her brother.

"I know, Mike, he was something special. He had only been in Nam three weeks. I even got mail from him today," she said as she held up an unopened letter.

"This god-damned government has us in a war we have no business being in," spoke Mike's older sister Kathy. "He was only 20 years old."

Mike leaned against the wall as the parlay card seemed unimportant at the moment. "How did he die?" Mike asked.

"He was guarding some god forsaken bridge and a sniper shot him in the neck," told the mom. "I hope they cherish that bridge. It cost dearly," she added.

Cuno and Mike turned and left. As they did, they gave Bill the winning card. Bill took it silently and stuffed it in his pocket while he took a big swig from a can of Bud. This was not the time for words or vices. The boys knew it and left the apartment. Making their way out passed the lobby door, Mike gave a glance back over his shoulder at the piece of brick that was chipped away from the old brownstone. He stopped and ran his hand over it and let memories and the harsh lesson of life seep in. The guy whose super fastball broke off a chunk from the building face is now no more, thought Mike. "Tomorrow never knows," he quoted from a Beatle song.

"No, it doesn't," answered Cuno, "and I don't think it even cares."

Even tragic news has a hard time dampening the resilient temperament of a teenager. The two youths had driven only a few blocks and their talk was about the winning parlay ticket and time to celebrate. They drove up to the local watering hole, a seedy dive called the Town Tap. Cuno got out and went up to the first patron that came stumbling out. Five bucks service charge for a 12 pack of malt liquor was the going rate and the boys paid it and then got going. They ran into Gino and Ace as they drove down the rut known as Roosevelt Road.

"Hey, bo shams, we got the suds," shouted Mike.

"Good. Let's grub. I'm starved," answered Ace, the man who could fart at will. They piled in and headed for

McDonald's in Forest Park. They shot the poop about the usual crap when Gino had a bulb above his head go off.

"Hey, I think I can get our grub for free," he stated.

"Oh, oh, watch it. Gino has a plan. Get your bail money handy," joked Ace.

"You know how McDonald's keeps their milk in the frig in the back? Well, you order and when they set it all down, you ask for some milk, and when they go get it, you bolt with the goods," explained Gino.

"You mean phantom Macs-- now you see them now you don't-- Big Mac's," joked Cuno.

"Yeah, just watch the expert and see how it's done," stated Gino.

Mike drove Rudy the Rambler into the land of the Golden Arches and parked as Gino and Ace went in. Cuno and Mike had a great view as they parked right next to the window. They intently watched as Gino and Ace placed their order. The people next to them started to stare at Ace, which meant he purposely blasted a buster in their direction. He did this to get some space and just for the hell of it. The boys in the car could see Gino place one long order as he pointed to nearly everything on the menu. Ace, in the meantime, was walking around crop dusting any and all that neared him. Finally, the man behind the counter walked up with helpers as they hoisted four huge bags filled with the over salted, grease saturated, artery-clogging goo everyone loves. The counter looked like Christmas morning with white parcels brimming and overflowing for all to enjoy.

The clerk asked if there was anything else needed and Gino, with a straight face, told a crooked lie. "Yes, four milks, please... sir." As the clerk turned and headed for the back, Gino and Ace calmly collected their booty and with the face of choirboys walked straight out the door. They got into the waiting Rudy, which was now facing the driveway, and they drove away with the Rambler's windows quickly steaming from the fast cooked food. "God bless America," cried out Gino as he dug into the bags of food.

"Dis kid did really good," replied Ace.

"You two looked like angels walking out of there," laughed Cuno.

"You should think about robbing banks. You're both too smooth at this," added Mister Mike.

They were heading down 1st Avenue when the familiar squeal of a siren sounded behind them.

"Oh shit, they called the cops," said Mike as he started to look for a place to turn off or pull over.

Gino glanced back. "Hurry, stick all the food back in and I'll heave it out the window." The blinking red lights were still a ways off, but gaining fast. Gino got the food and crammed it back into the bags that now were greasy-bottomed. He rolled down the window and threw all the stolen goods into the dark woods of Miller Meadow. The siren was screaming and lights filled the Rambler and its ducking heads occupants. Mike pulled over and rolled to a stop as each member looked at each other wondering which one would be their cellmate. The Rambler slowed to a stop and then, like a frightening flash, the siren and strobing lights whizzed passed the boys. It was an ambulance!

Four versions of mad swearing ensued, as the burger bandits had realized that once the panic button is pushed there's no reset. To make manners worse, the aroma of the speedy slop was still permeating the

Rambler like a hooker's cheap perfume as a reminder of what could have been! Like the last scene of "Treasure of the Sierra Madre," the four boys laughed greatly at their missed labor. They drove passed four, smashed, greasy bags laying on the roadside oozing an all beef patty sesame seed bun pickled swell.

Gino, being the eternal optimist, yelled out, "Let's try Pizza Hut."

"Gino, did your parents sue for damaged goods?" joked Ace.

There's something about a news bulletin that finds its way through the clatter. Sure enough, amongst all the yipping and babble the dry urgent message shot in the ears of the lads as the ticker machine tapped in the background. "We interrupt this program with a bulletin... flash dateline Madison Wisconsin... a small private plane carrying musician Otis Redding and his band has crashed into Lake Monona and sunk... rescue efforts are underway... there are said to be no survivors..."

"Fuck. God dammit. Some night this is turning out to be. We just saw him at the Kinetic Playground. He was the best," shouted Mister Mike as he slammed his clinched fist into the dashboard.

Mike sharply pulled his '66 six-cylinder beater over. He jerked open the glove box and grabbed a can of lighter fluid. He waved the dripping container. "I'm totally inflamed and Rudy shall bear witness to my hostilities," he declared.

"Solemn dis," shouted Ace. With his best 'friendly Mel' hand salute he glared into Mike's eyes.

"SOLEMN," and Mike looked towards Mr. Excitement for the ritual reply.

"Witness," responded Cuno feeling the mad energy build.

All the boys ran out of the car and to the hood of Aunt Ruth's pride and joy, the beloved "Rudymobile." Mister Mike poured the fluid on the hood in the shape of a large "R."

"All hail Rudy... king and ruler of all roads and alleys."

The sound of four malt liquor cans opening in unison is a beautiful thing. The renegades all took huge chugs from their beers as Mister Mike lit a match and threw it on the hood of the car. A small explosion shattered the winter night and when it cleared, a perfectly flaming "R" stenciled the front. The boys all madly dashed back in the car and Mike dropped it in gear. The flame with its blue light and majestic glow was something to behold. Rudy roared down Roosevelt Road in full glory. People in their cars all looked at the passing Rambler in awe and amazement. One entire family packed in a van pressed their noses against the dirty windows to get a better look at the infantile insanity. The yelling inside the ride had gotten ear splitting as Cuno plugged in The Doors "Light My Fire." The flaming letter "R" still burned longer than anyone imagined. Rudy went down 18th Avenue as Mike laid on the horn and Cuno sprayed even more lighter fluid that created a mobile bon fire. The Old Kid and Michele both popped up from the GTO and cheered on the passing fireball.

"Long live Otis, Ike and Rudy," yelled Mister Mike at the top of his lungs. The car briskly disappeared like a fading comet into the cold, humid, Midwestern sky.

Chapter 9
Peabody's Tomb

The arrival of the Christmas break gave the tension at Proviso a much needed pause. The icy fingers of winter had reached the Midwest and held a firm, chilly grip. The Windy City becomes a torture chamber as the north wind howls off the lake and sticks its pins into the faces of Chicagoans. There have been recorded temperatures of 20 below zero with a combination wind chill of 50 below. When this happens, squirrels run out from their hibernating trees and jump around in mad circles trying to escape the frosty vice. A diesel engine will lock up as the fuel freezes even if the car or truck is running. This harsh weather seems to temper the spirit with a toughness and indelible fortitude that gives the locals their brash, outgoing character. Chicagoans are a fun loving lot, but yell a little too loudly in a bar and draw a little too much attention and your shoulder will be tapped as well as your face. Winter in the Midwest is not for the faint hearted or the frail. Your hardiness will be tested each and every day as you feel the ice chips bounce off your face from scraping the car window outside and in.

The Brothers were in force at the tar pit in the late afternoon hours of the first weekend of winter break. The cold weather kept the boys in their cars only to walk out to write their names in the snow. The harsh weather made this yet another sport, as the contest was to see who could produce the most steam rising from their pee.

"This should be an Olympic event," said Punkwille.

"Truly a visual spectacle," added Chief as the boys watch Musclehead and Sweet Daddy etch the white snow with a yellow font.

A big ass 1959 Buick Roadmaster came sliding down into the school lot. It was an old friend, Angie, better known as "The Big Guy." Angie was a party commando, but found The Brothers to be just a little too wild so he only checked in from time to time. He was also quite rich and spent much of his time and money on the babes. His dad was connected with the mob and "Nice Guys with Ties" sat in unmarked cars in front of his house monitoring his every move. Angie went to St. Joe's, a private Catholic school in neighboring Westchester. He closely resembled "The Great One," Jackie Gleason, and for a teenager Angie was something of a fashion plate dressed in the finer styles.

The Big Guy pulled his red and black Buick next to Wilbur's Cobra and powered down his window. "How's it hang'n men?" he asked.

"Bend over. I'll drive you home with it," wisecracked Punkwillie.

"I hear there's going to be quite a party tonight in Hinsdale. P-lid is throwing it."

Hinsdale was one of the riches suburbs in the nation and had the mansions to prove it. Without saying, it has nothing but hot hunnies hopping around. In fact, many Playmates in Playboy have come from this perfect little community. Pam Liddy, aka P-Lid, was a blue-eyed blonde that was built like a brick shit house. She seemed to like Gino's parties and mixing it with The Brothers. Rich girls like to put the tease on from either side of the tracks, which was the general feeling the boys had about her. The truth really was that The Brothers knew how to have a good time and her snobby friends were crashing bores with their daddy's BMW's and being mommy's little chauvinist.

"Well, cool beans all around," exclaimed Punk. "This calls for our finest Boone's Farm vintage."

The Old Kid knew this was the boys night out and had already told Michele he was going with his Bo-Shams. She, being an understanding and typical girlfriend, gave him the short, snippy answer drill, followed by the early hang up procedure, a customary and mandated routine governed by the laws of nature that all relationships abide by. This technique is applied to all boyfriends, so they have a cloud of guilt hanging over their heads no matter where they go. The Kid did feel a little badly about not being with her and wondered if this was the seed of marriage beginning to sprout in his soul. The thoughts of being a beer gutted, old fart with a wide ass wife and snot nose kids running around made the kid tremble a little. "Anyone have a brew?" he shouted out of nowhere. "I need a drink," he stated.

"Kid, what's wrong? You look a little pale," questioned Wilbur.

"Did you see a ghost?" asked The Hams.

"Yes, I saw a ghost alright. The ghost from Christmas future. Ahhh... I need stinko material!!" he yelled.

Wilbur flipped opened his glove box and handed him a miniature Jack Daniel's bottle. "Here. I keep this for dire emergencies," said Wilbur as he handed him the bottle.

The Kid twisted the top off and chugged the sour mash whiskey as if it would extinguish his internal raging fires. "Dis kid is feeling much better," he said followed by a world-class belch.

The boys decided to load up for the party which meant a trip and raid to Wisconsin Farms, a small deli that made the best hot corn beef sandwiches known to man. Wilbur worked there part time and knew that Friendly Marty was at the helm today. The muscle cars all roared up like synchronized swimmers into the Farms' lot. The boys all got out and filed into the little store. Friendly Marty looked up and just said, "Please go easy. The owner's getting hep." The gang filed passed not even looking at Marty and the purge began-- crunching sounds from bags of chips with all textures and varieties being the first items to be pilfered. This was followed by the clamoring of frozen meats wrapped in styrofoam and plastics. Paper bags filled fast with condiments from hot sauce to cold cuts. No one said a word except for The Old Kid's yumming out loud at the olive loaf he was packing away. Like a close order drill team the boys about faced and marched out of the shop. Friendly Marty stepped back as the passing hands plucked out the Marlboros, Salems and Mister Mike's favorite, Swisher Sweets. Quicker than a Nazi blitzkrieg, the assault was over and engines roared away. Next stop Clark gas station for some of that 99% octane, the atomic fuel that could make even Rudy burn rubber. The Brothers generally were not a law-breaking group of thugs, but then again, they weren't choirboys either.

The raid on The Farms was more of a semi annual event. The owners never said anything, suggesting that the store was probably a front for some mobsters and was expecting to lose money. Once filled up with atomic juice (gas) and plasma (oil), The Brothers were now on their way to the wonderland known as Hinsdale, Illinois. The bright, multi-colored Christmas lights from the houses made a fantasy appearance against the falling snow. Winter may be a son of bitch to deal with, but snow gives the dark ghoul of the frozen tundra a dream like picture. The radio stations were playing the new Beatle's album, "Magical Mystery Tour," and songs like "Strawberry Fields Forever" added to the enchanted environment. The caravan of American prowess snaked its way onto Route 83, the barrier from the haves and has it all's.

There is a barren stretch of land that is owned by a Monastery called Peabody's Tomb. The fable goes that the monks once kidnapped a boy and imprisoned the child and he died. His body is on display in a glass tomb. Punkwillie looked out at the brooding tower of the monastery and sat up in his seat. "Hey, let's check out Peabody's Tomb and see if it's real."

Wilbur, who was driving, swerved the Shelby alittle. "Waaaaa... are you crazy?" Wilbur then nodded to The Old Kid sitting directly behind the Punk. The nod was a signal for a traditional face squeeze. Punkwillie was looking straight ahead when two fists flanked his face and started to close like a power vice with a simultaneous yelling of "NNNOOOOOO." The Old Kid and Wilbur pressed the Punk's face so hard he couldn't move at all and became a squash-pussed prisoner. After a few torturous moments, he was free to be his usual, idiot self.

"Hey, man, I think he's right, man," spoke the Chief. "Let's see what's going on there. I've heard the rumors my whole life, man."

The idea started to appeal to Wilbur as he turned off the major highway and onto the unlit, little road that led to the dark, towered monastery. The other cars followed as the Cobra pulled off. "We're going to see Peabody's Tomb once and for all," laughed Wilbur.

"Sure, OK, why not?" laughed Cuno in his Camaro.

A procession of four cars rumbled down the road and up to a cathedral-like building and parked. The site sat on a gentle rolling hill that was very uncommon for the flat prairie land. The 16 teens got out and made their way up the wide concrete stairs that led to a Gothic, wooded chamber door. Even with all the trimmings of Christmas that the surrounding towns featured, this area felt more like Halloween. They all felt as if prying eyes were upon their every move, but no sounds or sightings of monks had transpired.

"This place gives me the willies," stuttered The Hams.

"The Punkwillies," said the Punk. "Those are the best kind." No one laughed.

The Old Kid who was the unelected leader of the group walked up to the 15 foot, double hinged door and just when he grabbed for the iron knocker, the door slowly creaked open. Amazing bright lights from inside slit the darkness and the boys found themselves face to face with a group of hooded monks. "May we help you?" asked the monk closest to the door who was quite physically imposing.

Punkwillie stepped out of the black leather crowd in his white jeans and tried to peek inside the monk's hood while explaining. "We are with the Proviso East school paper and would like to interview you about the story of Peabody's Tomb."

"Do you have an appointment with the Monsignor, gentlemen?" asked the faceless monk.

"Well, no. We just figured you guys weren't all that busy on a Saturday night and..."

Quiet laughter from the monks interrupted Punkwillie's BS story. The first monk took his hood down and revealed a rather handsome looking man in his 30's. "Well, gentlemen, believe it or not we do have our activities here, but I see no reason not to be cordial and grant your request. Please come in, gentlemen."

The Brothers all looked a little surprised that the Punk's bull got them inside. "Hey, man, we're being set up, man. We're gonna be the next rumored tomb, man," Chief cautiously whispered. The boys all walked inside the aged cathedral and were taken by its beauty. The architecture seemed to transport the boys to the 15th century. The elaborate tower was adorned with huge paintings depicting angels and cloud formations with rays of sun beaming through. The boys quickly noticed that other bands of monks were gathering to see their uninvited guests. "Hey, man, stay together, man, or you'll end up on the menu, man," spoke the spooked Chief.

Suddenly all the monks stopped in their tracks and the entranceway became ghostly quiet when up upon the grand staircase a figure appeared dressed in a white robe with a golden sash around the mid section. All the monks slowly bowed towards the figure who, too, was hooded and rendered faceless. The Old Kid looked at Punkwillie for his estimate of the sitch. "Is that God?" wised the Punk which caused a rippled chuckle from the teens and not even a flicker from the nearby monks. The figure walked down the staircase inspecting the group of teens with each step. Everyone stayed still except for Chief who baby stepped his way closer to the door. The great figure had finally descended and lifted his hood back. There in front of the lads stood an elderly man who seemed to radiate a warm and charming glow with just his physical demeanor. His hair was as white as the snow falling outside and his eyes smiled with an internal wisdom he seemed to possess. The boys, to be honest, were a little nervous because they realized that no one knew they were in the monastery and with one finger click from God they could find themselves chained to a wall with a pit and pendulum nearby. The great figure leaned into the boys and looked them squarely in their questioning eyes.

"Welcome, my sons. We all welcome you to our place of worship and to our home. Please allow me to ask gentlemen... How 'bout those Bears?" This busted the ice into pieces and the boys cheered and smiled back at the grand man. All except Chief who still believed the Trojans had invited him into a horse. "I'm Monsignor De Angelo and these are my brothers. Please feel free to ask your questions for your school paper." This stunned the boys a little since the monsignor wasn't around when the lads stated their reason to visit, but no one tempted fate.

Punkwillie stepped forward and spoke. "Monsignor, there has been a story going around for years about a glass tomb with a child inside."

At this time, the other bands of monks in the hall and balcony dispersed and went about their chores. Monsignor De Angelo smiled and looked at the youths. "Yes, that is true, but we did not kidnap the child. We know the story, too." He gestured towards the chapel. "Come with me, my sons, and I will explain." The boys followed the leading leader through the large hall and into a divine looking temple.

The heavenly beauty of the room commanded silence and even Chief let down his guard although he let slip a whispered, "Holy shit look at this man."

That comment caused some glaring from everyone except the Monsignor who seemed to know the ways of his flock and gave a forgiving glance.

The diminutive church was astonishingly as clean as it was holy. Italian white marble covered the walls that featured brilliant, stained glass etchings of the holy family. The Monsignor proceeded to the front altar and genuflected to the symbol of the cross and made the sign of the cross. This caused the clumsiest attempt in the great history of Christianity as 16 boys attempted to respect their host's sentiment. Part of the group went to one knee and collided with those who had never been in a Catholic church-- again, a backward, forgiving glance from the shepherd to his vacillated herd. The boys seemed a little nervous as their imaginations ran wild with what they were about to witness. All the stories and tales of a captured child being on display were a hard concept to grasp. The last thing any of them imagined was that any of it was true, yet in a few moments all questions were about to be answered, but at what cost? Chief started to mumble about the possibility of them seeing the victim and now having to pay with their lives for the story to be safeguarded. Monsignor stopped and pointed towards the floor. "Behold gentlemen the Child of Marso." The clan hurriedly gathered around a smaller altar off to the right of the pulpit. The sacred table was outlined in shimmering, gold plated layers and all four walls were, indeed, crystal glass, and inside lying on satin red and white pillows was a child-size skeleton. The most startling aspect was that the small, weathered remains had a doll's wax face on it. The boys all stared in complete silence except for Chief who was flicking his head 360 degrees scrutinizing the trappings. He was convinced that he was among mad monks and at any moment they would rush out of the shadows with axes and chains with spiked balls attached.

The Monsignor looked at the youths. "Gentlemen, let me explain the history of the Child of Marso. 75 years ago our order of the Franciscan Brothers in Rome went into a deep catacomb and retrieved the remains of a boy that died around 1000 A.D." The Monsignor had the complete attention of the herd, even the lost sheep, Chief. "They sent the corpse to us as a sacred gift in remembrance of those who passed before and we have preserved the skeleton in this air tight case. We used to give mass in this small chapel every Sunday years ago and I believe that the small children who attended rewrote history with their imaginations. Somebody thought it would be a good idea to put a wax doll's face on the remains to give it a more tender feel. Well, the intention was good, but to a child this is all a little overwhelming." The Monsignor surveyed the boys carefully. "May I ask, where are your writing materials? What sort of reporters just commit to memory?"

"Ehh, Father, we forgot to bring our paper and pencils, but we will never forget what we just witnessed. Thank you for straightening out the myth. We can tell everyone to cool the hysteria. We know the truth now," stated the stately Johnny Hams.

"Well, gentlemen, if that is all, then please let me show you to the door. We have a mass to prepare for."

"Well, good, Father, because we have a party to prepare for, too," said Cuno.

The elder priest led the procession back the way they came and once in the hallway the other monks appeared to give a silent good-bye to the young visitors. Chief was closest to the door. "Well, gentlemen, our door is always open for you at anytime and if you ever want a tour and to experience what our brothers do here, feel free to join us."

Punkwillie once again stepped forward. "Ehh, Father, I haven't noticed any women here. Where are the babes?"

The Monsignor surmised the flock and said, "Funny... I was about to ask you the same thing." This made the entire mob of hooligans chuckle as they left the dark tower.

The Old Kid looked back as they all descended the long, cement stairs. "Well, The Brothers have finally met The Brothers."

"Amen, man," quoth Chief.

The gang assembled once again and started to caravan to the original destination, P-Lid's party in swanky Hinsdale. The full winter's moon now peeked through the silhouetted clouds giving the sky a haunted but majestic look. The snow filtered down as the temperature did the same. The cars finally pulled into Hinsdale as the town was nestling into a peaceful slumber with hearths glowing and cold winds blowing. The Brothers drove passed the three story, massive house of P-Lid and noticed that other cars were everywhere. "Some shindig tonight. Her folks must be in Florida again," said the Musclehead. After parking a block away the boys all got out and carried their booty from the Wisconsin Farms to the blow out. The house and entire neighborhood was in full holiday costume with lights outlining the homes and huge animations of Christmas figures.

The band of boys went up the front steps flanked by illuminated candy canes. The familiar sounds of mayhem and music came through the aluminum storm door. The boys had been here before and knew a few of the locals and regular P-Lid groupies. Mister Mike knocked on the locked door and waited. No response. He repeated the gesture. Still nothing. This time he gave the wooden, handcrafted door a hard kick and yelled, "Hey, let us in. We got the eats."

"Fuck you. Go away," came a rude dude retorting from inside, followed by laughter and muffled taunting. The house looked crammed and the boys had no idea who was giving them grief. The boys looked at each other and without a word spoken went to Plan B, a walk to the back door. They went into the wooden fenced yard and saw that the kitchen area was even more packed than the front. The fun sounds from inside were lighting up all party cylinders and The Brothers were becoming a 16 headed monster that would not be denied. This time Cuno pounded on the back door and got similar results, only this time a girl looked out the kitchen window.

Cuno yelled to her, "Where's P-lid?"

The girl flipped up her middle finger and said, "It's the white trash from Broadview... eeewwww."

Cuno looked at his mates. "Fuck'n rich bitch."

The mood went to Defcon 4 as the boys walked back to the front door. Once more they tried to enter and this time the entire front window filled with the snobs and snobettes of affluent Hinsdale. The Brothers now stood on the front stoop being ridiculed by the brats inside. The bags of stolen groceries were set down and at that very moment a loud sound of breaking ice and metal came from the side of the house. The boys all looked and noticed the long piped, drain spout was shaking side to side and the hanging icicles were falling and dropping like little bombs. Even the teasing teens inside became quiet and pressed to see what was going on. Suddenly the drain started to break apart and fell into three sections on the ground, and like a Roman warrior carrying the spear of Caesar, Mister Mike came around the corner with a ten-foot section of white downspout in his arms. This site brought a rebel yell and battle cry from his pissed off partners. The collective gasps from inside the house could even be heard outside. "Dis kid is totally inflamed," shouted Mister Mike as he built up speed and turned straight for the three panel, French front window. The crashing sound of glass and metal dominated the winter night and horrified screams from the people inside quickly followed. The door flew opened and the battle line was formed right in the doorway. Cuno and The Hams met the brunt of the assault, but the powerful twosome of Musclehead and Sweet Daddy smashed any face that showed to the door. The boys were more than holding their own at the Battle of the Bulging Doorway. The sounds of the backdoor flying open and yelling young men told The Brothers they were about to get outflanked. Mister Mike then grabbed the drain spout and pulled it back from the shattered window. He had trouble with this maneuver as the Christmas tree had become entangled on his lancer. The front yard quickly filled with combative teens and the boys were severely out numbered. Mister Mike started swinging the long drainpipe like a helicopter blade and all and any stayed cleared. The drainpipe was a mixture of razor edged metal, chipped glass and Christmas tree branches-- some weapon indeed! The boys on the stairs quickly regrouped on the front lawn and knew the street fighting strategies of a united front. The two gangs seemed to slow down for a moment and the Hinsdale youths just about surrounded The Brothers. There was a rumbling sound from the house as all eyes looked again to the front door. There in the doorway stood a mountain of a man with only his pants and shoes on. The terrifying screams of a girl were heard in the background and now the boys knew where P-lid was.

"You fucking bastards," said The Mountain who had muscles layered like a Greek sculpture of Hercules. The Hinsdale teens all let out a cheer as The Mountain made his way down the stairs towards the boys. With each step he became even larger. The sound of police sirens began as none of this went unnoticed by the neighbors. "Who do I kill first?" asked The Mountain as he headed straight for the tightly formed Brothers. The Mountain kicked one of the fallen wise men from the destroyed nativity scene. The boys were in a bad sitch-- out numbered, out muscled, and surrounded with the bulls charging. When the human monster came within five feet of the boys, The Old Kid rushed forward. The bright glint of polished metal caught everyone's attention. He was wielding a jack knife. This was a desperate time and it called for desperate measures. The Kid always carried his four inch, swing out, saw toothed blade for many reasons and protection was one. The massive lad stopped dead in his tracks and glared at The Kid. The two boys gave each other a gladiator stare down and the air became anxiously tense. The steam shot out of The Mountain's nose making him look even more Taurus-like. He wasn't about to back down in front of his worshipers and calculated that The Kid didn't have the stones to really use the blade. He was wrong. As soon as he took a step towards The Old Kid, The Kid lunged out and cut a ripping seam down the large lad's pants. This stopped the battler in his tracks and he jumped back at the same time a huge gasp shot out from the crowd. The Mountain's pants waved in the wind and a huge, open slit could be seen. This startled the entire mob as The Mountain felt for blood he surely thought was there. The Kid held the knife out and it nervously vibrated in the air like a rattlesnake's warning shake.

"Let them get out of here," some diplomatic voice cried from the house.

P-lid could see things getting even worse as the cops were fast approaching and a jittery teen was holding a deadly weapon. Like Moses and the Red Sea, the Hinsdale brats parted giving a clear path to the street and freedom. The Brothers made for the exit with both sides giving til we meet again stares. Cuno reached and picked up the plastic figure of the Christ Child that was still in one piece and carried it with him. The boys had just reached their rides when Hinsdale's finest arrived like the moral janitors they were. The caravan boogied its way out of Snootville and back to the other side of the tracks. The cars headed once again down Route 83 and once again turned to the darkness of the monk's monastery. The cars quietly drove up to the front door and a lonely lad got out and placed the figure of baby Jesus in a manger on the doorstep. The boys left their calling card for their holy, new found friends.

The hour was late and the teens were just finishing what brew was left. They all enjoyed telling embellished tales of the fight at P-lid's. They all knew it was The Old Kid once again to the rescue and admired his courage and tenacity. He had a feeling now on how great chiefs became leaders of their tribe and it wasn't a role he relished, but knew it was yet another of life's challenges. Everyone was about to call it a night when The Hams spotted a police car sitting down at the tar pit. He peered closer and noticed it was empty. "Hey, Musclehead, pull by that roller," he shouted as the other cars followed.

Lo and behold it was Officer's Moody's Chevy Biscayne sitting unattended and unprotected. "Hey, let's give him a royal salute," said Hams. The boys all knew the drill and quickly surrounded the patrol car. The beer filled bladders of the boys were only microseconds apart from blasting and spraying the arch rival cop's car. The pee pump on a teenager is something to behold. It can shoot a stream of 98.6 degree piss in a seven foot range with little effort. "Get the top, too," yelled The Hams as he leaned back creating an almost artistic bow of rising steam. 16 portable fire hydrants rained down on the once white Chevy and all the cheap booze and beer covered the car bumper to bumper. The boys all zipped up went back into the warmth of their wheels and watched Mother Nature turn the young urine into one, huge, frozen peesicle. Moody's wheels quickly became a yellow cast block of ice.

"Sure like to see him chip at that for an hour or two," laughed Cuno, but everyone had enough fun for one night and it was time to recharge. The boys all went home to their beds and sticky pages of Playboy magazine. All slept well that night pleasantly reliving how they left their calling cards throughout the western suburbs of Chicago.

Chapter 10
Achtung K-Mart Shoplifters

The winter break was enjoyed, as it should be. Cuno had been on a real winning spree and the bookies at Sportsmen Park horse track became impressed with his betting skills. They wanted to meet the young gambling phenome who had won four football parleys in a row. He and Gino drove out to the track with Mister Mike's brother, Billy, and his bookie, a skinny, rat-faced man in his 30's named Shaky. Shaky had a nervous disorder and was always twitching in little spurts of jerky motions. He told Cuno that he could have a $30,000 line of credit to cover his bets. This would be a stepping-stone on the path to being a high roller, something Mr. Excitement rather fancied. Cuno was a brave soul for being only in his teens and making deals with low-level gangsters. Ask any cop and he'll tell you it's the wannabes that are the more dangerous hoods. They have an image they envision and will do anything to achieve it, no matter how ill conceived. The men and boys shook hands and as they did, Cuno could not help but notice the black handle of a .38 pistol in Shaky's shoulder holster. Cuno could now call in his own bets and even bank some wagers himself. The risk of a risk taker can be more daring than risky.

The holy night of Christmas Eve is full of tradition and festivities that are celebrated by the entire world. The Brothers, too, do their part in observing this sacred time of year with a night that is anything but silent. There is the annual party at Billy Q's house where his family opens their doors for all to join in and become their extended family. The boys all show up at the residence intermittently to wish everyone a Merry Christmas and raise a toast with the "Q's" and friends. Getting a kiss from one of Billy's sisters is a nice perk, too. This year would be no different as The Old Kid made his appearance with his flame, Michele, joined by Stevie and Evie. Gino was belting carols so out of tune that it was hard to know which song he was singing. The world famous Bobby-G was there dressed like a wise man complete with a walking stick.

Michele pointed to him and tugged on The Kid's arm. "Look at that guy in a costume."

The Old Kid looked down at his girl. "That's no costume. He really dresses like that. It's a hippie thing. If it's a fad, Bobby-G is all over it." Michele studied Bobby-G in amazement wondering just how many crackpots are out there. "It's how he gets chicks. Guys will do anything to get a chick, even look like that," sneered The Kid.

The Christmas Eve bash is well known to all Broadviewians. It's a time to stop by and wish the best to the best. Bygones are bygones as the spirit is such that no one brings up anything negative. Old bets, hurtful feelings, cheap shots, have no place at the "Q's" Christmas party. The true meaning of this holiday permeates like the sandalwood candle that gently flickers above the family fireplace.

The mood was already festive and alive, but when good old Mister Mike pulled up with a flaming R on the hood of Rudy the Rambler, the gathering got goofy. The shots of Schnapps were hoisted and the bells jingled as the ancient yule tide carol was trolled. Mister Mike and his cousin, Punkwillie, were five sheets to the wind as they fell out of the Rambler. They both carried their own personal bottle of blackberry brandy, apparently a Christmas tradition that "dated back hours ago" claimed Punk. Wilbur noticed a decent dent on the side of Rudy and asked how the contact got there.

"I hit a sleigh and killed all the reindeer," wisecracked Mike.

"Really man?" chimed Chief.

"It's possseeeble," laughed the cousins together.

Wilbur broke out his pig sticker and started to write his initials on the side door of the beat up beater. The Old Kid followed his lead with his saw tooth buck knife that still had some pants material stuck to it, courtesy of the human mountain. Mister Mike looked over and shrugged his shoulders and joined in with his Swiss Army knife that featured a well-used corkscrew attachment. Everyone now took turns leaving their names to be immortalized for all time on the once pride of Aunt Ruth. Even the quiet, reserved Michele engraved a short message: "The Bizarre Brothers of Broadview."

She had just finished when Sweet Daddy came flying up in his 427 red hot Chevelle. He rolled down his window and barked, "Hey, get to K-Mart. There's a riot going on. No one is paying. Everyone is leaving with the goods." A new world's record was now being established for getting in a car and roaring down the street as the participants of the Christmas Eve wingding jumped ship. The trip to K-Mart was short and fast as the muscle cars muscled their way into the crowed parking lot. The frantic sight in front of the teens was amazing. There were people wildly scurrying in all directions. Those coming from the store had their arms filled with anything not bolted down and those empty handed running back for more. The teens rushed to the doors and joined the human melee. People were crashing into each other carrying the latest electronics, appliances and other goodies. One person was even running with a table full of merchandise with the blue light still attached. This was Christmas Eve and all hell had broken loose as shoppers became angry waiting in long lines and just started walking out in droves and the security cops gave up and stepped aside. Once in the store the group spilt up and went everywhere and anywhere there was something to find. Kids rode bikes up and down the aisle as footballs and basketballs flew through the air and out the door. Punkwillie ran over to the music department and since his friends were the first whites to arrive, there were plenty of rock eight tracks left. He grabbed every Beatle tape he needed to complete his prized collection. Michele and Evie left the store empty handed. They just couldn't bring themselves to stealing, especially on Christmas Eve. The boys on the other hand had little issue or conscience concerns. This was one big corporate present as far as they were concerned. Even the display Christmas trees were getting yanked.

"Guess the needy really need a tree," joked Cuno as he made his way through the smashed jewel cases that had long been picked over. The only place that was guarded by the workers was the back room storage.

"They're keeping that for themselves," shouted Mike.

Hit by this avenging swarm of locusts, the low cost department store was wiped out faster than Custer at Little Big Horn. The boys all headed back into the cars with arms so overloaded they couldn't see where they were going.

"I'm done with my Christmas shoplifting. Everyone on my list is getting something I could never afford," said Punk.

They filled the trunks with everything from batteries to golf clubs. Someone even snagged pink, hi-cut panties for someone real, real special in their life. The youths climbed in and asked "Now where?"

"Midnight mass is about 30 minutes away. Let's go there."

It was a perfect transition from looting to the Lord with a quick stop off at the party to get another shot of cheer and beer. St. Eulalia Catholic Church in Maywood holds an annual midnight mass in its huge parish, filled with families and worshipers from all walks of life. Some of those walks include the local teens that are a little too full of life and alcohol. The Brothers did many things together-- sporting events, social events, fighting, rioting, chasing whores, all the usual and unusual occasions-- even going to church together. What better place to ask for God's forgiveness and mercy while checking out the hot hunnies, rosary beads and all. The boys stumbled in as best they could without raising too much suspicion. After all, any family member could be in attendance. They sat somewhat scattered in the church with Punkwillie and Mister Mike sitting behind a splendid Aryan family-- Mom, Dad, junior, and sister, all blonde, blue eyed, clear skinned, no slouching, healthy glow. Hitler's dream realized. The two boys sat quietly but the heavy odor of cheap blackberry brandy gave away their real condition. The Aryans were appalled and sent mean, un-Christmaslike glances to the youths.

"Hey, stop firing homelies at us, please," directed Mike at the sour Krauts.

Punkwillie looked around at the trappings of the holy church and gave heavy thought to his feelings. The Stations of the Cross were a blow-by-blow recounting of the slow torture of a man who resembled the hippie he met in Olde Town. The sacrificial altar in the front made him wonder about just what was being sacrificed and why all the depression. He thought about all the holy rollers he had met and how sure they were they knew everything there was to know about God. He wasn't into the incessant preaching of a doctrine that was force-fed to him his whole life. "Why not eliminate the middle man and just talk to the real good Lord himself?" He pondered on how many people had been killed in God's name by religious fanatics. The confessional off to his left reminded him of all the times he had to confess his imprudent guilt. What sins could a ten year old possibly have? Was licking the creamy part of an Oreo and putting it back a venal or mortal sin? He smirked at the time he made up treeemendous transgressions in the confessional booth to shock the shit out of the priest. Tall tales of sex with nuns would surely make the padre's head swim with suspicion on his next visit to the convent! Just as he was trying to clear his worldly thoughts that drifted on blackberry clouds, the lights went out in the capacious church. This was yet another traditional observance of five minutes of darkness until the midnight hour. The boys sat as patiently as they could listening to the ritual coughing and baby whining that takes place at all public gatherings. The minutes counted slowly by as the congregation sat in obscure dimness. "What are they waiting for... Christmas?!!" crackwised the Punkie brat. He thought it was one of his best lines, but the Nazis and surrounding parishioners glared otherwise. He had had enough and scooted down the pew to the aisle just as the lights came up and the holy procession began walking straight at him waving the chain pot of incense. Punkwillie was not interested in any more witchcraft and pushed the altar boy carrying the crucifix out of his way. Symbolic and untimely as it may have been, he was out of luck if only the Catholics were to win the heaven sweepstakes. For he was now a man without a religion, but more than happy to walk that dogma!

The great star of Bethlehem shined down on the little village of Broadview as it slept in heavenly peace. Santa and a sleigh of reindeer flew by with gifts and presents for all... courtesy of K-Mart!

Chapter 11
Chance Dance

The next big event of winter break was the annual New Year's blow out at Gino's. This party was like all the rest except Gino had a wild tradition of setting off a brick of firecrackers inside his house. This made an ear splitting amount of noise, but stirred the senses to an animal level of behavior. This year's party was even made more special when Big Chuckie, Ace's biker brother, stopped off with 50 pounds of prime rib. His gang, The Renegades, had a yearly tradition of stealing some steers from a farm in Iowa and putting them in a U Haul truck, then killing the beasts and feasting on tons of the best corn fed beef in the world. Chuckie was an imposing figure at 6'6" 250 pounds. He looked and played the rebel character to the hilt. The truth was, he was quite harmless. He and Ace had a terrible childhood and, like most bikers, joined a gang for some sense of family in his life. He was also into heroin, something The Brothers did not want around them. So, he, Stevie and Evie went upstairs to "Ride the Serpent."

When the countdown began to bring in the New Year, everyone gathered in a circle. The song "Time has Come Today" by the Chamber Brothers was a ritual dance that the kids of Broadview wildly observed. When midnight kicked in, The Old Kid and Michele swapped spits and hugged as everyone cheerfully wished each other a Happy 1968. Wham Bam Pam ran around the house kissing everyone and drinking everything in sight.

She even poured up a boilermaker in an almost empty Windex bottle. This girl could party like an Indian warrior. She could bury anyone under the table and not even appear to be drunk. This was a legendary talent indeed. She had her sights on the Punk boy, but he was a pro player deluxe and seldom swam in the same pond twice. The Old Kid and Michele, however, were becoming known as Mom and Dad. They seem to be constantly together and the teasing got The Kid unnerved at times. He knew he was heading down the tunnel of love without a paddle and his worst fears about being chained down couldn't save him. This girl had him in her magic spell and he was powerless. They both did their best on having protected sex, but some nights passion overthrew reason, the very reason most of us are here. Gino blasted his fireworks, they all gorged like lustful Vikings on pilfered prime rib and a tribal dance to "Time has Come Today" was passionately performed. Ring out the old, ring in the new, as Dick Clark saluted yet another year into the books.

School resumed at Proviso after the break and the whole student body was captivated with the school's powerhouse varsity basketball team. Led by Papa Jim Brewer, Proviso East had talent that got the attention of all the major colleges and pro scouts. The games served as a great social function that got the kids' minds off the differences they had. Cuno was making fast greenbacks with side bets on the game. Over and under was the most popular among the young gamblers. Mr. Excitement was starting to feel rather invincible as he was still riding quite a roll. He tried hard to get bets against the Green Bay Packers in Super Bowl II, but no one believed the reigning NFL Champs were going to lose to the AFL's Oakland Raiders and the Packers' defense was led by Proviso East alumnus Ray Nitschke which made a bet even harder. Hes spotted 15 points, three more than Vegas was giving, but no takers. His biggest venture was posting book on Evel Knievil trying to jump the fountains at Caesars Palace in Las Vegas. Cuno had been to Vegas with his parents and knew what a Herculean effort it would take and the long odds of making it. So on New Year's Day a small group of bettors gathered around a smuggled pay-per-view signal at the Broadview American Legion. Cuno yelled he was giving three to one odds Knievil wouldn't make a clean landing. He got his action and was holding around a grand as the jumpy image on the small TV screen showed the stuntman taking a warm up run up the ramp. "Last call for bets, gentlemen, last call before the big fall," he yelled.

The cash sat high on a table as the announcer blared out. "This is it, ladies and gentlemen. Evel Knievil is making his final approach at the ramp and should throttle it up." The small group of men became deathly quiet as their imaginations ran wild with what they were about to witness. Evel Knievil soared up the wooden, white ramp and zoomed off into the heavens without wings. Like being shot out of a cannon, he lifted into flight at an amazing altitude for a motorcycle. For a brief, tranquil moment it looked as if he was free and clear as his flight zenithed high over the cream colored statues of the great palace. Mr. Excitement was rather excited when he noticed the front wheel degree to the left. He now realized that a huge, horrific accident was about to unfold and a man could lose his life in front of an awe struck world audience and he would gain from it. The motorbike look like a toy as it slammed into the hard, unforgiving pavement and Mr. Knievil became a rag doll with limbs flaying and thrashing uncontrollably. Everyone viewing tightly squinted in moral anguish, but no one looked away. The motorcycle went one way and Evel the other as if in slow motion. It seemed every bone and joint in the man's body cracked apart. The announcer was not announcing as the atmosphere became eerily calm. They all got their fill of morbid curiosity as the flicking image of a lifeless body lay in the bright Nevada sun.

"Wow, I've heard of losing it all in Vegas, but damn," joked the eternal jokester, Punkwillie.

The silence was broken by the sound of a large pile of moola being scooped up by the ever excitable Mr. Excitement. "Drinks on me, boys," he yelled. The bartender leaned over and reminded him you have to be 21 to drink. "Who's drinking? I'm just buying," he said stashing a double sawbuck in the barkeep's shirt pocket.

After the Christmas holiday life gets a little dull with the weather getting even drearier and Midwest melancholy sets in. Cuno wanted to liven things up a bit so he hosted a casino night in Gino's basement. He invited students and former alumni to his affair. He had transformed the wet bar into a crap table. Mister Mike brought a slot machine over that his dad had for years. Beer, pizzas, cards, dice and a porno film to mess with the gamblers' concentration was all the preparation needed. The Brothers all showed up as well as some black kids from Maywood. Fast Eddie was a good friend of the boys and often partied with the Broadviewians. He got tired of seldom getting the hot, blonde, white chick and had to settle with the heavy hitters. He brought his girlfriend, Bootsie, over and some Maywood gang members. This all made the mood uneasy, but everyone was there for one purpose and this was not the time or place for any social confrontations. The only color that mattered tonight was "Mr. Mean Green."

Michele stopped by with Wam Bam Pam, but she left. Pam, however, stuck around. She seemed to have some interest in Fast Eddie and his gang. Cuno started a poker game at one of the tables, but then quickly handled the house duties at the craps table. The basement quickly filled with the gray pewter smoke from Marlboro Country and the "Looks." The black kids liked to smoke menthol cigarettes and Kools were most popular. They called them "Looks"-- Kools spelled backward. Fast Eddie was throwing the bones and rolling hot. He had four passes in a row and was rattling ice in his hand with his partner Darnell Coles yelling "same address" hoping for yet another pass. Eddie flung the dice down the table and they danced in the air and landed with a nine as his point. The table was completely surrounded and most bets were on the come line meaning if Eddie made his point, most bettors won and the house lost... big! Once again Fast Eddie shook his hand and let the cubes fly. "Same address" echoed once again.

"11. Craps! We have a loser," belted out Cuno as he caustically swept up the moola laid out on the lines.

"These dice are loaded, man," bitched Eddie.

"The only thing loaded around here is my heater and don't put it in a bad mood. You sure weren't complaining when you were winning," bitched back Cuno.

The night pretty much went as expected with the gamblers actually having moments of brilliance, but never really knowing when to fold them. That's the secret of why the house always wins-- it has a slight advantage in the games, but the players hang on too long. No one leaves a game when they are on a roll and Lady Luck is on their shoulder. The truth is Lady Lucky is a whore and leaves when the money is gone. Cuno clearly remembers what his grand pappy told him about gambling. "When you're red hot, all you can do is melt. It's not if, it's when!" He always dreamed of running his own saloon with a hot game in the back. Don't take chances, he believed. Take other peoples' chances.

Gino cranked the stereo with The Watts 103rd Street band's "Do Your Thing." This appeased the black players and betting got hotter and heavier as the Looks burned away. The night burned away, too, and around 4:00 AM only the truly hard-core gamblers remained. They all sat at the card table playing dealer's choice. Mister Mike called out his favorite game, "Rap poker."

"What the fuck is that?" asked Fast Eddie.

"You play poker until you feel you have the best hand and when you do you rap the table and everyone gets one more turn. You can raise at any time."

"OK, deal," said The Hams.

Cuno knew the trick in this game was not to get too greedy. The first five cards he got were nothing special-- Queen, 10, 8, 5, 2. He discarded the 2 and drew a Jack. Gino and The Old Kid made their usual bluffing faces while Eddie and Wham Bam Pam were busy playing footsies. Bootsie, Fast Eddie's girlfriend, was passed out on the couch, snoring up a storm. Mister Mike raised the pot $15 and Cuno called as he drew another Queen in trade of the 5.

"Baby, I don't mean maybe, but I do mean soon," shouted Punkwillie as he fanned himself with his cards. This made Darnell Coles and Fast Eddie laugh. The Punk's humor seemed to be more of a black person's type, casual and carefree. He had always gotten along with black students at Proviso better than most whites due mainly to his appreciation of their general outlook on life. White people seemed a little rigid to the Punk and white racists were true idiots that didn't have the courage to make this a better world. All The Brothers saw Fast Eddie during the riots as he saw them. Both parties understood the whys and held no grudge. Martin Luther King had stated that he dreamed that some day children from different races would sit down at the same table and be friends. This dream was now being realized even though it was a card table. Well, at least it was a start! The game continued with the pot being built up to the $375 mark. Everyone had pretty good hands at this time. Cuno felt he should play his pairs of Queens and Jacks, but vibes told him the full house was in the next deal.

"Rap," yelled Wilbur, followed by a collective moan from all the just around the corner players. The young card sharks all drew and dealt their final cards as the taxing chill of the basement grew upon them and seeped into their bones. Wilbur's turn arrived and he laid down four Kings. "Look at my cowboys girls and boys. YIPPIE KIE IE AH," yelled the usually soft-spoken lad.

Punkwillie looked at Will's cards. "Well, out fucking standing, but cry me a river my bo-sham," as he threw out a 10 high straight flush. Cuno was mentally kicking himself, as was everyone else for waiting so long for the perfect hand. Greed comes in all shapes and sizes. Yet another lesson learned. Now sparks flew because no one was sure if four of a kind beat a straight flush.

"It's a tie. One tie all tie," yelled Darnell Coles.

"Your mammies drawers, Darnell," snarled Wilbur. They all argued for some time, but the consensus was that the straight flush won.

"Come to papa," sang out Punk as he swooped the pile of cash.

"Everyone hates a winner, ya know," quipped Mike.

"Hey, don't get nervous because I won a game. I'll give you a chance to get it back," answered the Punk brat.

So they played well into the night, changing games with each deal-- games like "Spit in the Ocean" where the flip card and all ranking cards are wild, "Cincinnati," a hold 'em game, but with bets placed with each card dealt, "Shotgun" and "Three Card Poker." They finally were about to wind down as the ebb and flow of winning and losing played out. Cuno realized the house was just a little ahead for the long evening and decided to play "Blackjack." The only members remaining now were Mister Mike, The Old Kid, Fast Eddie, and Gino. Wham Bam Pam went upstairs with Darnell Coles. The integration movement was at full speed. "Go make some little albinos," crackwised Punkwillie as the couple headed up the stairs to Shangri-La.

Cuno dealt the cards out and "21" began. The ashtrays were full, beer cans empty and cigarettes gone, but the gamblers stayed knowing that Lady Luck was going to sit on their face anytime now. Cuno became uneasy as Fast Eddie got on a roll and a half winning six hands. He seldom took a hit on anything over 12 and the house was sinking faster than the Titanic. The rest of the crowd had it and the game was between Fast Edward and Cuno, the house. On his seventh in a row winning hand, Cuno threw out a challenge knowing that the odds of eight winning plays was highly unlikely. Eddie, tired and worn out, surprisingly accepted and laid all his winnings in the pot. Mr. Excitement threw the first to himself face down and the next card was a 9 to Fast Eddie face up. The turn card to Cuno was a face up Queen.

"The lady stops by to say hello," joked Cuno.

The next card to the ebony youth was a 2 of spades, for an 11 total. Quick Edward was hoping for an

Ace or picture card as he signaled a hit and got smacked with a 3 of hearts.

"14 to the man," quipped Cuno.

Fast Eddie thought to himself how he usually rides the low numbers and lets the dealer take him out. "That's the trick," he told himself. "Don't take yourself out of the game. The dealer can always bust!" He was anything but fast now. His nickname came by the speed which he played pool. He shot like a machine gun in billiards, but with a heap of molten moola staring him down, time was not going to rush him into a bad play. He dragged hard on his Looks and flipped his finger for another daring hit. He thought when you gamble you should do just that— gamble-- and hitting on 14 was just that. The shiny card flipped out and landed face up. It was a 4. Eddie knew good and well a picture card was due and quickly ran a fist over his cards.

"Stay," he whispered.

The ball now moved to the young entrepreneur of the establishment. The pot looked to be around $1.200, not a bad sum for high school kids. Cuno flipped his down card and revealed a 6 of hearts.

"16," spoke the house owner.

He needed yet another hit to over come Fast Eddie's strong 18. Cuno dealt the next play, an Ace of hearts. The picture card that everyone knew was around the corner finally arrived. This was mass suicide but the house had to hit again and Mr. Excitement was now a little too excited, as his hand drew the card but it hit the table and dropped to the floor. A one eyed Jack was lying on the stain covered basement floor. This card would have given Fast Eddie the win.

"What's this bullshit?" yelled Fast Eddie. "You can't be fool'n around, sucker."

"Sorry, the card is dead. It was an accident," yelled Cuno trying to be sincere, but Eddie had hit the temper button.

"Hey, man, you a mother fucking liar," he shouted, waking up his honey, Bootsie.

The tension rapidly replaced the chilled air and all eyes went to Eddie's hands to see if he was reaching for a heater that he was known to carry.

"Hey, man, that's how it goes," stated an agitated Cuno. "You in or out? I'll call it a dead pot and give you back your money."

Eddie stood up and glared at Mr. Excitement. "Man the only thing dead around here is going to be your honky white ass if I don't win this pot." The Old Kid came in the picture and leaned on Eddie as a reminder of just where he was and who surrounded him. "OK, deal the next mother fuck'n card goddammit," said Eddie as he also had his eye on The Old Kid. He knew The Kid's reputation as a warrior and didn't want to get into that sitch. Everyone calmed down as best they could and sat back at the table. Cuno reached for the deck again and this time slowly drew and flipped out a 5 of spades.

"BUST! You BUSTED!" screamed Fast Eddie as he jumped like an M-80 went off in his underwear. Cuno stood there silent and crushed as he saw his house advantage being swept up in the pockets and wallet of one Fast Eddie. Eddie started for the stairs and turned. "Hey, man, let me know when you crazy mother fuckers want to do this again."

The Old Kid stood up and stared straight at the black teen. "Call me a mother fucker again and I will crush your balls into pulp."

Eddie's wide smile got real narrow real fast and he was in no mood for battle. He had just won a ton of fun. He wasn't stupid and realized he needed to show his friends from the other end some class. "OK, boys, I didn't mean anything by it. Just don't lose my phone number." He started up the stairs yelling, "Hey, Darnell, get your lazy black ass up and out. We got to get some Beefeaters, the good gin."

The party was over and the house actually lost money, about $900 to be exact, but, Cuno knew that in gambling the best way to get your money back is to double up on the next bet and so on. Eventually you have to win. Don't you?

Chapter 12
Big Mac Maniac

The winter wore on like a funeral procession: dreary and slow. Snow may brighten the landscape and make it look dreamy, but after the fourth month most people have had enough. Waking up to chilly bedrooms and stepping outside for an Arctic wallop tends to set one's mood to the bitter side of life. Midwesterners endure this and seem to develop a better sense of family traditions because of it, partly due to the fact they are stuck inside with each other and must find ways of coping. The most pleasant form and undoubtedly the favorite activity is cooking. No matter whose house you're in, each family has a special meal or two that is exclusively their own. Punkwillie's mom, an Irish colleen, made one hell of a spaghetti sauce that even her Italian neighbors envied. "Cook the meat in the gravy and add olive oil to soften the meatballs" was her primary secret. Mister Mike's mom made the best damn chili this side of the Rio Grande. She blended tomatoes with succulent peppers and tender turkey. Turkey was the most absorbent meat that sucked up the sauce and held in its victuals. The Hams' mom made burritos with sliced beef and diced potatoes. The barbecue award went to The Old Kid's mom who made a special burger called "Juicy Lucy." The twist on this cheeseburger was that the cheese was inside the patty, not an easy task. If the two patties were not sealed correctly, the cheese would leak out. This was a great treat because a person could add their favorite condiment to the cheese. Sliced olives or onions were a popular choice as well as bacon bits. Food was not a pleasure overlooked by The Brothers, but with their bizarre sense of humor they turned even eating into an event.

The early part of February is a time when most Chicagoans get cabin fever. Even though it is the shortest month, it seems to last forever. People seem to get a little crazy around this time of year and The Brothers were no exception. Cuno was taking book with anyone in the halls of Proviso that The Old Kid could eat more Big Macs than anyone within 30 minutes. Cuno had seen The Kid when hungry and it was almost inhuman. Once the boys went to an All You Can Eat crab legs buffet. The owner had turned off the air conditioner and it was a hot, muggy day in the summer. The Old Kid was dripping sweat like a waterfall, but had eaten so many crab legs the owner threw him out. Cuno knew that when it came to devouring food, only a Grizzly fresh from hibernation could give The Kid a run. The tournament was to be held at the Forest Park McDonald's on Des Plaines Avenue, the same McDonald's that was victimized by Gino and his phantom Mac attack. Several takers showed up and even the lovely Michele, who wanted to see just how big a pig her boyfriend was. There were six participants in all each paying a fee of $25 in this winner take all event. The contestants were The Old Kid, Musclehead, Sweet Daddy, Lunchmeat, a pool shark named Partial, All the Way Jose, just known as "Way" to his friends, and a tough, big German thug from Berwyn named Karl the Kraut. Cuno laid out the ground rules that mainly stated eat as many Big Macs as you can in a 30-minute time limit and no post puking. Cuno's take was twenty percent for being the event promoter, a field he intended to pursue after high school.

Each man was handed his first Big Mac and with a three, two, one, count down the challenge was on. All members easily polished off the first Mac with little effort. The strategies started to show when the second triple stacked burger was attacked. Most took a slow deliberate pace, not to show panic, but a brains not brawn approach. This tactic was not employed by The Old Kid or Karl the Kraut. They seemed to show everyone else that a call of the internal wild beast was going to win this contest. The Old Kid even bit his little finger hard enough to draw blood. This caused a look of great concern on Michele's face, as she looked stunned at her lover boy turned jackal. These two boys were handed their third Big Nasty as the others looked from the side of their eyes with great interest. Remarkable as it was, Karl the Kraut crammed this burger in just two legendary chomps. The Old Kid paid little attention as it was clear he was now detached from this world and in a carnivorous state. This was a place known only to the primitive and manic assailants that unmercifully devour their helpless victims.

They had all hit the 20-minute mark, but it became clear that this was a two horse race. Sweet Daddy's face was a massive mess of special sauce and pickles as he slowed to a stop at number three. Musclehead was hanging tough and becoming the people's choice as his face told the tale of gut grief. "Come on, Muss, get those jaws moving," cheerleaded Gino. The noise level in the restaurant rose with each burger and even the help came out to witness. Gino held his hand to hide his face as one of the clerks seemed to remember this bandit of burgers. All the Way Jose was holding his own and was a real dark horse to win. Jose was handed his fourth Mac with only ten more minutes left on the clock. Karl and The Old Kid both hit the wall at the same time as they took a breath of air and a glaring stare at each other. Then a fifth Big Mac was given to them with only four minutes left.

"Look at their guts," yelled the Hams as the swelling became evident in the bloated tummies.

"Come on Old Kid," screamed his babette, Michele. "Sock it to 'em."

These words fell mute as The Kid was in his transformation level of existence. Trained monks of Tibet have mastered the art of mind over matter, as they are able to generate body heat and dry wet clothing on their back. The Old Kid had gone transcendental as well as he put mind over red meat. His eyes rolled back like a great white shark on the attack when he crammed another chomp. Everything went into slow motion for him as his body began dealing with the overdose of slop it had to digest. Cuno raised one finger in the air and the backward count down began. Both combatants took one, last, desperate stab at the remaining all beef patties special sauce lettuce cheese pickles onion on a sesame seed bun burgers and gave it their best shot.

"Time!" shouted Mr. Excitement and he quickly noted that both The Old Kid and Karl the Kraut had completely eaten five Big Macs in their entirety. All the Way Jose had his head down on the table next to a half eaten fourth burger. "This is a dead heat and now we must wait the required 15 minutes to see if either contestant will hit 4th degree.

Neither man had much to say as Michele tried to get her boyfriend back to the planet Earth with a deep shoulder massage. "Danny, how did you do it?" she asked.

He was blurry and tried to focus her in. "After the third one, the love of Macs kicks in," he answered with a lettuce garland smile. The crowd became quite restless and impatient within minutes.

"Hey, the hell with waiting. Let's just have a shoot off like in soccer," shouted Punkwillie. The crowd approved with a rousing "YEAH." Again neither contestant said anything, but looked at each other with a "let's do it, pal."

"OK, we will go until one throws in the bib," said Cuno as he grabbed two more big burgers and handed them to the stuffed boys. The two grubbers lifted the styrofoam lids and burnt burger aroma made its way up their noses. This was too much for Karl the Kraut as he clenched his fist over his mouth and rapidly doubled up.

"Oh, oh, look out below mates... he's phoning Earrrllllll," yipped the Hams.

No sooner was this spoken and Karl made a half hearted attempt to the bathroom, but his newly found excess weight bogged him down like a lead belly. Everyone scattered in all directions, as Karl became a human fountain of fast food.

"He's erupting! Save yourselves!" shouted Punkwillie running out the door like a scared squirrel.

Cuno proclaimed The Old Kid winner and champion of Macdom. A slight smile came to the bloated lad who was still sitting in his seat with only the puking Karl the Kraut as a companion.

Chapter 13
St. Valentine's Day Massacre

     Valentine weekend had arrived and The Old Kid got Michele to convince her parents that she was going on a retreat in Wisconsin with her friends. The ruse worked as three of the lil foxes played along as well. The trusting parents even signed the fake permission slips allowing their young, innocent daughters to cross state lines for a weekend of good, clean, wholesome fun, with a lil booze, drugs, sex, and general debauchery thrown in. The girls made up a retreat name and said it was in a remote part of Wisconsin with no phone service. Each one told the tale how someone else's parents were going to drive them there. This would work because they gave their parents Wham Bam Pam's private phone number. She, of course, conveniently took it off the hook. So, the girls Michele, Sinful Cindy, and Wham Bam Pam all packed their bags and kissed their trusting parents adieu and parted. The plan almost fell apart before it was ever hatched as Michele's mom started to unzip Michele's carrying case to place in some in case of an emergency tampons. Luckily, Michele re-entered her room and dashed to her mother's side. "Oh, Mom, I'll take those. Thanks so much," she said trying not to sound nervous. Had her mammy opened the case, she would have spotted not only the packs of cigarettes, but a couple of skimpy nighties she had hidden as well. Michele breathed a sigh as her mom left the room with a reminder of how to wear a hat in the cold weather. The teen chuckled to herself as she wondered if she would even see the outdoors.

The girls rendezvoused with The Old Kid and his Goat. Michele climbed in and found good old Stevie and Evie in the back as the eternal party continued. Wham Bam Pam hooked up with Punkwillie and his shiny silver Nova. Sinful Cindy went with them to feel a little more secure. Sweet Daddy in his Chevelle SS and Musclehead's Mo Par Plymouth GTX rounded out the caravan to the north woods. Wisconsin is called the great escape for Chicagoans because it is such a sharp contrast to Illinois. The greater Chicago area is as flat as a steamrolled pancake and with its gently rolling hills and farmland, Wisconsin is another planet. The teens destination was to be a small ski resort near East Troy called Alpine Valley. Skiing is not something indigenous to most Chicagoans, but partying at the lodge is something they excel in. The cars made their way onto the money sucking Illinois Tollway. Usually the plan was to party once they all arrived at the journey's end, but the plan didn't last long, as usual. Punkwillie pulled into the automated tollbooth and deposited his 30 cents in the mesh basket with two empty bottles of Boone's Farm strawberry. The empties lay in the basket like a sign that a major stinko was under way. The pace quickened as the landscape opened up.

"Ahhhh, fresh air," quipped Sweet Daddy. "Smells great...ahhh."

"Nah, Sweetman. I just farted," replied Ace the human fart machine.

"I'm going for the triple crown tonight, fellas," claimed Gino. "I'm gonna kick some cheesehead ass and puke on him."

"That's the easy part, Gino. What about the nookie?" asked The Hams.

"I got plans for Cindy's glands," answered Gino.

"Well, get in line. Way in the back," cracked Hams.

"She'll be soooo loaded she won't know what the hell is going on," remarked Gino as he gulped some rotgut wine called Paisano.

"That's your move?" remarked the Hams. "Get her to pass out? Some Romeo. Why not just walk up and punch her lights out?"

"Now there's a Hallmark moment," joked Sweet Daddy.

The Old Kid was psyched about going to Alpine, but that strange feeling of being too tied down was rolling in again. He knew that a good party was talking place in the other cars with the boys and what if there were hot horny babes at the lodge? Then again what if there weren't? At least he was assured of prime poon-tang. He was learning the balance of life. Everything has its pros and cons. Stevie was lighting up a Whacky Tabbaccie and passed it to The Kid who took it like a falcon on a field mouse. Michele had noticed that her beau was getting more into the weed thing. His hair was getting a little longer, he was not dressing as sharp as he once did, but he was easier to be around. He seemed to be mellowing. She had figured that everything in life had its pros and cons.

She turned to the backseat lovers and asked, "You ever notice how life is in a balance?"

This got Stevie's attention for he loved a good philosophical discussion, especially when a little stoned. "What do you mean?" he asked.

"Well, when you think about it, to have light, there must be dark, and to have good, there must be evil, and to have life, there must be death," she so eloquently said.

The Old Kid looked at her. "Wow, heavy stuff. Maybe you're getting a contact high, huh?"

"Yeah, she's out there for sure," added Stevie.

"To have love, you must have hate, right?" chimed Evie.

"This is major heaviness for sure. I might have to pull over," laughed The Kid.

"And to have lows you must have... highs, like the one I'm getting now," joked Stevie.

"How groovey is that?" added Evie.

The portable party finally arrived at the rural ski lodge located in the scenic southeastern portion of Wisconsin. They went as a loud, boisterous group into the knotted pine lobby. The hotel clerks gave each other the "Here's another traveling circus from Chicago" look. The locals know that these punks from the windy city come to raise hell and have a good time. They are well trained in ignoring the misdemeanors and not provoking the drunk brats into anything that could get out of hand. The entire state puts up with this rude behavior, not for their love of Chicagoans, but because there are big bucks in it. The gang walked up to the desk already smelling of cheap booze and Hi-Karate.

The lovely, young lady behind the counter greeted her guest with a smile and obligatory, "Hi, welcome to Alpine Valley. Do you have a reservation?"

"Yes, we are the Smiths. All of us," crackwised Punkwillie.

The Old Kid had to butt in and take control, as usual. "We have a reservation for Capone." This was a joke he loved to play on the cheeseheads. It seemed to get things done faster.

"Ahh, yes, two rooms," replied the clerk. "There are only two queen beds in each room and there seems to be so many of you."

The Hams leaned in. "That's alright. We don't plan on doing much sleeping."

The clerk gave a cute smile as she handed them the keys. At the same time Musclehead pointed to a banner over the desk: " Congratulations World Champion Green Bay Packers."

"You take that down or we do," he said.

"Sir, let's not start off on the wrong foot, please. The banner stays or you don't."

"WOLF COOKIES... WOLF COOKIES... Muss just got served a batch of WOLF COOKIES," shouted an excited Punkwillie. He just loved a fellow wise ass. The gang loved the come back from the cute clerk, but she was not to be spared by the King of Cracks and Comebacks. Punkwillie leaned over the counter and stared at the cute clerk's breasts, which weren't very prominent. "Hmmm, not a good representation of the dairy state, ya know," as he slightly pointed at his line of sight. The girl just turned away, just like the manual says.

The group went back out to their cars to unpack. The trunks lifted open and revealed a world-class collection of malt liquor and cheap wine and not much else. The only suitcases belonged to the girls. "Where's your luggage?" asked Cindy.

"It's on the next flight," quipped Cuno as he lugged two cases of Old Style. "Come on, boys, time to get fully 'Kraeusened.'"

"Ahhh, the great outdoors," said Gino as he clapped his hands briskly together. " Where are our rooms? It's fucking cold out here."

The groups tried to split up as best they could in the two rooms but it was more of a roulette wheel of occupants coming and going. The Old Kid realized that any chance of nookie in private was going to be a difficult task at best. Finally things settled down and most of the gang went to the slopes to try their hand at skiing. The Brothers for the most part were pretty athletic, but skiing was not a strong suit of theirs. Punkwillie even had big trouble just using the towrope as he somehow lost control and fell, splitting his pants completely at the crotch. While most kids using the slopes were dressed in nice and tight fashionable ski attire, The Brothers wore their traditional greaser uniform of baggy work pants and a black leather jacket. Heaven forbid if they had earmuffs or even gloves. None of them really had any real skiing experience other than hanging on to the back bumper of a car as it drove through the snow, so this lent itself to be a real adventure. Surprisingly, most of the boys caught on rather fast, but the pressure was on, as all four of the girls glided down the snowing slope gracefully and effortlessly.

Once again it was Punkwillie demonstrating just how perilous a novice can be as he blasted past any and all skiers down the hill. He didn't realize that you must turn to both sides to control the run. He thought snow skiing was like water skiing-- straight and upright-- and when it finally dawned on him that this was not the case, it was too late. He tried hard to make some kind of a swish, but to no avail. He could hear the wind whistle by his ear with shouts of "Hey, watch it dude" or "Lookout, runaway train." His speed was ever accelerating, as was his heart rate. He even tried to fall down, but his legs were locked and beginning to spread wide apart. The freezing air flowed through his ripped pants crotch and he feared his balls might crystallize. His legs were now spread beyond any stretch point he ever encountered before and thought "What a way to go... split in half!" He imagined the impending wipe out that would probably accrue at some point. Wild thinking of Evel Knievil's splintering face plant filled his head as he shot passed the screams of the four girls who took off a full ten minutes before him.

"Oh, God," he murmured, "I knew you were going to get me good." His thoughts of how sorry he was for all his wrong and sinful acts raced through his head. For some odd reason a bad practical joke he played on Wham Bam Pam entered his mind. He'd given her a birthday card and a condom filled with Jergens lotion stapled inside and a written "Thinking of You." Unfortunately, she opened this with all her family gathered around the cake. No sooner had a fraction of a second passed when he noticed that the run had a turn in it. "Oh, crap. OHH!" Even though this was a green diamond course, it was still a decent hill and who knew what lay beyond the fast approaching drop off. He felt his ass begin to pucker as he rocketed up and out into the silent air. When the human mind is overloaded on adrenaline, events seem to unfold in slow motion. Such was the case as the Punk looked down to see what his landing zone was going to be. "Plat" was the only real sound the youth heard as his skis broke off as designed. He knew he had landed and was now taking a rapid damage control inventory of all body parts. He felt no real pain except for his chest, which took the brunt of the crash landing. In fact, he quickly realized he was not injured at all and rolled over on his back. "Well if this doesn't take the peanuts out of the shit," he joyfully shouted. He hurriedly reached into his ripped crotch pants and felt around "The twins are fine. They are not ice pellets." This was a big, big relief as he remembered watching a film of how a rose can shatter like glass when in a frozen state.

The swishing sound of skis came over his head as the ski patrol came zooming up followed by the four girls. "Whoa, dude, you're lucky. You landed in our man made drift. It's here for clowns like you." The ski Gestapo helped the Punk up and out of the drift with a warning that he will be booted out if he is seen doing that again.

"Don't worry, gents. The only place you'll find me from now on is safe and warm between her legs," he said pointing at Wham Bam Pam. That statement caused Pam to make a face of discontent. He walked passed her and whispered "and I'm sorry about the card, but it really was Jergens, I swear!" This caused a double dip of discontent, but she did love her Punkie boy so!

The sky glowed a beautiful, amber red as the sun set behind the snow covered rolling hills. The lodge of Alpine Valley was brisling with activity as the fireplace crackled and the sound of laughter permeated off the knotted pine. Musclehead, Ace, Mister Mike, and Sweet Daddy decided to cruise over to Lake Geneva in Musclehead's GTX to go babe hunting. "All the talent here are taken and the ones that aren't should leave their ski masks on," complained Mister Mike. So the horny hunters climbed into the powerful Plymouth and headed to the land of milk and hunnies.

Gino had disappeared with Sinful Cindy long ago and had not been seen all afternoon. Wham Bam Pam was in her room seductively showering when an unannounced nude Punkwillie joined her. "Hmmm your compass is pointing due north I see." she slyly noted.

"Don't worry, baby, you're safe. Just don't drop the soap." The luxurious bathroom's mirror steamed to a dripping wet infusion of hot humidity and distorting images of two naked figures embracing like twine around a stiff tree branch. Tranquil sounds of running water, gentle gasps of pleasure and rhythmic sharp slapping of human hide, deeply penetrated throughout the water closet, thrust fully interrupted by an oatmeal cake of soap crashing upon the bottom drain.

"Shhhhh, we must be quiet. Stevie and Evie will hear us," whispered Pam.

"If those two hear us they will want to join us," laughed Punk. "Besides, they are out cold. They've been stoned all day and are fucked out," added the excited boy.

"Wait. I'll be right back. I need to get the ice bucket. I want to show you what a properly placed ice cube can do," said Pam as she stepped out of the shower and into the bedroom.

"Oh, I'll be right here, dear, just reloading for round two," answered Punkwillie as he punked on his willie, glad his beanbag was in working order after the spill he took earlier in the day.

Musclehead and his group were making good time on the road to Lake Geneva and everything was strictly low sparks as the Elvis was eight track'n away. "Hey, check this out," exclaimed Mister Mike. The car came to a braking halt and parked near a roadside stand that had a sign, "Home Grown Cherry Juice," with a smaller print "Mixes great with Vodka." The boys piled out and quickly noticed the stand was empty, but the snow footprints to the house made a logical path. The small group went up to the farmhouse door and loudly knocked. Within seconds a muffled "OK... OK, I'm coming" was heard. The door squeaked open and there as if he had just walked out of "American Gothic" was the quintessential dairy farmer-- Oshkosh jeans, John Deere hat and all.

"Howdy, boys, what can I do ya?"

The teens all looked at each other with a "get a load of this hayseed" in their eyes.

"We would like some of that world famous homemade juice of yours if we could, please," wise cracked Sweet Daddy.

"Well, I don't know if it's world famous, but we do have some," retorted the farmer.

"Hell, yeah it's famous. All you hear in Chicago are stories about your juice and how it mixes with vodka," Sweet Daddy cracked again.

"Really!" answered the weathered-faced farmer. "Ma! Ya hear that? We famous."

"Oh, yes, I came all the way from Booger Glob, Sweden just for this," joked Ace.

"Well, come on in, boys. Are ya all hungry, 'cause we also sell homemade sandwiches we like to call Bombers."

"Well, yesssssir, we do have a slight case of the munchettes, but just what's a Bomber?" asked Mike.

"Everything from Eyetalian beef to black forest type ham on home made French bread." responded the Farmer.

"Well, then, BOMBERS ALL AROUND!" shouted Mister Mike.

The old woman in a dark corner started to stir as the ash from her cigarette hit the ground. Musclehead looked down at the floor and noticed just about everything known to man had hit the floor at one time or another. Ace went back to the GTX and grabbed a full bottle of Smirnoff and raced back in. The boys sat around an aged, wooden kitchen table as the farmer brought out a huge jug of bright red homemade juice. "Here ya go, boys. One gallon for five dollars and four Bombers four dollars each." The old woman served the massive sandwiches as the old man poured up some juice. Ace opened the Smirnoff's and they all feasted.

When the meal was about complete, the old man stood up and asked ,"Hey, you boys over 21?"

"Of course we are pops. Why?" asked Sweet Daddy.

"Well, I got some homemade kickapoo juice you may want to sample."

"Well, hell yeah. Go gets it," laughed Mister Mike.

The old man opened up a pantry and brought out another jug with a clear liquid. "Go easy now, boys. This stuff will fry the freckles off a French faggot. You're sure you're over 21 now?"

"Hey, our ID's are in the car. Want me to get 'em?" asked Musclehead.

"Nah, I guess it don't matter none," said the old man as he pinched the old woman's behind when she passed by. "This is on the house, boys, for your nice company." They all poured some homemade moonshine into the homemade cherry juice and stood up for a homemade toast. "To a good crop next spring," boasted the old farmer.

"And to us gett'n laid tonight," stated Ace.

"By the way, you don't have any of those world famous farmer's daughters running around, do ya?" joked Mike.

"Nah. The old woman is the only feline under this roof," answered the farmer.

"Nope. Can't get that drunk," laughed Musclehead as the light from her match glowed against the old woman's sneer.

"Moonlight is burning, Bo-Shams. Let's go," said Ace. The boys headed out the door and thanked the earth-toughened old man for his hospitality.

"Keep it groovey and homemade, Pops," said Musclehead.

The boys got back in the GTX and drove off down an unfamiliar, ice slicked country road. While driving, the boys quickly noticed the strong buzz they were getting from the moonshine and laughed about it. Ace turned up Elvis singing "Jail House Rock" and the mood picked up rapidly. Musclehead started power shifting his muscular car and picked up some serious speed.

"Dis ride can beat any sleigh out there," bragged Muss.

"Nah, Rudy would blow the doors off this hog," claimed Mike as he felt his head get heavy.

"Rudy couldn't beat my little brother's red wagon," retorted Muss.

"It's possseeeble," cried out Mister Mike.

"Solemn dis," shout Ace.

"SOLEMN," shouted back Mike.

"WITNESS," cried out Sweet Daddy.

"Dis tub of shit can't even hit 100," said Mister Mike.

"OH, YEAH?" answered Musclehead as the drunken teen stomped on the accelerator like it was a spider. The Plymouth let out a T-Rex roar as the 440 V8 lifted the car stoutly above the pavement. The speedometer started to rise rapidly and the higher it got, the more the stinkoed teens yelled!

"Come on, Muss, gun this bastard," yelled Ace. The needle went from 55 to 90 in seconds and the fence posts became a long, white blur. "95... 96... 97...," shouted Ace as his eyes fixed on the dash.

The car sunk briefly as the road slightly dipped. The subtle rise in the road was all the launching pad the powerhouse GTX needed to become airborne. This major rush was diminished in microseconds as the occupants of the muscle powered wingless plane could see that the road veered sharply right. Once again the slow motion clock started to tick in the alcohol filled heads of the teenagers. They all saw the telephone pole that stood directly in the path of their immediate future. It's amazing how a person can sober up when the heart is on overload. The beefy car sensationally smashed head first into the stalwart, wide, wooded pillar. The propelled Plymouth was still a good five feet off the planet when it hit with such a ferocious force that all the windows shattered and blew out. It's young passengers immediately followed. All the flying teens blacked out at the identical moment, a defense mechanism the human body has in traumatic times. No big blast was heard-- no screams or words-- just four, motionless bodies lying on the frozen field surrounding a crumpled car and its draining liquids. The only sound came from deep inside the twisted wreckage as "The King" himself asked "Are you lonesome tonight?"

The Old Kid was sitting in his lodge suite looking out a frosty window, pondering the moon that shown so brilliantly in the winter sky. There was a soft glow around it and his mind drifted to how amazing it is that we float through space on our own planet. This made all the trials and tribulations of man trivial and extremely immature. He thought of the time when he shook the hand of Proviso East graduate astronaut Eugene Cernan, the second man to walk in outer space. How amazing it must be to look down upon the entire planet. He wondered what sound the earth made as it revolved. This was one peaceful moment and the slowly falling snow had such a light, hazy blue glimmer that it lifted all his teenage stress up and out of his body and mind. The mood was perfect with a Moody Blues lullaby softly playing, as the glow from the fireplace filled the pine-wooded room with flickering warmth. The Kid was waiting on his lovely Michele who was in the bedroom "slipping into his Valentine present" as she put it. He was sipping his glass of merlot when the bedroom door gracefully drew open and out stepped a slender figure into a misty magenta shadow. Michele was a true vision of female, with class, character, and like all elegant women, a style all her own. The Old Kid was now transcending to a place that many men spend their lives seeking. Between the beautiful ambience of the suite and the lovely vision that his girlfriend was presenting, he felt for the first time in his young life what it meant... to be! He realized that humans are not just material beings, but possess an ever-flowing stream of cosmic energy. The Kid even reached above his head to feel the glowing halo that he felt surely surrounded him. Michele stepped into the subtle light and revealed her special choice of sleepwear, a lavender, transparent negligee. The Old Kid was finding it hard to breathe, as this was the first time he had seen her not smashed into a back seat or at a party in a room so dark that he wasn't always sure of what he was grabbing. She sensually stood there taut and perky as nature intended. The Kid was mesmerized by the silky whiteness of her breasts; they looked like they had never seen the sun, because they never had. He walked over to her and they embraced in a cuddling, affectionate hug. She reached her hand inside his shirt and probed his husky back. They began a long passionate kiss with him gently massaging her temples. She opened her mouth and accepted him in. The hormonal endorphins shot through their bodies like arrows from Cupid, creating a true physical bond between the two lovers. Nature has many expressions of erotic, sensual instincts and now, as two joined as one, the sexual rivers overflowed into a sea of love... intensely deep... desirable... ecstasy-blessed. The winds of the north woods called through the forest and swirled upon the timbered lodge as if to celebrate the generative union taking place under the stars and ponderous moon. All the correct ingredients were present for the making of love... and love was made! The young lovers slumbered off in each other's embrace and rested from their long day of travel, adventure and passion. Their sleep was heavy with dreams and peaceful visions.

Then a loud and ardent banging at the door put an end to all this bliss, as The Hams called through the door. "KID, KID, WAKE UP! THERE'S BEEN A TERRIBLE ACCIDENT!"

Shaking his head and trying to get his bearings, The Old Kid quickly deduced the sitch and sprang for the pounding door. When he opened it, he found Gino and

Johnny Hams with fire in their eyes and excitement in their voices. "What happened? What's going on?" asked The Kid.

"We got a call from Ace. Musclehead's GTX had major contact on some farm road," shouted Hams. "They're at a hospital in Geneva. We've got to go!"

"How bad is it?" asked The Kid.

"All I know is that they all lived, but the Musclehead is in bad shape."

The Kid grabbed his leather and told Michele to stay with the others and he would call her from the hospital. They fled in his Goat and fishtailed out of the lodge's lot. All the boys had severe hangovers and had to roll the windows down to get fresh, cold air, or to puke. There was little talking in the car except for Gino who couldn't make out the map. The Hams grabbed it from him and bitched, "Gino, this is a map of Indiana. Do you even know what fucking state you're in?" The road signs gave the boys all the help they needed as they peeled down unfamiliar routes. "We're about ten minutes away," said The Hams looking at the correct map.

"What's that?" yelled Gino as the car rapidly approached a huge collection of swirling lights. The Kid lifted up on the gas as the car came upon a scene of mayhem. Police cars, both county and state, as well as a tow truck and bright red, pumper fire truck were there.

"Oh, my God. This is where it happened!" shouted The Old Kid. The teens all looked at the horrific scene as they did their best to check their emotions. The area looked like a complete Twilight Zone with liquids puddled everywhere.

"Jesus, look at that," pointed Gino. The crumpled remains of a once big and beautiful Plymouth GTX were now squashed like a box that one could put their arms around. The boys stayed quiet, but silently knew that there had to be serious injuries and even deaths involved. They did not ask the police anything or want to draw attention to themselves.

"Look at all the blood. It's everywhere," said The Hams. "Let's get going."

The Kid drove off with his hands uncontrollably shaking from the tumultuous commotion. What were they in for at the hospital and how bad was it going to be? The Goat finally arrived in the charming, little town of Lake Geneva and The Kid followed the signs to the hospital. They parked and walked into the emergency entrance and already felt ill from the strong odor of medical alcohol that permeates every clinical hospital. There is nothing more orderly chaotic than an emergency room at night. The Kid did a quick scan of the sitch from a guy hunched over in his chair holding his head to a kid crying in his mother's lap about not knowing a tractor could do that. The boys all looked at each other with a "What's our next move" look since there didn't seem to be anyone from the hospital around.

Then a voice rang out. "Hey, you guys, hey." It was Ace and he was walking towards them.

"Ace, what the hell happened," shouted The Kid as they all ran to meet in the hall.

"We had major contact. I'm still in shock, but I'm fine," said Ace.

"We saw the car. How can you be fine? How are the others?"

Ace looked at them in amazement as they braced for the worst. His eyes watered as he said, "We all lived. In fact, Mike and I were barely scratched. Sweet Daddy has a broken arm and Musclehead's face is a mess, but everyone is fine."

"How can that be? We saw the car and there was blood everywhere," shouted Hams.

"That wasn't blood. It was cherry juice we were mixing with vodka," smiled Ace. "We hit the pole with such force that the windows blasted out and we each followed in four directions. If we had been wearing our seat belts, you would be at the morgue right now," told Ace.

"The gods surely smile on us," exclaimed Gino. This statement was frightfully true as The Brothers were involved in many wild car wrecks and received very little physical damage.

"Lady Luck has a crush on us," was Punkwillie's explanation for their good fortune.

Since this was something of a country hospital, restrictions were lax and the boys went in to check on Sweet Daddy and Muss. Sweet Daddy was not in a good mood, but very happy to be alive. Muss just laid in bed with an IV tube and his entire head wrapped in bandages and gauze. The leaking blood told of his injuries, but he was drawing air and that was a good thing! Mister Mike had one entire bandage on his hand for his end of the trauma and Ace complained that his balls hurt a lot. "We'll have a nurse rub some Ben-Gay on 'em. You'll feel much better," joked Gino.

This was truly a miracle, but the boys took it in stride. Between the unauthorized crossing of state lines with juvenile girls, Punkwillie flying off a cliff, and Musclehead's GTX getting totaled, this was just another weird weekend in the ongoing saga of the boys from Broadview.

The Old Kid drove back to Alpine to fill everyone in on all the events. It was decided that even though it was early Sunday morning, it would be best to go back to Broadview. Cuno would pick up Muss and Sweet Daddy in Geneva and The Old Kid would sneak the girls back to their houses. On the way out of the lobby The Old Kid looked up at the banner about the Packers hanging above the checkout desk. He remembered how Muss wanted it torn down. With a dead man stare in his eyes, he walked behind the counter and grabbed the large green streamer, and with one mighty yank he ripped it off the wall. "We're leaving and so is this," he said crumpling it into a small ball. "HAPPY VALENTINES," yelled an irate Old Kid. The well-trained clerk did nothing as the pissed off kid threw the gnashed globe into a big hearth near the entrance door. They all loaded up and headed home as the wise, old desk clerk reached down into a long cabinet drawer and pulled out another "World Champs" banner from a large stack.

The ride home was much more sober than the portable party on the way up. Stevie and Evie, however, were not deterred and continued with their never-ending quest of excess and experiences. Musclehead and Sweet Daddy stayed behind in the hospital and dealt with all the police issues. The passengers involved in the crash were all way, way over the legal limit, and way, way under 21 years to boot. All that crap of court dates and counseling had to be dealt with, but they were alive and full of jive. Nothing else mattered!

Surprisingly, the ruse the girls planned went without a hitch as the trusting parents gave their precious daughters a hug. Michele's mom was so happy to see her angel and told her how worried she was after she heard about some Broadview boys being in a bad accident.

"Oh, how terrible. Are they alright?" asked the acting daughter.

"I hear they are OK, but it could have been worse. Drinking, too, can you believe it?" said the upset mother. Michele played her part perfectly and went orderly to her room. "Funny," her mom thought. "She never asked who they were. Oh, well, back to my coupons."

The remaining boys didn't get off as easily as the networking parents of all the parties knew what had happened and who was involved. They all faced severe consequences for their lost weekend that would thereafter be known as "The Saint Valentine's Day Massacre."

Chapter 14
Scar Face

The winter snow was stubbornly covering the ground as March approached and the boredom meter hit red for the youths. The lucky survivors of the Wisconsin wipeout were not so lucky with the aftermath. All the boys were grounded except for Ace whose mom was seldom seen around or anywhere else. Sweet Daddy didn't care as his arm needed to heal, but his folks were slowly driving him nuts. Musclehead was by far the most injured and 175 stitches bore his battle scars. Since he was behind the wheel, he did not jettison as cleanly as the other passengers. His face was deeply cut by a portion of the driver side window that splintered and remained in the frame. His amazing resemblance to Elvis had been jeopardized with this facial wound. He was warrior tough, though, and felt like his gash was a badge of honor. His folks had the ambivalent duty of punishing him for his actions and taking care of their son. He did wrong, yes, but what teenager hasn't crossed that line? Musclehead accepted his just sentence of being scarred for life. His biggest concern now was getting enough insurance cash to buy another beloved GTX. His parents slammed that idea by presenting him with their new insurance rates. Thanks to the accident, they would have to pay triple for the same coverage. Oh, the joys of parenthood!

The Chief, Cuno, and Punkwillie were wheel'n around late on a Friday night when the Punk kid came up with what he thought was a grand idea and certain boredom beater. "Hey. Let's go over to Mt. Carmel Cemetery in the morning and dig up Al Capone's headstone. Just imagine how cool it would look over my dad's bar in the basement." This was without question one of the stupidest thoughts anyone could have and the scary part was the other two teens agreed with him.

Al Capone is to Chicago what Beethoven is to the piano. Although Capone was without question one of the most notorious gangsters in the history of the United States, he was viewed as somewhat of a Robin Hood by many Chicagoans. When the Great Depression hit in the late 20's and early 30's, work was very, very hard to find. Men had to resort to all kinds of schemes to get food on their families' tables during those desperate times. Al Capone was one of the few employers that provided many with good paying jobs. Illegal work, yes, but when your kids are half starved and freezing, what's the big deal to drive a truck from Canada full of beer and booze? Probation came at a time when the country needed a drink the most. The powers that be had a pipe dream that if all alcohol was declared illegal, no one would drink and all vices would magically dissipate. Just the opposite happened as people went to great lengths to quench their thirst for hootch and if one had to use a bathtub to brew toxic gin, so be it. Al Capone's empire flourished under this new amendment and crime became organized, ruthless, and powerful. While the government struggled to provide basic services, Capone hosted soup kitchens for any and all that needed a hot meal. Yes, he was evil and would kill anyone in his way, but he was a man that came from a blue-collar world and he knew how to give what could not be gotten, legally at least.

The boys drove the usual rounds throughout the snowy night and went to Chief's garage around sunrise to pick up a shovel and pick axe. They ate some breakfast, and at 8:01 AM the grave robbers drove through the just-opened gates of Mt. Carmel. This sprawling cemetery is the final resting place of many famous and infamous Chicagoans. You can find the mausoleum of the "Black Hand" gang ruled by the vicious Genna brothers, a group of mobsters so cold that they coated their bullets with garlic believing it would cause gangrene. There lies the grave of Dion "Deany" O'Banion, boss of the tough O'Banion Irish mob. His main torpedo man, "Machine Gun" Jack McGurn, rests not far off. But, the number one attraction of all these tombs was the one and only Al Capone. For such a famous man he lays under a rather ordinary headstone-- just a flat, common marker that simply reads, "Alphonse Capone 1899-1947 My Jesus Mercy." This was the trophy the misguided teens sought as they drove up and parked just a few feet from the grave.

"Wow. No one is in sight. Let's do it," said Punkwillie ashtraying a Pall Mall.

"Hey, man, I'm not sure where it is, man," remarked Chief. A couple of inches of new snow had fallen over night and obscured any markers lying close to the ground.

"Let's take a gander," said Cuno as the lads all got out of the Road Runner and started to search the nearby turf. Each boy went his separate way, scouring the snow covered graves.

Chief started to think about the realism of standing upon rows and rows of dead, rotten corpses. "Hey, man, this place creeps me out, man." He stopped and looked around at the haunting landscape.

"Hey, man, you know something, man? I would like to be here during an earthquake, man."

Punkwillie just looked at him and questioned him with a "Why?"

"Hey, man, I bet you could hear all the bones rattling about when it hits, man."

This passed with no comment. The boys kept the search going, when Cuno halted quickly and shouted, "Whoa. Let's get out of here, now!" He seemed very frightened and shocked.

"What's wrong?" asked the Punk.

"I found Capone's grave," Cuno stated and began searching the grounds with fast head movements. The other teens ran over and hit the brakes hard, too. There, lying at their feet was the flat, simple headstone of Al Capone with all the fresh fallen snow brushed carefully off. They then noticed a series of footprints leading to and from the gravesite.

"Oh, my God. His tomb is watched and guarded," spoke a spooked Punkwillie. He, too, joined Cuno in a lighthouse scan of the area. With no words spoken the boys slowly walked back to the car.

"Thank God we didn't haul out the pick and shovel," said Cuno.

"Hey, man, if we did, we would become speedbumps somewhere, man."

The boys all realized that if the new snow hadn't fallen, they would had continued with their stupid, disrespectful plan and a price would be on their little, empty heads. They got into the Chrysler and drove slowly out of the cemetery searching, but not seeing, a soul, until they nearly reached the huge iron gate and noticed a man standing behind a crypt.

"Look at that dude," said Cuno. The man was whiter than the snow with a smile even colder. Cuno gunned the Road Runner and bolted out of the land of the dead before they would become permanent members.

Chapter 15
Riding the Serpent

The Proviso East varsity basketball team continued with its success as the team's schedule concluded. One of the biggest games of the year was the annual trouncing of rival Proviso West. This game had great significance to all the Proviso East alumni, as the blue collar, salt of the earth East school faced the richer, white jocks of the West. This year Proviso West hosted the event, which meant a good showing of white-collar conservatism, would be present. The Brothers were all attending this yearly massacre and Cuno had plenty of bets to cover with his healthy 15 point spread. This was also the first extra out of school activity for the injured Musclehead who still had his face taped up pretty good. The all white Proviso West squad was no match for the 75% black Proviso East team. The only real advantage the West team had was at the line making free throws. Everyone knew that the white kids were slower and less agile on the court, but as pressure shooters they excelled. The boys all hogged an entire row to themselves and immediately raised the attraction antennas. The usual visual treat was the parade of poon known as the Proviso West cheerleaders and this year was no exception. The boys became quite still, just like a dominant lion studying his pride of lionesses. Punkwillie became uncharacteristically still as his eyes fixed down at the West's cheer chicks screaming about their Panthers and usual rah-rah crap.

"Look at the Punk," said Gino. " He's becoming twitterpated." The poor boy was enamored with one the enemy's hunnies. She was a picture of health and beauty-- blonde, big boobs and brains-- who could ask for more? He knew she was smart as the other girls watched her to stay in time and in step with each drill.

"Forget it, Punk," said The Hams. "The only way she would go out with you is if she loses a bet." The Punk sunk a little in his seat, but his eyes stay fixed and true on this glass of wholesome milk.

The teams came out and the game began with Proviso West actually taking a ten-point lead. Everyone on East's side seemed rather unconcerned about this except a kid squirming like a worm in his seat named Mr. Excitement. Cuno had over extended himself on this sure thing and was holding around $900 in wagers. The quickness of Proviso East took over and by half time they took a seven-point lead. The half time was the usual nonsense of ritual chants and girls jumping around and spreading their youthful, lean legs. This is all in the name of raising school spirits, but it quite often raises other things as well, which is why some boys are reluctant to get up and walk to the bathroom.

When the game continued it became more than apparent that this was going to be another whitewash of the white guys. The Chicagoland area is one of the most fertile fields for basketball talent in the world. There is a wide and varied range of ethnic and racial talent. The inner city schools are comprised of mostly black kids who are quick as lighting, but lack discipline and defense skills. The suburban schools that are mainly all white are well-disciplined and good shooters, but are slow and clumsy. Teams like Proviso East had the perfect tapestry of racial makeup. Seven of the twelve players were black and five white, with combined components to give their team an unbeatable personality. When the game got out of hand in the last period, Cuno started counting his winnings. The rich, spoiled brats of Proviso West started a cheer directed to the working class Proviso East kids: "Your dad works for my dad. Your dad works for my dad."

The game ended with some pushing and shoving by the two teams and the extra police on hand quickly took control of the floor. All eyes were on the commotion taking place in the over heated, body-sweat smelling gym. Well, not all eyes, as the bewitched and bedazzled Punkwillie stared captively at his vision of perfect beauty. "I have to meet this cheerleader," he thought, "and maybe someday she will let me feel her pom-poms!" The crowd left and The Brothers were heading off to a victory party at Gino's. Punkwillie tried in vain to locate his lustful conquest, but she disappeared from the scene, but not from his dreams!

The gambling endeavor undertaken by Mr. Excitement had been going quite well, so he went heavily into the NCAA March Madness tournament. He prided himself on his extensive knowledge of sports and human nature. When trying to figure out what it takes to win, he'd throw the human factor into the equation. This means that even though an opponent could be an overwhelming favorite, one must chart many other intangibles such as recent events in the personal lives of the players, and the history of individuals and teams in big games and under pressure. Lots of calculating must take place. Cuno's favorite indicator was a new coach. He was always looking for the next Vince Lombardi, a man that could mold and motivate people into winners. College basketball had its legendary John Wooden and his UCLA Bruins. Cuno was looking for the next, great unknown to emerge. He thought he might have found him-- North Carolina's Dean Smith. This was an up and coming coach and he demonstrated all the criteria for a winner. Cuno followed this team throughout the entire NCAA tournament and Dean Smith's Tarheels looked like the real deal. Mr. Excitement played this team in each of its games and was winning. He was careful not to make the big mistake most gamblers make and feel too confident or invincible. This lad was wise beyond his years. Gambling could be a great high with lots of thrills and action. Young Cuno had been on a roll and everything was going just great. He had the world by the canollis. All he had to do was keep cool and keep winning. This simple plan hit a snag when for some unexplainable reason Mr. Excitement phoned in a rather large bet of $500 on two teams he knew little about. Houston, led by "The Big E" Elvin Hayes, was playing the Cardinals from Louisville in a regional semi-final game. Houston was a strong team and was laying 16 points. This was a hefty spread meant to send the novice and play-it-safers to a nice cushion of 16 points. Cuno had seen some of Houston's games and he knew just how powerful they were. Mr. Excitement felt this game was going to be a real ass whooping, especially when he read that some of the Louisville players had the flu. He took Houston and laid the points. Some of the boys came over to watch the game with him on his family's brand new, color television.

"Hey, man, this is like being there, man," commented The Chief.

The chips and other snackies came out, as well as Cuno's sister who felt the intense eyeballing she was getting. She had just turned 14 and had apparently grown since last seen by this crew. She sat for a short time realizing that basketball was going to be on for a while and was not too thrilled with it. Finally, she grew tired of visual probing and turned around with a "Take a picture you guys even smell horny" look. With that she left the room, with scrutinizing eyes on her thighs and other potential points of interest.

Cuno paid no attention to any of this as the score went back and forth more times than a congressman's convictions. The game was down to the final minute with Houston up by 17 and they had the ball. All they had to do was let the clock run out as it ticked the final few seconds' left. One thing about sports and is that people are involved, and when people are involved, anything is possible. The Houston guard was dribbling the ball up court and the Louisville defensemen were graciously conceding defeat as the clock ticked away. "In fifteen seconds I'll be $900 richer," shouted the kid gambler. Everyone started rooting for their friend and knew that if he won, he was buying, which is something to root for.

"11... 10... 9... 8..." shouted the gang of lads, when all fell silent as they watched in complete disbelief as the Houston guard inexplicably stopped dribbling and just handed the ball over to a Louisville forward who rammed and crammed a slam dunk as the clock ticked and the game ended. Houston won by 15! The room was completely silent, as the stunned boys could not believe what they just saw.

"What the fuck was that?" shouted The Old Kid.

"Hey, man, I ain't seen anything that weird since Oswald got shot, man," consoled The Chief.

Cuno stood utterly dumbfounded as he struggled to regain his cool and form a sentence. He just witnessed a $900 snatching from his pocket and it wasn't pleasant. The phone rang and Cuno's sister was up the stairs yelling that it was for him. "Yeah, I saw it. I know. Yeah..." spoke the shaken lad as he rapidly hung up. Everyone knew who was on the other end. It was the bookie from Sportsmen's Park called "Shakey" and he was giving a friendly reminder of what was owed. This wasn't the end of the world and Mr. Excietment knew the age old gamblers philosophy of doubling up your next bet, because you have to win sometime, don't you?

March comes in like a lion and leaves like a lamb-- the old adage about the first month of spring. The Midwest was finally starting to thaw from its frigid fellowship with nature and people's spirits seemed lifted. Activities at Proviso East were in their usual throws and the administration couldn't be happier. The varsity basketball team made it to the elite eight, but lost to the eventual champs Thornton Township High School from suburban Harvey. The atmosphere at Proviso was relatively calm and the race troubles of the fall were not very apparent. There were still more than usual fights between white kids and black, but those instances were more individual disputes. The only real action going on was Cuno's quest to make his money back. He devised a plan that he would study the daily races at the local Maywood harness track and follow some horses that would close to a lock. The main component to this was to get reacquainted with an old friend of his brother, Jack Slade. Jack was now a jockey at Maywood and had to have inside information on the condition of the horses. Cuno and Mister Mike paid Jack a visit one Tuesday night at the track and found him to be a rather nice guy, but definitely a boozehound. The boys were also surprised to see how much bigger harness drivers were than a thoroughbred jockey. The extra weight actually helped the harness's traction.

Jack told the boys to keep their eye on a new arrival named Gusty Wins. "This horses is a real up and comer," said Jack.

"Hey, Jack, how can we thank you?" asked Cuno as he reached for his wallet.

"Nah... nah, no money now. That would be illegal. Look, if the horse does well for you, great, and should I get hooked up with one of your teenage girlfriends, that's even greater," said the cheap whiskey breath jockey as he winked.

"No problem, Jack. We can take care of you there. Thanks again," Cuno said as he and Mike left the barn.

"Who you gonna find to get in bed with that sleazeball?" asked Mister Mike.

"Hell, Handjob Rita owes me for a few favors. She can wax his trombone for me," said the ever scheming, ever dreaming Mr. Excitement.

"America, the land of opportunity," laughed Mike as the boys headed home.

Three days later, Cuno read the Chicago Tribune's race result and saw that the horse, Gusty Wins, did indeed win, and by nine, convincing lengths. This was good enough for the boy and he made plans to be at the track next Friday when this up and comer was going to race again.

Most of The Brothers ventured out with Cuno to the track to see and bet on this horse. Cuno asked them not to lay any moola down on his pony because it would drive the odds down and affect his payoff. Gusty was running in the fifth race and hadn't moved in class, which meant he was racing the same grade of horse he walloped a few days earlier. Jack Slade spotted the boys and walked by giving a thumbs up. Turns out Jack was the jockey for Gusty Wins. The fourth race finished and not one of The Brothers had anything. Mister Mike even bet a heavy favorite to show and it lost out in a photo finish by a nose. The track announcer gave the opening odds and scratches for the fifth race. Out of respect for Cuno, no one placed a bet in case they won and he didn't, because they knew he was going to make a big play. The opening odds had Gusty Wins as the favorite with three to one odds.

"Damn, your horse is the chalk," said The Hams. "That's a good sign."

Cuno didn't raise his head from the Racing Form, but responded with, "The smaller the odds, the smaller the payoff. I'm gonna have to go thermo-nuclear and break the piggy bank."

"Five minutes to post. Five minutes to post," announced the announcer.

"Well, boys, wish me luck. I'm making my move." With that the young taker of chance took his chance and walked up to the betting window line.

"Three minutes to post. Just three minutes," blared the speakers as Cuno coolly dug deep and pulled out one, fat, leather wallet. He stepped forward to the betting window, which had a huge, white sign above it, which read: You must be 21 years of age to make a bet.

Mr. Excitement looked the mutual man dead in the eye and spoke. "$400 on Number 4 in the fifth to win." The man in the booth punched out the ticket and the youth laid out four c-notes and walked away with ticket in hand and hope in his heart.

The next man in line seemed puzzled and asked the mutual man, "That kid isn't 21. Why was he allowed to place a bet?"

The red, pin-stripe shirted man behind the counter lifted his head slowly and glared at the customer. "This is Chicago. You gotta problem with that?"

The complaining customer leaned forward. "I'll report this. You shouldn't have young kids running around breaking the law."

The mutual man motioned his finger at the just and concerned citizen to come closer. "What town you from, pal?" asked the mutual man.

"I'm from St. Paul, Minnesota," answered the honorable man.

"How would like to go home in a box, pal, 'cause here we don't break the law, but we do break the legs of accusers," spoke the mutual man as three, gorilla-type men silently walked over to the window with grins one gets when they enter the gates of hell.

The complaining man looked at the man in the cage booth as his face went through a montage of pales. "Five dollars on Number 7 to place in the fifth, please," and with that he disappeared into the winds of the windy city.

Cuno joined his mates at the rail near the finish wire to get a good view of the ending. He held his ticket like a baby clutches a bottle. "The horses are at the post," came the announcement as the large screen TV on the tote board showed the pace car entering. Harness racing is like watching a well-crafted ballet as all the horses get in position behind a spread open gate of the pace car. The horses don't gallop wildly like the quarter horses and thoroughbred races. A harness racing horse is called a trotter because it has been trained to run in a complete and beautiful synchronized gait. This motion looks extremely fluid and graceful as the horses pull a two-wheeled harness complete with buggy whipping jockeys. The pace car moved near the starting point as the ponies closely followed in perfect position.

"Herrrre we go, Bo Shams," yelled Cuno.

"And they're off!" spoke the track announcer as the pace car accelerated and glided away from the horses. "Bret Handover stays fast on top with Won To Three second and Blue Blues pacing third." Cuno and the gang remained calm, but desperately waited to hear the sound of wagered animals' names and position. The horses made their way up the backstretch as the announcer kept up with the fast and furious action. "Blue Blues now takes command and here comes Gusty Wins charging hard on the outside." This got the boys all excited as the horse went into the clubhouse turn and headed for the stretch. The horses were all tightly packed, but came into a clearer view with each step. "Here they come spinning out of the turn onto the stretch," cried out the track announcer. "Gusty Wins shows the way by two lengths, Won To Three, Dr. Jones and Kiss Me Miss Me rushing up."

"COME ON, WHIP THAT PONY, WHIP THAT PONY!" yelled Cuno as he crunched the ticket deep into his shaking hand. Jack Slade seemed to have heard the message as he cracked his whip over the horse's flanks causing a burst of acceleration as the horse charged down the home stretch.

The crowd noise swelled with a wave of emotion that only money can cause. The announcer was getting drowned out as he called, "Gusty Wins opens by four lengths."

"Come on, come on, " repeated Mr. Excitement as he pounded his fist on the metal rail. His horse was now a mere 25 yards from the wire with a huge lead. This is what a gambler seeks when his wager goes from fancy to fact. The lads could hear the whip cracking in the chill, night air and the hooves pounding on the soft, perfect turf as the jockeys swung their horses to the wire.

Suddenly, a rapid gasp filled the ranks as cries of "broke gait... broke gait" screamed out. Gusty Wins committed the deadliest sin a trotter can bear. He fell out of step and broke his fluent motion. Once that happens, all speed is lost and the harness swerves out of control. The other horses came up like freight trains and blew passed the broken down pony and rider.

Cuno stared out in complete disbelief, a feeling he was unfortunately becoming accustomed to. "I can't believe this luck I'm having," he dismally stated. His Bo Shams had little to say except for a consoling pat on the back. Every sportsman knows that things go in cycles and eventually the pendulum will swing back. The young gambler knew he had to stop his downward slide before it was too late.

"Let's blow this caboose," spoke The Old Kid. The boys watched Jack Slade getting off his broken harness while the trainers tried to calm the white-lathered horse. This was all was just too depressing for Cuno to watch as he turned and started to walk away from his nightmare.

"Hey, Jerkoff," shouted a voice from the grandstands. "You having any luck tonight, sucker?"

Cuno squinted his eyes to focus on the dark, silhouetted figure. He then recognized the high, shrill voice. It was Shakey. Things weren't bad enough for the lad. He now had to deal with a bookie he owed beaucoup bucks. Shakey walked into the light while fixing a solid stare on the beaten boy. "You got a week to pay up, dude," said the sleazy man with the mousey hair.

"Yeah... I know, I know," spoke Cuno trying to put on his no problem face.

The gangster got kissing close. "Don't get cute and try to stiff me, my little friend. I don't wanna give you a turban," said the twitching Shakey.

"What's a turban?" asked Mister Mike.

"It's how the doctor wraps your head with bandages for a fractured skull," answered Shakey. This war talk started to totally inflame some of the boys and they let the little man know he was surrounded by some teed-off teenage thumpers. Shakey surmised his situation and let his tan, leather jacket flap open a little, revealing a mirror chrome Smith and Wesson 38 resting in a shoulder holster. With that he walked back into the darkness from which he came. Cuno said nothing as the boys made their way out of the dreary little racetrack and into the Chicago night with its gusty winds.

Chapter 16
Shoot to Kill

Spring was starting to blossom and bloom as the bare, stark trees came budding back to life. The Midwest does not have subtle weather changes. The transition from winter to spring takes place in the matter of hours as the wind shifts and the warm, humid, gulf air dominates the region. The warming sun is very much a welcomed friend to the colorless landscape as the grass greens and birds sing. To lift the mood even more, the sports crazy town of Chicago becomes Shangri-La as the Cubs and White Sox start their new seasons filled with all the false hope of seasons past. The Blackhawk's were finishing a great year with a stellar line up that included the great "Golden Jet" Bobby Hull, Stan Mikita, and Phil Esposito. The new expansion NBA Bulls looked promising as well. The city was coming out of its wintry tomb and the air was filled with the sound of lawnmowers and barbecue smoke.

Proviso East had now become much more mellow as an almost peaceful calm settled in. The students seemed focused on the end of the school year. A newly formed black student union developed a forum for students to address their feelings regarding race or any other issues they wanted to discuss. Fred Hampton had made a few appearances with his advancement of socialism doctrine, which gathered support from many students of both races.

The Brothers were still firing homelies and playing chomps at lunch. The Old Kid and Michele were becoming a typical teenage couple as they fought, made up and made out. The halls were becoming a beehive of hormonal activity. Guys were pulling chairs out from girls as they sat down, which had to be the worst approach for attention ever. Girls became over-acting drama queens, standing by their lockers crying over who knows what. The yearly rituals of adolescent sexuality were now in full performance. Wham Bam Pam thought it would be a good idea to give Punkwillie an ultimatum about their relationship getting more serious or else. His only response was to pull out a pencil and point to the eraser. Mister Mike and The Chief were gathering up the boys to go watch a Blackhawk's game on Cuno's new color TV. They found Musclehead in the parking lot showing his newly formed scars to some girls in the library.

"Hey, Muss, is this your new pick up tactic? Wee, wee, poor me sympathy?" said Mike. Musclehead chose to ignore this and continued with his war story for the honey bees.

"Well, man, it's an improvement over your last move where you just literally pick the girl up like a caveman, man," teased Chief. Again the comment was tuned out even though it referred to a real event last year when the Chief was rapping with a sweetie at a party and Musclehead came over and carried the girl off over his shoulders. Both Chief and the girl were overcome with complete disbelief and it looked like this Neanderthal move just might work, until he set her down. The smack across his face was so piercing, it was even heard by Gino who was upstairs in his room with the door closed and headphones on. Musclehead finished his spiel to no avail and threw in the towel.

"We're going to Cuno's to watch the Hawks," said Mister Mike. The three boys walked down the hall passed Wham Bam Pam who was at her locker crying and being consoled by some girls.

"Hey, man, business as usual, man," said Chief. The only words the boys could hear from the sobbing chick was something about an insensitive jerk.

"Got to be talking 'bout Punkwillie," laughed Mike as the trio left the grounds.

The gang went over to Mr. Excitement's house even though it was a Thursday night. The boys wanted to give their pal some support for the dilemma he faced. He owed a bookie $900 and lost three months of car payments at the track. Mr. Excitement was facing the unthinkable-- selling his beautiful Road Runner, something he worked hard and saved for. This was worse than death. Musclehead had lost his awesome GTX and if Cuno lost his wheels, it would be like The Brothers missing their two front teeth.

All thoughts about his gambling trouble took a back seat when the game came on the cool, color TV. The Hawks were playing the New York Rangers in New York-- a great rivalry. The boys shot the bull and pigged out on snacks. Punkwillie talked about almost being caught for writing "sex education should be hands on" in his health class. Watching a game in color was really special. It just looked so real to life. No one dared ask the host if he made a wager on the game. May as well ask how someone terminally ill feels. The game was a hard checking affair with all the vicious violence Americans love so much. The color camera zoomed in on the colorful Pierre Polite as the commentator shouted that the Blackhawks had a breakaway. Chicago's living legend, Bobby Hull, was skating fast and hard towards the New York net and pulled his stick back to launch a blistering slap shot when suddenly the screen went blank. The dark screen was then quickly filled with that stupid looking CBS eye logo. The boys all looked at each other as the words flashed "News Bulletin."

"Oh, oh. This is it. World War III has begun," joked Punkwillie.

The set blared out "We are sorry to interrupt this program. News flash from Memphis reports that the Reverend Martin Luther King, Jr. has been shot. The first reports are that the wounds are fatal. Stand by for further announcements."

The room fell eerily quiet. Each teen was digesting what they had just heard. The Brothers as a group were not much into politics and current events. They just lived for the moment and the party, which was a typical teenage view of the world. They also knew what this assassination could mean to them and their community. Tension between the two races had finally simmered at Proviso, but this could easily ignite another full out riot.

"Well, here we go again," said Wilbur as he rubbed his nose, the very same big snout that took an umbrella beating a few months ago. Dr. King wasn't very well liked in the white community in general, but he was respected. The white youths at Proviso were learning to overlook their parents' bigotry as they witnessed first hand the utter frustration that blacks and other minorities felt. They had learned that all Dr. King wanted was what the constitution guaranteed, that all people in this country would be treated equally. The new, color television showed Walter Cronkite at his desk with people scurrying in the background.

"Guess that's it for the game," spoke Ace as it became apparent the hockey match was no longer important.

The phone rang and it was Mister Mike's mom. She was checking up to see that he wasn't out and about. She, like many in Chicagoland, were bracing for what could be a full out race war. Most of the boys decided it was a good idea to head home and help make sure everyone was accounted for.

"Well, fellas, see you at school tomorrow... battle stations, battle stations," joked The Old Kid as he and his amigos left Cuno's all wondering what the next day would bring.

That night the fears of the city of Chicago were slowly becoming realized as the city's predominately black west side erupted in a full scale riot. News of riots in many of America's cities filled the airwaves. The Old Kid helped his dad clean and load their hunting rifles in case unrest spilled into the suburbs. The night went by relatively quietly except for a few police and fire truck sirens.

The morning came and many parents made decisions on whether to allow their kids to attend Proviso East. The students were wise and veterans of the last outbreak. This was a matter outside of the school and many felt it would be treated as such. The Brothers still showed the good sense in not arriving in their hot, cool cars, except, of course, Mister Mike and his steadfast Rambler, Rudy. The boys all arrived together knowing about safety in numbers. The school took the precaution of having extra security present. The police seemed very edgy, as they were well aware of the trouble going on just a few miles east of them. The news of Chicago's trouble was downplayed in the media, but the blacks of Maywood, who all had relatives there, knew the real story. The Brothers banded together as they crossed First Avenue and on to the school grounds. The first observation was the lack of white girls at the school or anywhere in sight just as during the October riot. Once inside the doors any notion that this was going to be a normal day were dispelled immediately. Standing in the hallway was just about every black student the school had. The tension once again filled the air as the white students grouped together in whatever space was available.

"Well, another battle down memory lane, I see," laughed Punkwillie.

There came an announcement over the PA that school would be suspended for the day. This was an attempt by the administration to quell the brewing trouble. They realized that their hope of opening school wasn't going to work. The belief being that students could discuss their feelings in a forum, but the anger in the black community was beyond discussion. The mood with white students was that this wasn't their doing and they were upset at the King assassination as well. They also knew that the black kids just wanted someone white to pounce on and that wasn't going to happen without severe backlash. Another message came garbling through the speakers but was drowned out by growing noise and commotion in the halls and stairs. The police were trying to get more troopers in the school but there was no room for anyone. The school was literally full to the brim with people and hostilities. The Brothers all brought scarves and began to tie them around their nose and mouths in anticipation of mace and tear gas.

"We look like a bunch of bank robbers," said Wilbur. He was having trouble covering his large hooter.

There came a loud smashing sound from down the hall where the black kids stood and then even louder screams. The Old Kid looked back at his buddies and gave a "this is it" look. Something had started and it was heading the boys' way.

Mister Mike looked through the window of a classroom and saw Friendly Mel just sitting alone waiting for class to begin. "Where the hell are the teachers?" thought Mike. He went into the room and Mel gave his famous friendly wave. "Mel, get your ass out of here now. The shit is hitting the fan. You need to leave this school." Mel amazingly didn't seem all that concerned and just looked at Mike and said nothing. The scary sound of glass breaking mixed with hysterical yelling rang outside the door. Mister Mike ran back into the hall and gave a look over his shoulder as the geekie Mel quietly opened a book. Mike's mind ran the thought of how it was Mel with his top buttoned shirt and pocket protector that knew the right answer to all the discord. He was calmly and even bravely doing the right thing by just sitting there reading a book. He was not egging anyone on or inherently joining his tribe for battle and revenge. Friendly Mel was the only person in the school, city, state or even the entire country doing the right thing. Calmly sitting while the world around him exploded in complete chaos! Wave on, Friendly Mel!

No sooner did Mike step back into the hall when the entire crowd shifted forward. This was due to the police shooting tear gas from behind the white students. The halls once again clouded with the choking fog that burns one's eyes and air passages. The fire alarm was pulled which set off an earsplitting screech adding to the mayhem. All this was now a familiar routine to the battle tested kids of Proviso. A lunge forward took place and the boys all rode it like a wave. Within seconds the mass body of students had filed into the main corridor of the school. There was some fighting, but most of the black students were more interested in venting their feelings at the property of the school. Anything breakable was being broken and smashed. Punkwillie and The Old Kid were standing by the school's historic, glass trophy case when a huge, red fire extinguisher came flying through the air and crashed into it. This caused an amazing explosion of sound as massive amounts of glass smashed to the ground and then shattered into little razor-like pieces. Both of the boys were quick enough to cover their faces just before it hit and received small splinters of glass sticking into their hands. Had they not protected their faces, those sharp shards of shrapnel would have cut deeply into their soft eye tissues. All hell had once again broken out in the hallways of the high school. The boys all shot out the door as the riot-geared police came storming, swinging batons and spraying mace. The Old Kid and Punk were busy pulling the last of the glass out of their hands when a black youth came running at them waving a baseball bat yelling something about killing the killers of King. He was closing fast, raising his long, wooded weapon over his head for a death knell on Punkwillie's skull. The Old Kid instantly reached for the fire extinguisher that lay near his feet, aimed the hose at the assailant's face, and blasted a strong stream of white foam into the face of the bat-wielding attacker. This immediately blurred the black boy's vision, which caused him to stumble onto his back.

"Let's get the hell out of here!" shouted The Old Kid as yet another wave of angry blacks were charging their way. Both boys started for the doorway out of the school. Punkwillie came to a screeching halt and instantaneously reached down and picked up a huge trophy that had fallen from the destroyed case. The award was almost the size of the punk, brat boy. He struggled with it, but for some crazy reason he carried it along. The trophy was so big and clumsy that it looked like he was dancing with it as he made his way out of the school. "What the hell is that?" yelled The Old Kid.

"State Wrestling Champions 1948," came the Punk's reply. "Isn't she a beauty?"

Two Maywood cops came running up looking very mean and tense, screaming at Punkwillie to drop the trophy, which he promptly did. "What the hell are you doing?" asked one of the policemen.

"There will be no looting, godammit. We're throwing your punk asses in jail," said the other.

Then came a huge explosion from behind the school. Its concussion caused a sonic shock wave. The two officers turned to check out where the blast was coming from, and when they turned back to the boys, a five-foot brass prize trophy was standing alone and upright.

The Old Kid was running back to the parking lot with thoughts of how good it was his lovely Michele was not there. He didn't want to repeat that scene again. The boys gathered in the school lot around the venerable Rudy. Most of the white students had shot for home and there weren't many around. In fact, The Brothers were the only ones in sight. "Whoa, man. Look at that, man," shouted Chief as he pointed across to the school grounds.

The image was hard to take in at first because of its enormity. Black students had gathered in a great mass and were walking straight at The Brothers. None of the boys spoke. They were quickly getting the sensation Custer must have had just before his slaughter. The band of blacks grew and grew into a throng as it began to look like an endless sea of ebony. The Brothers each looked at each other knowing that running wasn't going save them. They each summoned all the bravery they could muster.

"Wonder what they will write about us," spoke Punkwillie as he stood next to his cousin, Mister Mike. The Punk wasn't the bravest soul and his hands started to tremble, but he knew he must stand steadfast with his blood brothers. He glanced at Mister Mike and could see that even in what could be their final moments, Mike had a slight smile in his eyes. He truly loved battle. The boys stood tightly together as the massive mob was now just a rock throw away. Police sirens were in the distance and sounded like the Calvary coming to rescue the pioneers. The Brothers were a unique gang in that they seldom used or even had weapons with them. Fist to fist combat suited them just fine, but at this time that just wasn't going to be enough. The black kids not only looked right at The Brothers, but seemed to be looking right through them. The time for wisecracks and jokes had passed as now the boys awaited the charge upon them. What seemed even more incredible was the fact that no familiar faces were in the crowd. The boys had black friends and knew a good many more, but as they searched for a friendly, life saving face, none could be found. The enormous sea of angry, mistreated, oppressed people were now just a few feet away still walking straight at the lads. The mob was remarkably quiet, especially for its size. It was apparent that this was not a spontaneous idea, but a planned assault. The boys braced for their demise, but still stood strong, their fists tightly clenched, hearts slamming, and sweat seeping. Half a league, half a league, half a league, onward! The walking wave of African humanity numbering well into the hundreds was upon the seven youths. Faces stared, as eyes met and the boys tried hard to grab a breath and stay stout. The Old Kid could feel a warm scented wind breezing on his face and realized it was caused by the multitude of expelled breaths in his direction. Waiting for the hammer to fall was creating another slow motion realm, something one can never get accustomed to even though The Brothers spent a good deal of time in this state. The voices from the blacks were still not loud. Their faces told of deep rage, but they were marching with spirits summoned from the cotton fields and plantations.

Incredibly, the endless stream of young blacks proceeded right passed The Brothers like a flowing river. These white boys were not the focus of this driven crowd. In fact, they seemed to be hardly noticed. Their fight was going to be with the Bossman himself, John Bull and the long, white arm of the law. This was a battle generations in the making and the killing of a man who preached non-violence was the last and final blow. The boys all looked at each other with great relief, as they knew they were spared and would live to fuck another day.

The boys piled into Rudy and Chief's Camaro as their stressful situation had lifted somewhat, but it was clear trouble was everywhere. The radio reports were about full scale rioting on Chicago's west side. Smoke could be seen billowing in the distance as the cars pulled on to First Avenue. "Hey, man, which way do we go, man?" asked Chief since all direct routes to Broadview were through Maywood, which was at a boiling point.

The cars didn't go far as police cars zoomed passed followed by a convoy of National Guard trucks.

"The sitch is serious," said The Old Kid. The convoy was right on the heels of the ever-growing procession as it looked like people of Maywood were coming out of their homes to join in. If the idea of bringing in the National Guard was to preserve peace, it backfired. The presence of the trucks escalated the crowd and the sound of destruction was filling the sky. Like a wildfire out of control, the spectacle in front of the boys unfolded. Rocks hurled through the air in all directions hitting the convoy and storefront windows. More police cars came up from surrounding towns and the soldiers tried to pile out of the trucks. The frantic racket of a mob gone crazy now permeated the scene and the boys had a ringside seat. Helicopters now hovered in the air and black Chevy Impalas hurried passed, driven by nice guys with ties. The once sleepy, little village of Maywood, Illinois was now becoming a war zone.

"We should get out of here," said Cuno. No sooner had he spoken these words when a sharp, popping sound was heard. The first thought the boys had was that someone was throwing firecrackers, but one glance at the sea of people beginning to scatter made it evident guns had entered into the mad mix. Chief downshifted his cool, blue Camaro as the tires smoked and the car jolted down First Avenue. Mister Mike's Rudy leaped forward, too, but it was due to Mike missing second gear.

"Come on, get our asses out of here, Mike," shouted Punkwillie.

"I am... I am," answered Mister Mike as he punched the Weather Eye logo on the dash as if that was going to make the car run quicker. Chief's Camaro was clean out of sight as the Rambler chugged its way out of Maywood.

The Old Kid looked to his right and yelled, "Step on it!" There on a side street was a small gang of black men all dressed in black berets. "Damn, it's the Black Panthers." One of the Panthers had a huge side arm and was pointing it at the slow moving target filled with four ducking teens. Mister Mike was driving with his head below the dashboard just hoping he would stay on the road. Suddenly, a loud blast filled the car and the rear window exploded in pieces.

"He's shooting at us! We took a hit!" screamed Punkwillie. Another surprising blast followed closely and the sound of air leaving the front right tire told where that round went. Never in Mister Mike's life did he press anything as hard as that gas pedal. They swirled, but he held onto the wheel and bravely glanced over the top to get his bearings. Police sirens quickly rose up and the squad cars roared by as Mike pulled the wounded car over. The boys all shot up in their seats and watched as the cops got out and returned fire at the fleeing gang. This was an all out hell fight as bullets zipped and ricocheted like killer bees looking to sting anything. The boys got out and ran in the direction of beautiful Broadview and safe haven. Mister Mike gave a backward glance over his shoulder for what would be his last look at his faithful and trustworthy Rudy.

The boys made it to Ace's house, which was known as the smallest house in the world. It was said you could open the front door and hit the back. Ace wasn't home, but his mom was, and she answered the door with her robe flopping open revealing Ace's first meals. She was a nice lady, but liked her drinks a little too much and today was no exception. "You boys seen Ace?" she asked.

"No, ma'am. We were going to ask you the same thing," answered The Old Kid.

"Well, if ya see him, tell him to get home. The niggas are restless and going to burn down Chicago," she said with a slight burp. Police cars and state vehicles were flying down the street pouring into Maywood. The boys asked if they could come in and call their parents to make sure everything and everyone was all right. The Old Kid called Michele, but her line was busy as usual. The boys thanked the lushie lady and left. They walked a few steps and Mister Mike pulled out a pint of gin.

"Where'd you get that?" asked Wilbur.

"It was on the counter at Ace's. She won't miss it," laughed Mike.

"After being chased, beaten, and shot at, I could really use a swig," said The Kid as he took one, mountain man gulp. The lads made quick work of the pint and got a nice buzz going. They were going to The Kid's house for his wheels, when Stevie and Evie came cruising on by.

"Hey, boys, you stay clear of Maywood. There's lots of shooting and looting."

"Really?" smirked Punkwillie. The two groups talked for a short moment and like homing pigeons the other Brothers came landing in. They decided to send word of a major blowout under the Roosevelt Road bridge. The Old Kid picked up Michele and Candy Miller while the rest made beer runs with a raid on The Farms to boot. Nothing can form faster and more clandestinely than a teen party. Under the bridge was perfect. The police had lots more to deal with than partying punks. The old gang got together as they drank, traded stories and philosophized about current events. Stevie brought some Columbian Red, which was now becoming a favorite among the teens. The world with its threat of nuclear holocaust, Viet Nam conflict, increasing divorce rate, decreasing moral standards, social unrest and assassinations was squeezing kids with unrelenting pressure. This was fast becoming a generation looking for an escape and drugs were the yellow brick road. The Brothers were a gang that when they went, they went big, and the world was easier to view with kaleidoscope eyes. Stevie started getting requests for anything he could get except smack. That was one road the boys didn't want to cross, not yet at least. Knowing full well all their parents were worrying like crazy about their darlings mattered little to the drunks. The sun had set as the high teens sat high on a man made hill. They were in a semi circle silently watching the hell-red glow from the fires that engulfed Maywood and west Chicago. The sounds of sirens and gunfire were faintly off in the distance while the stench from fumes cured Broadview like a smoked ham. "I wonder if this is how Nero felt," asked Punkwillie as he puffed the magic dragon, witnessing his hometown burn before his eyes. Wham Bam Pam nestled close to him and laid her head softly on his lap. The incongruity was compelling as the teenagers sat almost tranquilly all along their watchtowers, gazing at a world puking its guts out. Nothing is more resilient than a person with hope and a young heart filled with conviction of a greater tomorrow. The children of Broadview wondered about the world they were entering and if they could make it a better place. At least they hoped so.

The group broke as the chilly night air won out. Wilbur and Musclehead went to the local Shell gas station to fill up the Cobra. Buns Dunaway was working the shift. He was well known to the boys as one hard working dude. Buns walked up to the royal blue Shelby and nervously whispered to the boys not to leave him alone. Wil gave him an inquisitive look and Buns shifted his eyes over to a black man in an old army jacket leaning against the last row of gas pumps. "I called the cops. That dude has a shotgun in his back seat. Stay here until the cops show." Musclehead quickly got out of the Ford and took a look at the beat up Dodge Duster next to him. Sure enough, there lay a perfectly illegal sawed off Winchester pump shotgun. Muss knew it would be wise to not let the man near the car so he stayed put. The gas pump clicked off as the Duster's tank filled and the man threw his cigarette and began walking back to his car. Buns was very nervous as he was sure this was going to be an armed robbery. Wilbur climbed out and joined Musclehead as the black man with a huge Afro looked straight at them. He could tell the white boys were on to him. The three teens didn't budge when the Afro man neared his car.

"Say, man, can you step aside so I can get my wallet to pay you?" he said.

Wilbur, being the straight forward type, just blurted, "What's with the shotgun, mister?"

The black man stopped and faced Will. "That's none of your mother fucking business," he replied. Musclehead, never the diplomat, grabbed the man from behind with his forearm wrapped around the man's throat and stepped back. This put the entire body weight squarely on the teen's forearm, a classic chokehold. The man started to struggle and Will grabbed his arms and tried to pin him to the ground. This dude was a real scraper as he almost wiggled out of the grip. Musclehead applied so much pressure to the throat that blood started to flow from the man's nose. This all came to a screeching halt when the attention grabbing double click of a shotgun was heard. Everyone in the brawl froze and looked up as Buns was pointing the shotgun point blank at the stranger.

"Buns, be careful," yelled Musclehead who was directly behind the man and in the line of fire. Just then the squealing tires of Broadview's finest came on the scene. Officer Murphy came flying out with his gun nervously drawn. He was trying to assess the scene and ordered Buns to let the gun down.

"Hey, he's the bad guy," shouted the scared boy, pointing to the choke-held man.

Another squad came roaring up with veteran Lieutenant Rodermund behind the wheel. The lieutenant knew the first thing he must do is to keep all situations calm and under control. "What is going on?" he asked, pretending to be relaxed.

"This guy had a shotgun in his car," answered Buns.

"OK, let him go," ordered the lieutenant.

The boys stood away and the suspected robber sat rubbing his neck trying to form a sentence. "I'm... FBI," he stated between coughs. "I'm going to the riots in Chicago undercover."

"Let's see some ID, fella," asked the veteran cop. The black man dusted off his army jacket and walked to his car for his wallet and produced a weather tattered FBI photo identification card. "What the hell are doing, sir," said the lieutenant, "driving around with a shotgun showing when you're going to be undercover?" he added. Officer Murphy called in the ID and it checked out.

"Sorry for the trouble, but I wanted my Luella close by in case I needed her," said the black undercover man with the large Afro.

Wilbur extended his hand to show all was forgiven and when they shook he couldn't help but to remark, "I thought you guys all wore ties." No comment was made as the disguised dude drove off towards the bright red glow of a burning Chicago. The two policemen told the boys to get home because the riot in Chicago was getting bad and there was a possibility of ghettos emptying into the suburbs.

"Is there going to be a race war?" asked Wilbur.

"I don't know, son, but we are hauling out the big guns just in case," said the lieutenant. "Every police department around here has an arsenal of weapons from M-69 grenade launchers to water cooled 50 cal machine guns. We even have a small cannon," boasted the policeman.

"So that's how you keep the peace, huh? Kill everyone in sight," laughed Musclehead.

"Well, we can let them through to your house if you like," smirked the cop. The police radio put a quick ending to the conversation as it called for a rapid response to a 12-20 in progress. With that the officers went out on what promised to be a very busy night and the two boys left for home as Buns Dunaway went back to his scratch and sniff issue of Hustler magazine.

The next day, Saturday, was extremely tense. There were reports of mass rioting taking place in both Chicago's west side and Maywood. People were dying on both sides of the fence as sporadic gunfire could be heard in neighborhoods bordering Maywood. Looting was a huge problem. Windows of stores and shops were smashed and pillaged, plundered and ransacked of anything of value, even the brass knobs off bathroom faucets. Somehow, order had to be restored, and the tough, old, Irish Mayor of Chicago, Richard J. Daley, was the man to do it. He gave a proclamation to the police to "shoot to kill" any arsonists or looters. This was viewed by many community leaders as being too extreme and immoral. The Mayor believed this situation as a true danger to the entire city and desperate times called for desperate measures. Everyone was glued to their TV's for all the updates on the spreading turmoil. Mayor Daley was known as a street-smart man who didn't bullshit around. He was like most Chicagoans, extremely proud and very excitable. The rioting had him fervently inflamed and he provided a good laugh with a verbal boner. He held a live news conference and with cameras sticking in his face, he tried to defend the actions of the police with a statement that, "The police were not there to create disorder. They were there to preserve it." Laughter could be heard in every household and saloon in the metro area. For all the harsh criticism Mayor Daley received for his tough stance, the rioting came to a quick, if not immediate, halt. The deadly order restored order and for the first time in 72 hours, bullets and blood receded like a sweating fever. Chicago and Maywood had their guts ripped out, and the first steps on the road to recovery had been taken. The civil rights movement now had a martyr and the conscience of white America. A man was killed in Memphis, but a dream was born. America had to face itself in the mirror and ask hard questions of what it was seeing. Perhaps some answers would come this summer in the upcoming Democratic Convention being held, where else, Chicago!

For some weird reason The Old Kid and Punkwillie thought it would be exciting to drive through the west side of Chicago to see what it looked like. There was no law or declaration that white people couldn't go to the west side, it just seemed like who in their right mind would, and why? The two boys, being more full of adventure than sense, just wanted to experience what real carnage looked like. Maywood had also experienced serious rioting, but not on the scale of Chicago. They drove down I-90 in The Kid's GTO to the Western Avenue exit. Not much was very visible from the highway, but once they drove onto Western Avenue things changed fast. There was almost no traffic nor people to be seen. They drove towards Madison Avenue, the physical dividing line for the city. Everything north of Madison was called the North side and south of Madison was, of course, the South side. When they approached Madison and Western, an overwhelming stench of burnt city filled the air. The National Guard soldiers were about in Jeeps and the police in patrol cars. No one was standing in clear view presenting an open target. The bright orange Pontiac brought much more attention than the boys ever considered. "We better bail," said Punkwillie, and The Kid turned slowly on Madison and the boys looked down the throat of Chicago's once proud west side. There was not a building standing that didn't tell its tale of horror. The blackened, wooden structures stood as if a huge incendiary bomb had hit the city. For as far as the eye could see, devastation and repulsive destruction validated the horror that took place. The GTO turned and headed back to civilization as the boys studied the tired eyes of the troopers and police who were too exhausted to stare back. The cool looking muscle car was in sharp contrast to the gutted out buildings it passed, but nothing was going to get any emotion out of the spent sentries.

The weekend settled to an almost normal existence, as the locals were becoming veterans of social unrest. They knew the quicker they could make life feel regular, the better. The Brothers even gathered for the usual Sunday night grubbing at the Lazy Lion. Cuno looked over at Big Tuna Tony Accardo's table and fancied the idea of walking over and asking him to get Shakey the Bookie off his back. This was pure fantasy, as the mob boss really didn't know who Shakey was or would even care. Besides, it was reported that Mr. Accardo's house had been burglarized and every professional burglar in Chicago seemed to have disappeared. Why waste time asking questions was the Big Tuna's motto. Mister Mike was telling the story he heard about how all the security companies in Chicagoland were actually owned by the mob. "What better way to know where the alarms are when you install them yourself?" said Mike. Mr. Excitement was planning a financial comeback by staging a boxing match for any and all who wanted to participate. There would be a $10 entrance fee to cover the rental expense of the facilities. He had to work out the details, but from the reaction his mates gave him, this would be a cash cow.

The following Monday the high school was high strung as expected. Many of the white girls again were kept home, but there didn't seem to be any danger. The blacks were still very much upset about Dr. King, but they realized many whites were, also. If the hopes of Dr. King were to ever be realized, then it would call for compassion from both sides. Racism was not a one sided issue. Beating up students because they were white was only going to cause further division. Fred Hampton was doing his best at explaining that the real battle wasn't black against white, but rich against poor. Impoverished people needed to unite and create a strong and powerful political voice. There were millions of poor people which also meant there were millions of votes. Reverend Jesse Jackson, who witnessed the assassination, started talking about a "Rainbow Coalition" to help not just one race, but all in need. Proviso East once again had to recognize its role and place in the community. This was a school unlike most, since it had a 50-50 race balance, but was not an inner city school. Proviso had to show that blacks could live and work in middle class America. The Dr. King murder sent shock waves into the hearts and minds of many white Americans who were now seeing the injustices inflicted on blacks. They all saw the news footage of the troubles in the south, but that was about segregation. This was not an issue in the north. Now, for the first time in their lives, many whites realized that blacks were just about invisible in many well-off sectors. Chicago was one third black yet only five percent were on the police force. Figures like this were typical in all facets of society. This had to change and the killing and rioting shook America awake from its unethical slumber. Lincoln may have freed the slaves 100 years ago, but the chains still remained. Proviso East was at the focal point, and the first question was if it could even finish the school year peacefully. The future wasn't going to be determined by a panel of committed students, but by every student from Fast Eddie to Friendly Mel.

The first day looked promising and laughter could even be heard once again as The Old Kid waved a hamburger over his head. The one bite chomp was a definite world record. The burger was missing a huge portion that only a crazed hippo could have made. With all that was going on about them, The Brothers were not going to let a crazy world disturb their crazy world. Sometimes nonsense can make more sense. What better way to tear down the walls of tension than with a laugh? The halls still had an aura of hostilities, but no fights took place. The week went quite well and there were no serious issues at Proviso. Most of the black kids had been through so much they just wanted some sanity in their lives. Perhaps everyone was weary of the indifference and trouble.

Chapter 17
Pet Piranhas

Word had it that Chaino, the drug dealer, was renting a house and wanted to christen it with a blowout. Perfect timing as The Brothers were all getting spring fever and needed to get rid of some serious DG. The weekend rolled up and the gang rolled out to historic Oak Park, and to the wild lad known by one name, Chaino. Turns out Chaino had roommates that seemed to come from all over the world. One guy named Ricardo was from Argentina. He had a large aquarium with seven piranhas in it. This caused quite a stir, as Ricardo liked to throw lots of other little creatures in to watch the killer fish attack helpless prey. Ricardo was also a friend of a diplomat from Columbia and this meant he had access to a drug pipeline. "Diplomatic immunity is a wonderful thing," he stated. "My friend brings in suitcases filled with coke and weed and nothing is done or said." Chaino was all smiles with dollar signs in his eyes. "I can beat the system without the help of my diplomatic friend," Ricardo bragged. "All you need to do is pay off the people who clean the plane on both ends. They all have access to the plane from where it takes off to where it lands and while customs searches the passengers, the poor, ignorant, immigration worker walks straight passed, whistling Dixie."

"Wow. Amazing. Simply amazing. I'm so shocked," shouted Punkwillie. "I didn't think they even knew the song." This of course broke everyone up except for

Ricardo who didn't like being laughed at, even indirectly. He gave a glare at the crackwise kid who picked up on the vibe and relished it. Punkwillie always liked to get under the skin of people who talked too much. If there was going to be lots of talking, the Punk would be the one doing it.

"Time to feed the pillaging Pisces," proclaimed Ricardo as he reached inside a small, white, cardboard box and pulled a small, white mouse out by the tail. Michele and every girl there made a direct beeline for the kitchen. This was gross, guy stuff and no girl wanted any part of it, except for Evie who lit a cigarette and went back into the living room. Ricardo gave a short history lesson on how piranhas feed and just how vicious they are. "Look at their fins. They even bite each other just for spite." He held the mouse by its tail and the rodent scurried and flailed its paws in the air as if it was running away. Michele and the girls huddled in the kitchen and heard a ker-plunk sound followed by berserk, boy sounds. There is something very ritualistic and bonding to males when they celebrate the gruesome and hideous side of nature. The lil foxes shot outside in the yard to get away from the ecstatic, tribal bellows of the young bucks. There are many facets of attraction that females find in males, but this behavior reminds them of how primitive and disgusting mommy's little darlings can be. When the cheering finally subsided, the girls walked back in. Michele glanced at the aquarium and saw how red the water had become.

The Old Kid seemed a little embarrassed and realized that this was not the road to beloved nookie. Time to kick it back and let his babe relax as he played Marvin Gaye's "Heard it Through the Grapevine." Music can make the mood and the mood needed to mellow.

Chaino brought out a small glass bottle filled with a clear liquid of heavy viscosity. He asked Stevie to go get some sugar cubes from the kitchen. Chaino asked if anyone wanted to go on a trip?

"Where to?" asked the Musclehead, giving credence to the nickname.

Everyone knew what trip the young junkie was talking about, sans Muss. Stevie laid the sugar cubes down and Chaino pulled an eyedropper from a table drawer. "Ladies and gentlemen, meet Mr. Ellis Dee," he said as he put three droplets on each cube and watched them absorb. The drum solo had just begun on "In-a-gadda-da-vida," a perfect piece for the challenging experience that was presented to the kids. "Anyone want some acid?" asked Chaino. "Your first time is on the house." The Old Kid didn't even glance at Michele as he reached in and grabbed a sugar cube. He held it up to a black light on the wall and could see the ghostly glow the chemicals gave off. Being the trailblazer he was, the sweet, square morsel popped in his mouth and down his hatch. The other boys all followed suit as if they were united and were really going away.

"One goes, we all go," said Mister Mike throwing his cube in the air like it was a grape and catching it in his mouth. Wham Bam Pam and Evie were the only two girls indulging in the synthetic, social venture. Michele wasn't at all pleased with the way her boyfriend jumped into the fire with no concern for her opinion, but she wasn't going to play Mother Superior either.

"Hand me the phone," ordered Punkwillie. "I'll talk to King B before this shit kicks in." Chaino and Ricardo had no idea about the Punk's routine on radio, but they were about to find out. Punk sunk into a big, overstuffed couched and sipped on a bottle of

Thunderbird, the bottom of the wine barrel. Within a minute Ron Britain had answered and told his favorite fan that after the New Colony Six's "You Run Around" he was on. The punkster tapped his toes as Michele sat on the lap of her lover, The Good Old Kid. The Hams turned up the radio.

"Wella, wella, we have my old buddy, Punkwillie, on,'" said King B. "Punk, how ya doing, my man?" asked the DJ.

"Well, King B, by and large I'm doing fine, which is how I like my women... bi and large."

"Ok, Punk, keep it clean now," retorted Mr. Britain.

"Geez, Ron, that's what my mom says about my underwear."

"OK now, Punk, how's your love life going?" asked King B.

"Just great. I dated a girl from Phoenix. She had a dry sense of humor, though. I asked if it was hot there and she yes, but it's a dry heat. Whatever that means. Then I met a girl from Seattle and I asked if it rains there all the time and she said yes, but it's a dry rain." This broke up King B and the gang at the house except for Ricardo who didn't get any of it. "Yea, Ron, I was also with an English hooker and I asked what it cost to have sex and she said three pounds, so I gave her the Sunday paper and said here's four, keep the change. Hey, Ron, I'm going to visit my eccentric uncle in Wyoming. He has 50,000 heads of cattle. No bodies, just the heads!"

"Punk you're awful," laughed King B.

"Hey, King, did you hear the one about the mom who was waiting at a gate at O'Hare for her daughter who was coming back from Africa?"

"No, Punk, can't say I have."

"Well, she saw her daughter walking down the ramp and the daughter got all excited and ran up to her mom and said, 'Mother, I want you to meet my new husband,' and up walked a black man wearing a towel, with a bone in his nose and holding a spear. Her mother jumped back and started screaming, 'No! No! I said marry a RICH doctor.' This got King B and the house guests roaring. "And, Ron, never forget what they say," spoke the jokester punk as his voice started to falter followed by dead air silence.

"Yes, Punk, don't forget what?" asked King B. The comic fell silent as the LSD had started to kick in and the young lad just had a blank stare in his dilated eyes. "Don't forget what?" asked the DJ trying to figure out what was going on.

"I don't remember... better go ask Alice," mumbled the stoned boy as he dropped the phone with a dull thunk going out over the 100,000 watt transmission towers to listeners from La Crosse to Kokomo.

"Mmmmm," said King B, "I hope my pal is OK. Sounds like he went on a magic carpet ride," and without missing a beat the veteran disc jockey played Steppenwolf's "Magic Carpet Ride."

As if a magic wand waved throughout the room, the experimenters were receiving their trial by fire. What really transpires when one takes a drug like LSD is that a certain amount of strychnine enters the blood system causing a hallucinated reaction. Vision becomes distorted and a person loses their ability to focus both physically

234

and psychologically. Objects blend in with nearby lights. From the beginning of man's history, civilizations have employed the use of masks in ceremonies. Archeologists have discovered bizarre and wildly painted disguises in every corner of the world. When one enters into a hallucinated state, artwork takes on real life qualities. The six arm figures that adorn paintings from India become animations. The arms appear to be moving as well as the head. Masks become the real faces of gods or spirits. The sitar loses its high-pitched twang and transforms into a sonic stream of constant energy much like a flame. The Brothers were all experiencing this makeover at the same time.

The Chief walked over to a black-light poster and was just simply awestruck. "Hey, man, this is blowing my mind, man," he said trying to poke his fingers into the poster as if it had dimension. The Old Kid was sitting next to Michele with a dumb struck glare. He was starting to trip and was glad she was around. He knew she was straight and would guide him and his friends out of real danger.

Chaino, who was always tripping, saw that his guests had loaded the bus and were ready for a ride. "Well, how does everyone feel?" he asked surveying the room. The silent responses told him all he needed to know.

Ricardo, who was the only male not on acid, stood up and walked around the room. "Well, now you know how a rat feels when it's about to die. Rat poison is 100% strychnine," he proclaimed. This didn't sit well with the experimenters. Negative thoughts and images are not very desirable for someone who is soaring on Cloud Nine. This can cause a bummer and Chaino warned his Latin guest of this.

Wham Bam Pam walked over to the window and pointed to the trees outside. "Look at this," she said. "Look at the rhythm of the trees. They are swaying together like a choreographed dance."

Chaino, who had taken the role of tourist guide, walked next to the stoned girl. "You're starting to notice the harmony of nature now, huh?" he asked.

"Yes! Birds even sound like they are talking to me," stated Pam.

The hours passed as Chaino completely entertained the crowd with an amazing demonstration of strobe lights and incense. The stoned teens even watched a White Sox game on TV and were amazed at how different it all seemed.

"Sports and competition are so war based. It's us against them-- beat them, kill them, win... win... win," spoke Mister Mike.

"Listen to us," laughed Sweet Daddy. "We sound like a bunch of hippies... peace and love... flower power," he added.

Michele was sitting through this experiment just as a casual observer and nightingale. She asked if anyone wanted anything to drink as she headed for the kitchen.

"Yeah, I could use a beer," answered Cuno, which was followed by a number of the same request.

"Guess you guys are coming back down to earth, huh?" she responded.

The stoners were starting to come back to reality and all the demands of nature started to kick in. Michele walked into the good-sized kitchen admiring how nice older homes were. "They really didn't scrimp like home builders do today," she thought as she ran her hand over the wood crafted cabinets. She opened the frig to grab some beers for her friends when a face popped up from behind the opened door.

"Can I give you a hand?" asked Ricardo in his Latin lover voice.

"No, thanks. I can manage," replied Michele in her go catch the next bus voice. Ricardo gently ran his fingertips down the bent over girl's back.

"You're very pretty, I think," he said with a gentle slap on her firm ass.

Michele sprang up like a Jack in the Box. "Look, dude, keep your greasy paws off. My boyfriend is in the next room and all I have to do is yell," warned the angry girl.

"Oh, your boyfriend is one of those tripping hippies, huh? Well, they are so stoned they won't notice if we went downstairs to do the forbidden dance." Ricardo was not use to American girls. He always got his way in Argentina and this was something foreign to the foreigner. "Well, don't be angry with me because I find you attractive," whispered Ricardo, trying the I'm under your spell approach. Michele stood up arms filled with brown, bottled gusto as Ricardo lifted her chin with his hand. "You have the most beautiful eyes and I mean no harm," he softly spoke.

"WELL, I DO!" shouted a voice from behind the Latin lady-killer. Ricardo whirled around to see the intruder and met a powerful blast in the face from The Old Kid's fist. WHAM came the sound followed by a succession of loud thumps. Ricardo over played his hand and like any bad gambler, he paid the price. Michele screamed her protest, but to no avail as her totally inflamed beau did a tango on the poor playboy's puss.

The Old Kid grabbed Ricardo by the pants and lifted him high over his head and walked into the living room. "One Don Juan coming through," shouted The Kid as his friends all laughed at the sight. Ricardo started to scream as he realized just where he was heading. The Hams cleared out of the way as The Old Kid gave a two-step run followed by a massive heave ho, Herculean toss. The Latin visitor became airborne as he sailed up and over the couch filled with astonished onlookers. Flailing his legs as if that was going to give him extra distance, poor Ricardo faced his fate head on... literally. He let out a Spanish squeal when he crash landed upon the glass aquarium, filled with his pet piranhas. The smashing sound of glass was horrendous and equally matched by the roar from the observers. Ricardo lay on the floor softly moaning in a pool of water and flopping fish.

"Wow," yelled Musclehead. "This really is a trip."

Michele just stood there as if she was the one stoned out of her mind. She couldn't begin to form the words of what she just witnessed. Chaino came over to help the beaten up boy. He knew he wasn't about to scold anyone from this mob after just viewing a soaring senor. Ricardo was more shocked than hurt and just laid there checking his condition. The Old Kid walked over and stood directly above the drenched dude. "Welcome to Chicago. Drop in anytime," he laughed, echoed by even louder howls from his amigos. Everyone knew it was time to vacate and all got up except Wham Bam Pam who was transfixed on the dying piranhas.

"Shouldn't we help the fish? They didn't do anything."

"Fuck the fish. This is pay back for the mouse," laughed Mister Mike as he stepped on the tail of the aquatic killer making it snap its razor teeth.

Michele grabbed The Old Kid's arm. "Honestly, I can't believe you, Danny. You didn't have to do that," she said, escorting him out as the rest of the crew followed. Poor Ricardo just sat there on a heap of blue aquarium rocks tending his dying fish and injured pride.

"So much for diplomatic immunity," joked The Hams as he slammed the door shut.

The ride back to Broadview was anything but pleasant in The Old Kid's GTO. Michele started to scold The Kid for being so obnoxious and violent. Stevie and Evie were in the back seat gobbling the spat up-- nothing like a front row seat at a heavyweight event. "You know, Danny, I can take care of myself. You didn't have to jump in like that," she ranted.

"Yea, Michele, all I saw was him holding your face and you weren't exactly jumping back protesting. In fact, the only thing you seem pissed about is me breaking it up," retorted The Kid. "If you want, I will drop you off back at Ricky Ricardo's, your Bob-a-Louie," snapped The Old Kid with veins starting to appear on his neck.

Michele was looking out her right side window. "Sure, why don't you? Then you can score some more acid and melt your brains away, what's left of them. Rat poison, Danny. Is that what you're down to now, RAT POISON?" she bit back.

"Well, now, it's that, huh?" cracked The Old Kid gripping the steering wheel even tighter. "Why don't you just make a list of what I should being doing, or maybe you should go date another girl 'cause I get the feeling guys are not your type. I don't need your permission to do anything." This was met with casket cold silence for the remainder of the ride. Stevie and Evie were wild eyed and dead quiet as Evie looked at Michele for a reaction on the girl question. The Old Kid punched the gas as the tires cried out the driver's anguish down 18th Street to Michele's house and came to a screeching stop. Michele got out without saying a word and the obligatory squealing of the tires came as the GTO peeled out. Any points The Kid had with her parents went up in tire smoke in front of their home. The Old Kid made the turn onto 17th Avenue so fast that Stevie piled on top of Evie and crushed her in the corner.

"Do you two ever fight?" asked The Kid.

"We used to and sometimes still do, but I think we are on each other's vibe pretty good," replied Stevie.

"Yeah, as long as he stays hard, I'm easy to get along with," laughed Evie.

"I hope I find a chick as cool as you, Evie," said The Kid.

"Oh, you got one, babe. Michele is a great girl. She isn't into the biker lifestyle, but she lets the little things go and that's important," answered Evie as Stevie put her hand down his pants.

"How come you let my little thing go?" joked Stevie as he began pumping his crotch to her hand.

"Stevie, are you ever serious? Is sex the only thing on your mind?" asked Evie.

"Hey, I cut the bullshit out, babe. Other guys will ask a girl, my place or yours, I will ask, my face or yours," giggled Stevie.

"Well, I hope Michele gets used to me being a little wild. I got some seeds to sow," said The Kid as he lit a cig.

"Danny, to be honest, watching your boyfriend take acid for the first time and then throwing a guy into a fish tank filled with piranhas does take some getting used to," said Evie.

"Yeah, I guess you're right. Next time I'll throw him into an aquarium filled with mermaids," joked The Old Kid.

"Hey, throw me in, too," stated Stevie.

"Me, too," smiled Evie as the bright orange Goat headed down a typical, busy, suburban street on a typical, spring night with an unusual, fish story. This was a typical ,unusual weekend.

Chapter 18
The Underdog Glove

Cuno had to tell his parents that he needed to borrow money for his gambling debt and they responded by immediately putting his cherished Road Runner up for sale. He paid the bookie off and made his car payment. Now he had to come up with $900 to get his car out of hock. He had rented a small warehouse in Broadview's vast industrial section. Mr. Excitement was a very enterprising young man and even chewed down the landlord from $300 to $100 for the one night event. He had made his car payment, but was severely in the hole from his losses at the racetrack. He had a grand plan to become a small-scale fight promoter. The catch was to make the spectators either combatants or bettors. Hopefully, both! He went around Proviso and let word out about the tournament; it was key not to get too much exposure, otherwise the police would find out.

All The Brothers signed up and paid the $25 entrance fee. Kids from every section of the Proviso Township also wanted in. The roster of 50 battlers filled faster than anticipated. This sort of sport seemed to have a bright future to the young organizer. The event was set up for two divisions-- heavyweight and not so heavyweight. The deciding factor was the 200 pound limit. The prize money was $400 for each division, winner take all. After the rent, Mr. Excitement cleared a cool $450, and with side bets, he would make his lost $600 found. There was a clever counter measure

drove the poor Willie boy back and the crowd up as blood curdling screams filled the old warehouse. Buns continued his onslaught with a haymaker to the staggering Punkster who was trying to clear his head. Buns came in for the kill as he tightened his underdog glove into a tight knot of fist and muscle. He ran up to the helpless Punkwillie who was nothing more than a sitting duck with a bull's eye painted on his face. Buns pulled his fist into a grand wind up to complete his kill.

"TIME!" yelled Cuno who also managed the clock. The three minutes were up and mercifully saved King B's biggest fan from the gallow's pole. Even though both fighters did not exert much energy in the bout, neither lad was anywhere near boxing condition. To dance around a ring throwing and ducking punches takes lots of stamina. Getting tagged and the stress of fighting also drains a fighter and the two amateurs showed it. Punkwillie was in his corner breathing like a bus was on his chest, while Buns was coughing up something green and slimly. Still, action was being played on both. Many believed, based on the first round, that Buns Dunaway would be victorious. The bell saved the Punk and the smart money was going on Buns with his underdog glove. Mr. Excitement walked back into the center of the floor as the cigarette smoke created a haze that made breathing even harder.

He clapped his hands together. "Round Two," and he walked away.

Both boxers got up from their respective corners as Mister Mike yelled encouragement to his cousin. "Come on, Punk... sicum." Buns had a bright look of confidence in his sweaty eyes as he knew a few more smacks with that light glove and Punkwillie was toast. Buns fired a wild left followed by an even wilder right.

This time the Punk brat was ready for the assault and leaned back, but kept his feet in place. Now with Buns seriously off balance, Punkwillie quickly leaned forward and slammed a nice combination of left hook to the jaw and right uppercut to the chin. This sent both Buns and the smart money players reeling. The wide-eyed look of supremacy had now shot into Broadview's wisest wise ass. Mister Mike nearly popped the bulging veins in his neck from cheering so loudly when he saw the command his kin showed. Buns regained his balance and looked up only to meet two more lightning fast punches to his reddening mug. Punkwillie was becoming a reincarnation of Willie Pep, one of the greatest lightweights of all time. His punches were crisp and instant with the footwork of a dancer. His tap dancing lessons were paying off now. Buns was as spent as used rubber. He hunched over and tried to bear hug his opponent. This was a serious logistical error. Buns head was now down near Punk's gut when the new Pepwillie slammed a vicious right to the head and ear of Buns. This punch caused the lad to grab his ear and pile down like a horse turd on the oil-stained floor.

"AHHHHHH," yelled Buns, rolling and tightly clutching his left ear.

Cuno jumped in and bellowed, "Fight is over. The fight is over!" No need to declare the winner as Punkwillie was being lifted in the air while Buns Dunaway was being lifted to his feet. Wild, celebrating cheers of the winners drowned out the moans of losing bettors. Punkwillie was still gasping for air as he hoisted a cold, malt liquor and sucked it down like a vacuum cleaner.

Buns was still bent over and still holding his ear that was swollen and red. "I can't hear out of this ear," he complained.

"I think you punctured your eardrum, Buns," said Musclehead who had had every injury known to science.

The damp, dark building became silent out of concern for the injured pugilist. The concern ended when Fast Eddie started yelling, "Who's next, mother fucker?" Howlers for dollars filled the air as booze, beer, and bets transformed the dank room into boyhood bliss.

Cuno dug into the "Heavyweight" sack and pulled out two slips of squashed paper. "The Old Kid and Jimmy the Greek will do battle on this day," shouted Cuno as murderous screams of wagers shot off the beams. The Old Kid was well known and had a reputation throughout the western suburbs as one battling bastard. The Greek was from neighboring Westchester and more than once made it known he would like to kick The Old Kid's ass. This battle was a promoter's dream come true. You couldn't have drawn it up any better, which led Gino to look in the "Heavyweight" sack and notice the papers were all blank. It was Cuno pairing the bouts all along.

"Who gives a shit," thought Gino. " This is better than any lopsided matches," so he kept quiet.

When the signal to begin came, it was readily apparent this fight was going to be different. There was no feeling out of anything. Both teens were over six feet and weighed in the 220 range. The Greek was the bigger of the two and had a deep, five o'clock shadow. He had been shaving since he was twelve. The Greek liked to think he was the biggest bad ass around and resented any idea to the contrary. He had been gunning for The Kid for sometime, but never got around to cruising into

Broadview to settle it. The punches came fast and hard from both teens as footwork was replaced with just reaching back and letting go. The first real indication of just how war-like this match was going to be came when The Old Kid threw an overpowering right that the Greek just barely ducked under. The sure size of The Kid's fist and the violent velocity behind it made the air swoosh like a warning shot for all in its wake. This was serious duking and neither fighter seemed concerned about future rounds or setting a pace. This clash was going to be decided at breakneck speed with a possible neck breaking. The audience was quiet as they all stood with mouths and eyes wide and wild. The two young gladiators traded slams and whaling wallops as sweat, spit and blood sprayed onto the slimy floor.

"Come on, Kid, kick his fat ass," screamed each of The Brothers as the Greek's backers cheerleaded with curses of their own. This caused the mood to agitate in the ranks and Mr. Excitement was quick to quash this uprising.

"Hey, man, this is what it must have looked like when the dinosaurs fought, man," said Chief.

The Greek landed a thunderous blow that lifted The Old Kid and made his eyes cross. Like a great white shark smelling blood, the Greek made his move inside, but The Kid wildly whipped his arm around backwards and sent a blow to the Greek's face that halted any advancement. Even being knocked senseless, The Old Kid could still muster up a counter attack, a sure sign of a gallant warrior. The temperature in the decrepit depot began to rise dramatically as the rambunctious crowd became intoxicated with the savagery. The intensified heat caused the two combatants to secrete sweat in tributaries of salty swill that burned into their eyes and parched mouths. Their lungs searched for air with gasps of repentant mercy as staminas weakened and wills strengthened. The Kid left his body and mind as he fell into the trance that Indian braves endure from sweat lodges as if his soul was being ritually purified. The crowd noise was a background blur to him and their faces were obscure masks. The sound of Cuno's voice giving the 20 seconds warning was distant and isolated. Jimmy The Big Fat Greek was standing at The Kid's bow with a face of mash potatoes smothered in red blood gravy. The Old Kid saw the underdog glove coming for him like a hammer from the gods. He dug deep into his courage and instantaneously summoned the inherent beast of survival. Like a rattlesnake uncoiling its venomous assault, The Old Kid swung his hardened fist with every cell of brawn and muscle he possessed. The resounding slam blasted into the Greek's face with so much force that the birds outside shot into the sky from the frightful sound. The Greek's head completely twisted back as his mouth opened and his eyes closed. Down to the bitter ground went the boy, with his body in the warehouse, and his mind in Tennessee fishing with his grandfather. The Old Kid raised his hands high into the air for a victorious salute. When he lowered his sweaty arms the crowd gasped as a bloodied single tooth sat imbedded in the glove like a lone tombstone, testament of a teenage hoodlum's holocaust. Once again the formality of patting the winner on the back and getting the loser off his back took place.

The night went on with clashes being fought and money switching hands. The final bouts were to take place, but many of the previous winners were in no condition to carry on. This included Brothers Punkwillie and The Old Kid. Mister Mike, however, being a born battler, stepped into the final heavyweight bout. His opponent was a giant black kid from Maywood named Roller Coaster Jones. He went by R.C., of course. No one seemed to know his real name nor did anyone care. He was called Roller Coaster because of his wild mood swings. He recognized a lot of the night's participants from Proviso, but bore no grudge. He stood a good foot over Mister Mike and was built like a steel shithouse. Many of The Brothers tried to talk Mike out of the contest because of the size difference. The underdog glove wasn't nearly enough of an equalizer. There wasn't much side betting due to the fact that no one thought Mister Mike had a chance. In the preliminary bout Roller Coaster had come straight down upon the head of a Dago from Melrose with such force the kid's knees buckled and sprained the lad's neck. Cuno announced that the winner of this battle would get $400, not bad for a long night's work.

The fight began with both adversaries staggering some from the incredible fatigue that boxers endure. Mister Mike, being the scrapper he was, came at Roller Coaster with some surprising success. Several hard combinations found their mark and the wise, white kid retreated quickly from any retaliation. Roller Coaster looked perplexed as he soon realized that this was not going to be a cakewalk. Both fighters danced the dance of tiptoed tactics as they tried to emulate Muhammad Ali. This performance didn't last long as no punches were thrown and a lot of energy was blown out. The creepy old building was a true hellhole with high, intense temperatures and the stench of a dead man's crotch. Somehow the onlookers were still in their bloodthirsty mood and vented like Roman citizens perched in the coliseum demanding carnage in its purest form. Roller Coaster Jones rammed two successive blows on Mister Mike that literally sent the poor boy spinning like a weed whacker on ice. Roller Coaster pursued his victim for the grand finish and, just as in the other bouts, the hunted became the hunter in a flash. Instinctively, Mike went into survival mode and resorted to his real talent. The lad was a natural born wrestler. He had once beaten the Illinois state champion in a training exhibition. Mike just didn't care for all of the crazy workout regiments a wrestler must go through. Working out in rubber suits to sweat the pounds off was insane, especially when you step outside and lock up from the icy, winter wind. His situation now dictated an all out assault as he flat out dove on Roller Coaster and bounced him off the ground with a bone-crushing thud. The mob watched in awe as a "Half Nelson" went full and the "Fireman's Toss" was followed with an "Olympic Roll," all this performed with boxing gloves. An absolutely astonishing demonstration of grappling skills stunned the crowd as well as Roller Coaster Jones who was rabbit punching a crazy horse.

"What the fuck is this bullshit?" cried out Fast Eddie. "This is supposed to be boxing, not motherfuck'n wrestling. Every time I deal with you honkies, I get jive served on rye."

Mister Mike had Roller Coaster in a vice grip that was choking his windpipe. R.C.'s eyes slid straight back and Cuno jumped in. "Fight's over... the fight's over!" He pulled Mister Mike's arm off R.C.'s neck and lifted it, shouting, "and the winner is from Broadview-- Mi..." Those were the only words audible as most of the gamblers were in complete disagreement. "Hey, this was a fighting event. I said in the beginning the only rule was no weapons." Everyone except Mike's amigos, The Brothers of Broadview, booed this down. There was definitely trouble brewing as the other neighboring towns out numbered those that agreed with Mr. Excitement's decision. The Hams saw the oncoming storm and slipped outside. He walked across the street to a newly built office building and threw a rock clean through a huge window. This triggered motion alarms and a signal to one of the most overloaded police forces in the country. The gang inside the old warehouse heard the alarm and sirens. The only thing that mattered now was to clear the area fast as possible. Everyone knew the Broadview police weren't about to bust their own thugs when so many other foreign hoods were available. Fast Eddie was especially aware of his presence in all this. He and his hombres got Roller Coaster to his feet and out the door. The decision of the fight was now not important as car doors slammed and tires squealed.

When Officer Moody arrived first on the scene, as usual, he saw no one, but the pile of empty malt liquor cans and Mad Dog bottles told him who was there. He walked into the empty, dank building and saw the blood on the floor mixed in with freshly crushed cigarette butts. His attention turned to a pair of boxing gloves lying dead center on the floor. He picked up the smaller glove and wondered out loud, "Is there one normal bone in any of their bodies?" He dropped the sweaty, dilapidated bag mitten and walked out, stepping on a sack of blank papers and a bloody, Greek tooth.

Chapter 19
The Evie of Destruction

The end of the school year was clearly on every student's mind as spring blossomed away. Trees that stood stark and dark just weeks earlier waved the green flag of nature's return. The big school was getting uncomfortable with the sun burning through the classroom windows. Being the always-sarcastic optimist, Punkwillie noted, "When the heat is on the rise, we see more thighs." The mini skirt was all the rage and so was the hormonal male response.

Michele, however, was still serving The Old Kid a healthy portion of cold shoulder, basted in a nice, scorned-eschewed sauce. Her only words in weeks to him were about his swollen face from the fight night at the old warehouse. She was truly amazed that even with all the violence of the last riot, her boyfriend was seeking even more physical rampage. "No wonder the world is in such turmoil. Look who runs it--men!" she thought. Even though she avoided her beau, the relation radar was squarely fixed on his position. If The Kid was going relieve his "DG" sitch, she would know who, when, where, and why. Baseball, football, and basketball are games of sport for males. Romance, love, and relationships are the games of sport for females. Every teen magazine or romance novel is nothing more than more ammunition in the war between the sexes. While guys read about their statistical heroes, girls study proven methods in interrelations and man management.

The male species is aggressive by nature, and females use this hostile behavior as leverage. Judo is an ancient martial art based on using your opponent's aggression against him. Michele was going to throw her much larger adversary for a huge loss. The harder he tried to let her know that he was mad and she was being punished, the more he realized that she didn't care and he was being punished. When he saw her laughing it up with Johnny Hayley, the school's All-State jock, circuits blew like fuses made in China. The poor boy was sorely out matched. To make matters worse, he wasn't even sure what the spat was about, but what the hell, the world has gone to war on those merits. The Kid had his pride and no one was going to infringe on that. She had him right where she wanted him!

The month of June seems like a ship that is pleasantly sailing along with homeport dead ahead and in clear view. The mood is as light as the drifting cottonwood seeds that float down upon the green grass and glowing, yellow dandelions. The sky seems bluer, clouds puffier, and breezes softer. The morning of the 5th, nature was giving the Midwest a kiss on the cheek as the birds sang out a glorious good morning. The Old Kid drove into Proviso's parking lot with Barry Mc Quire's "The Eve of Destruction" blasting on all eight tracks. He had just replaced his stolen player with a state of the art RCA model he purchased from Maxwell Street, home of the Blues and other stolen goods. The Kid got out of his Goat and immediately sensed something was wrong. The usually noisy lot was quite quiet. The boys were gathered in a small group huddled around Wilbur's Shelby with the radio on.

"What's the word, fellas?" asked The Kid. "It's like a funeral parlor around here," he added.

Ace lifted his head from the group. "Haven't you heard? Robert Kennedy was shot in the head last night."

"What? Another Kennedy? I bet a titsoon did it for revenge of King," exclaimed The Kid.

"Nah, they caught the dude. He's some camel humping asshole with the same first and last name," explained Musclehead. The boys continued to listen to the unbelievable news that another cool American was violently executed. The once pleasant June air now had the familiar taste of bitterness and shock. The days of Dick Clark and American Bandstand were truly over. No one seemed interested in going to the malt shop and listening to the jukebox anymore. The madness of the world was driving this generation of teenagers from drinking coke to snorting it. The stress and pressures of the Viet Nam War, the Cold War, the war on poverty, the war on drugs, the war between the sexes, social wrongs and civil rights, sent kids seeking sanctuary anywhere they could find it, from Strawberry Fields to a land called Hannah Lee. The look of confusion was in the eyes of students as they made their way through the day. Teachers did their best trying to explain this latest nightmare, but how can you make sense out of the senseless? Robert Kennedy was becoming a voice of reason in an uncertain time. Like his brother, President Kennedy, and Martin Luther King, he worked to unite people and insure freedom for all, but as word filtered out that he died from his wounds, spirits sunk to an all time low. The flag outside the school was once again lowered to half-mast.

"Why not just leave it there?" asked Evie who seemed to be more bitter than most about this latest disaster. She and Stevie had decided to return to Proviso and try to make up for lost ground. Their absences were at a world record status, but they both demonstrated gifted intelligence and the administration was willing to work with them. Quite often it's the smart people who become disenchanted with the world. It's no secret that many of the homeless winos on skid row were once accomplished people. Stevie and Evie had always seemed to be ahead of their peers. They met as freshman and instantly hit it off. The two often climbed into deep philosophical debates on many worldly subjects. They also experimented and experienced many facets of life. While kids their age were busy popping zits, Stevie and Evie were busy popping pills and seeking thrills. Their stories of their sexual escapades dropped the jaws of other teens that were just learning the dirty words. The two lovers were more like adults or even parents to many of the other kids, always friendly and knowledgeable.

That Friday night they both watched the TV news together on her sofa. The somber image of a train carrying Bobby Kennedy's body back to Washington D.C. was just too touching for Evie as tears ran down her cheek.

"Hey, come on now, Eve, you're taking this just a little too hard," said Stevie as he gave her a comforting hug.

She just stared at the flickering screen. "I don't know, maybe this isn't worth it," she mumbled softly.

"What? I didn't hear what you were saying, babe," said Stevie. She wiped her tears and gave her lover a stare that reached deeply into his young soul.

"Maybe this isn't worth it. The longer you live, the more pain you receive, and for what?" she asked.

Stevie's knee jerk reaction was to console her and give the standard "Ahh, cheer up" speech, but these two were never ordinary or conventional and he said nothing.

"Stevie, sometimes I think we weren't meant for this world. I mean, we definitely seem to be at another level than anyone else I know," said Evie as she got up and turned off the depressing news program. Stevie remained silent as his great intellect was telling him where she was going with all this. "Do you ever think about what happens to you when you die? Where do we go? Or do we just disappear from the universe, end of story?" she added.

Finally Stevie spoke. "I read a poem once that went: You awake in another world and find you are not scared, because there is no one there."

"Stevie, my love, do you think life is worth living or that this world is heading for the Apocalypse? I have to tell you that I'm so tired of the daily kick in the head and I think hell, I'm just starting out. I'm going to end up like my parents, exhausted and eternally hung over from the stress," said Evie lighting up a cigarette. "Look, Stevie, we have already experienced just about every pleasure life has to offer. Do you ever think it's all going to become quite boring and we will become wasted little junkies with dark eyes and sunken dreams?" she added blowing smoke straight up in the air.

Finally, Stevie turned his head and slid in just one inch from her mascara-running face. "Evie, just what is it you're trying to get at here, my sugar-kissed dear?" he spoke in a soft, yet deep, voice.

"I think you know already. You always seem to know and that's why I love you so fiercely," answered Evie in an angelic whisper. "I believe we weren't meant for this world or this world wasn't meant for us. I truly want to take the final voyage together."

Stevie looked passed her eyes and into her heart. "I know how you feel about this world, but don't you want to see what sort of little brats we could have running around tearing our house up?"

"The greatest gift I could give my children is to not put them through all this bullshit and with all the drugs we have done, who knows what deformity they would possess. Our children would be paying for our sins and that I couldn't handle."

"Well, then I have to admit that I have shared these thoughts, too, and it doesn't surprise me that we both are, once again, off track and on target," said Stevie licking the sides of a newly rolled joint. They both just sat in a spacey, shadowed silence and contemplated the somber conversation and grave proposal. Stevie never lit the reefer as he wanted his head clear for this commitment. He looked at his "amante" and thought of how innocent but commanding she looked when they first met. Evie was a girl with a rare courage and deeply intense interest in life and its meaning. He thought of his own life and the hopeful plans he once had, but now a sense of non-fulfillment and floundering seemed to preside in his dreams. He knew that he and Evie had an artist's creative outlook on the world and there was little chance they could actually realize this lifestyle. The rows of factories in industrial Broadview and throughout the western suburbs gave warning of the impending, depressing future that would likely be his. His intelligence was a blessing and a curse, for he clearly understood the toil of a 40-hour workweek times 52. Stevie knew his strengths and his shortcomings. He was aware of his creative skills, but also of his lack of determination and commitment needed in an industrial age. "Damn Indians had it right all along," he thought. "No traffic, no taxes, no time and half, just sit around and get high and live off the land. Just how did the white man think he was going to improve on this?" He sat staring out into space when he noticed Evie was fixed on her own moonbeam. He looked at her face and asked, "So when do you want to take this magical voyage?"

She turned her head ever so slowly and met his eyes. "Tonight," she whispered.

Stevie gazed at her with steadiness and conviction. "My bags are packed. I'm ready to go," he said hiding a quiver in his voice.

Evie leaned into her lover and they kissed with all the passion and emotion spiritually possible. When the unimaginable is imagined and final realization sets in, one's body enters a process of self-removal. The two teens went into an automated response to their deadly decision. They almost stopped communicating verbally as the plan for their demise materialized. Stevie walked into the connected garage and found a garden hose and sawed it to his best estimation of what was needed. He told Evie that he was ready and then after a soul-searching pause, they turned to walk towards the garage door.

"Are you going to say anything to your parents or leave a note?" asked Stevie who felt the inner battle of his conscience screaming in his mind.

"Wait one sec," answered Evie as she saw a deflated, old, beach ball lying on a hook. "Lets blow this ball up together and I will leave a note saying that our last breaths are in this ball and sometime in the future let that trapped air flow freely on your face and you will remember us with a smile." Stevie smiled with approval and put his mouth on the plastic valve as Evie grabbed some paper and pen. When she finished writing, she, too, added her breath into the ball and taped the note to the colorful sphere. She set it on her dad's abused, dusty, workbench and the couple headed out of the garage. When they neared Stevie's yellow Beetle, Evie's mom rapped on the window and both teens turned around and looked up at her. She was peering through the curtains and gesturing to her watch-- the universal signal for don't stay out too late. "Mom," was the only word Evie could summon from her emotionally choked throat. The teens got into the car and drove off into the dark night as the window curtains came down and closed shut.

"Do you think Muhammad Ali could beat Cassius Clay?" asked Musclehead as he munched on a soaked Italian beef from Carms.

"Musclehead, they are the same person," laughed Gino sitting on the hood of Sweet Daddy's Chevelle SS. The Brothers were gathered in Lindop's lot per usual for a Friday night. Gino and Musclehead just loved to lock horns about anything and everything. Each was completely convinced the other was an idiot and a half.

"I know they're the same person, ass wipe. I'm wondering which was the better boxer."

"Musclehead, only you would waste time on something that strange. I still can't get over you last week at Home Run Inn when the waitress asked if she should slice the pizza eight ways or four, and you answered four, 'cause you didn't think we could eat eight!" This, of course, sent off the overload of laughs that Musclehead was more than accustomed to hearing.

Punkwillie was thumbing through a newly published magazine called Rolling Stone with his hero John Lennon on the cover. "Look at this ad," he stated showing a page where a male hippie was giving a peace sign between a naked woman's legs. "Wow, what's the world coming to?" he asked.

"I don't know, but as long as it's coming," laughed The Old Kid.

"Was that supposed to be a joke?" asked Mister Mike as he picked stems and sticks from a nickel bag. The Brothers were slowly becoming hippified like the rest of their generation. The boys were all growing their hair longer, which looked good on them, except for Mister Mike whose extremely curly hair looked more like a lion's mane. This was a splendid summer's eve and the boys were more than ready for another adventurous weekend as they pursued the blessed quest of the "Triple Crown." The Big Guy even cruised by showing off his new Caddie De Ville with power everything including stereo FM radio, a real novelty. The weekly debate began in earnest about where to go and which vice to abuse. Votes for Olde Towne and Lady Madonna seemed to be the people's choice. Cuno felt a visit to neighboring Cicero's bars was a good call, because they never carded or cared, as long as you had the scratch, you got the snatch. There was a vibrant rumor that Nancy Knockers, once a popular Proviso cheerleader, was working the brass pole at "The Kat's Meow" in Cicero.

The boys all seemed up and ready for some good, clean, wicked behavior, except The Old Kid. His mind and heart wanted to be with the lovely Michele. He was becoming a real casualty in this battle of the sexes. No word came on her latest whereabouts and he knew any wolf out there could scoop up a girl like her.

Wilbur pulled up with his usual, wicked smile, which meant he had some major stinko material. "Hey, Bo's," he shouted from his cool car as he popped the latch on his trunk and ooohs and ahhhs sounded. Four half-liter bottles of Crown Royal wrapped in their cloth sacks sat in a wooded box like jewels in a treasure chest.

"Whoa, Bo, where'd you score that?" asked Punkwillie.

"Ah, my brother knows a guy," laughed Wilbur, meaning the less you know the better. The Old Kid dove right in and grabbed a bottle, and with one motion he twisted the top off and took a healthy hit of Canada's finest. No one said anything because they all knew he had feelings he wanted to entomb. The rest of the lads followed his lead and like the Viking warriors they so much admired, hearty shots of blended whiskey were gulped. No one noticed the sound of the police siren as it shot down 17th just a block from the boys. Then came a series of cop cars and ambulances shooting passed the boys at serious speeds.

"Damn, someone is having a bad night," joked Gino as yet another squad blasted by. The sound of all the sirens made the night seem as if the sky was screaming like hellcats in heat. The boys went back to their bottles and grab-assing.

The Chief produced a pipe filled with Panama Red. "Hey, man, this grass from South America is like the smooth booze from Canada, man." He was starting to light it when a figure of an approaching adult came out of the dark and down to the lot. This got more than the boys' attention as the figure held up his hand, waving.

"Hey, boys, don't shoot. I'm just checking." The figure came into the light and sight of the teens. It was old man Momber, a German immigrant who was well respected by the crew.

"What's up, Moms?" asked Cuno.

"Vell, boys, I heard on my scanner that some teenagers were found dead under the Cermack bridge. I was seeing if it was any of you lads." This news stunned the fun right out of the boys as they could sense it had to be someone they knew. The Old Kid took another massive chug from the bottle as he had wild thoughts that Michele could be involved.

"No, Mr. Momber, it's not any of us, but thanks for the concern. Would you like a tug from the jug?" asked Punkwillie. Surprisingly, the old man took them up on the offer and downed a sizeable swig.

"Vell, be careful out there, boys," spoke the old man as he walked away with an aged tremor in his step.

The Old Kid went straight for his Pontiac and the rest saddled up as well. The question of whose last night this was had to be answered. The caravan turned onto Cermack Avenue, blowing through red lights since they knew where all the cops were. The short distance to the bridge was covered like a jet as all four muscle cars slid onto the gravel under the bridge. This episode startled the already startled cops and paramedics on the scene. The Old Kid got out of the Goat and the question of who was answered immediately. There in the middle of the circle of police and twirling lights sat the yellow, beat up, Beetle Volkswagen of their friend, Stevie, with a sawed off garden hose coming out of the tailpipe. The boys all climbed out and were quickly met by Officer Moody and two detectives.

"What happened?" asked Mister Mike.

"That's what we want to know," retorted one of the detectives.

Moody walked up and asked, "Who was with these two last?"

"What two?" questioned The Old Kid. "Stevie and Evie?"

"Yeah, the druggies," smirked Moody. "Apparently, they wanted a double suicide, but even fucked that up," said Moody as the detectives stepped in front of him and his belligerent behavior.

"Why? What the fuck happened to them?" yelled Punkwillie as he pushed his glasses up with his middle finger while staring at Officer Moody.

The taller detective looked at the youths and spoke. "Well, it looks like they ran a hose from the exhaust to inside the front window and they both passed out. The boy came to and realized he didn't want to go through with it, but I'm afraid it was too late for the girl. She succumbed to the fumes. I am sorry. You all lost a friend."

The boys stood in silent shock trying to deal with the terrible news. Thoughts of Evie filled their heads and looking at Stevie's Yellow Submarine just made those memories even more vivid.

"Where's Stevie now?" asked Sweet Daddy.

The detective pointed to an ambulance leaving the scene. "He's going to the hospital now. He's suffering from the exhaust poisoning, but should pull through," answered the dick.

"He's going to be charged with involuntary manslaughter, and from the smell of all your breaths, he's going to have company in his cell," added Moody. "I want all of you to go home now, and if I see any of you driving around, you're busted. One death is enough for tonight. We don't need any others," said the shorter dick. The boys all took a look at the VW and then went back in their cars.

"Wow, this is something. Those two were always out there, but wow," remarked Gino.

"Should we go to Evie's house or Stevie's?" asked Ace.

"Nah, there's nothing we can do right now. I just wanna sit down and reflect. Let's go to Cicero and see if Nancy Knockers is there," said Cuno. With that, the band of brothers left the crime scene and sought refuge from their shock and pain in a saloon where women dance naked. Not even death can curb the ultra sonic hormonal urges of a teenage boy. The Brothers were indeed crushed and saddened, but life goes on and what better way to have their spirits lifted than to be hypnotized by a beautiful woman's eyes and thighs. The boys gathered around a table in the smoke filled bar and hoisted their glasses in a toast to a girl who would completely understand and appreciate the setting of a salute in her honor.

"To Evie... a cool girl and good friend... until we meet again... until we meet again," cried out Punkwille. The glasses all clanked as the whiskey was drank and a neon sign flickered above the door, but to see Evie's smiling face or hear her sweet laugh... quothe the raven... nevermore!

The following day the boys all had serious hangovers to get over. There was no word on Stevie's condition or where he was. The buzz about the botched double suicide was all over Broadview with parents interrogating their kids on what they knew.

The Brothers felt a little guilty, but they had to all get together to formalize their new softball team they called "The Bummers." Softball in Chicago is a religion and, of course, Chicagoans have to have their own brand of ball. The rest of the world uses a 12" ball as a regulation softball. Chicago has a 16" ball, due, in part, to the fact that many of the crowded city parks are small and the large ball can't travel as far. The larger ball, however, makes every play exciting. There are no routine plays with a 16" monster. No gloves are used, so to catch this substantial sphere takes complete concentration and positioning. The real winners here are the beer-gutted jocks from days of old as the game favors the beefier heifers. Mister Mike came up with the team name in honor of the Brooklyn Dodgers nickname, "The Bums."

"That's what we are. A bunch of Bums," he remarked a few weeks earlier.

Punkwillie thought "The Bummers" would be cool since it was a new buzzword regarding bad LSD trips. This weekend was long ago planned to be their first practice at Schroeder Park. The boys all made it, even though the realization of what happened the night before was sinking in. The battle plans and logistics were laid out-- what kind of uniform, who could they get to sponsor them and, most importantly, who was playing where. Ace, The Hams, and Punkwillie were in big trouble because they were too thin for this fat man's game. Cuno was perfect as a pitcher because that position called for a cagey guy with shifty moves. The pitcher makes several fake tosses in 16" before actually making an underhanded delivery. His pitch also had a nice, slow arch that looked very tempting to the batter, but was very hard to hit. Practice went pretty well for their first one, with no real injuries, just some 4th degreeing by the party boys. They had just finished when Sinful Cindy and Candy Miller stopped by. The boys all wanted to know if they had heard anything new on Stevie since Cindy's dad was on the city council.

"Stevie has been charged and will be released from the hospital tomorrow. Evie's parents are having a private funeral and made it clear Stevie is not to attend," reported Cindy. The girls were very distraught because it all seemed so senseless. Everyone knew that they were an unusual couple with all their experimenting and solitary ways. To the other young adults discovering their world, this was one dark episode, but to the more nurturing females it was truly traumatizing. The teens sat for a while and chewed some fat. Gino thought it would be a nice thing if they all went to mass Sunday and lit some candles for Evie. Normally anything to do with getting up early and going to church was something these party commandos seldom contemplated, but agreeable head nods signaled approval. The Brothers planned to stop by Stevie's house to pay their respects, but the flood of relatives' cars and even some police squads put a delay in those plans. The idea of going to Atsa Nice, Broadview's only Italian restaurant, was going to be the extent of Saturday night's plans. So around a nice heaping dish of antipasto and a four-cheese lasagna, The Bummers once again toasted life and whatever the hell comes after it.

Sunday was a splendid, early June morning and pews in Saint Eulalia's had more souls than usually seen. Father Hamer knew of the local situation involving the suicide and would address it ever so eloquently in his sermon. The Brothers, who prided themselves on merits of character, showed up in force at the church. They mostly sat with their families and knew that this was a serious time and shooting a homely or pointing to a hot hunny was not in vogue. The Old Kid knelt on the thinly padded pew bar and focused his thoughts on Evie and Stevie, but the pain in his knee kept creeping in. "Damn Catholic Church just wants to punish you even when you pray," he thought.

Father Hamer began the service with the usual rituals of bowing and genuflecting. The sunlight beamed in the church and spirits seemed to lift with brilliant rays. Father Hamer was well respected and had been Monsignor for the past fourteen years at St. Eulalia. He spoke about a great tragedy in his own life when he was a priest at Our Lady of Angels in Chicago in 1958 when the entire school burned down and 93 children and 3 nuns were killed. He said he questioned God about how He could have let that happen, but realized matters like that were beyond his scope. "Why two young people would choose such an action is something we all ponder. Life and the world have many issues," he stated. "But it's a gift, and facing the challenges of this gift takes strength, and should you ever feel over burdened, just reach out. Reach out to God, reach out to your family, reach out to your friends, and you will find the love and understanding to guide you through your dire times." The priest's voice rattled with conviction as he was trying to send a message to the youngsters in his congregation.

His words were finding their target as The Old Kid was on his knees, head down, gazing at his family's rosary. He truly felt badly about Evie and said a little prayer for her. His attention was solely fixed on the miniature holy beads that he ran through his fingers, when a petite, tender hand gently seized his clenched fist. He glanced over and saw his flame, Michele. She had come to comfort her beau and to be with him in this difficult time. He did not speak, but his smile said everything. He was always aware of her class and character. Now she truly demonstrated how insightful she truly was. After the mass they both walked in the rectory garden and talked about their feelings. Their spat now seemed so childish and The Old Kid apologized about his behavior and promised not to be the jealous boyfriend again. The wind played in Michele's long, beautiful hair and she laughed slightly when she thought how funny the Latin lover Ricardo looked lying in a pool of water with piranhas flapping about. The dark clouds brought on by Stevie and Evie caused a time of self-examination and soul searching. The Old Kid and Michele felt they grew ten years during their promenade in the garden. They once again were embracing and filling their world with much needed love. The other Brothers were a little lost as well, but they had each other's humor to bring back the sparks. What's done was done and the time to mourn and remember was there, but as Bobby Kennedy and a young, curious girl ascended fore, the world kept turning as the sun kept burning... quothe the raven... forever more!

Chapter 20
Graveside Suicide

The next few days went calmly by as Proviso East prepared to graduate its class of 1968, a class that saw more turmoil and strife than all the other classes at the historic school combined. The prom was held, but had the lowest attendance of any. Many seniors such as the brat Punkwillie were not allowed to attend due to any trouble they may have caused during the riots. The Punk felt he actually saved the mammoth State Champion Wrestling Trophy of 1948 from being destroyed and thought a plaque in his honor would be fitting.

The days blended by and The Brothers were busy whipping themselves into shape with daily softball practices at Schroeder Park. Thursday's day practice was a little on the slow side as the Midwest was letting out a sticky, humid forewarning of the torturous days ahead. One of biggest debates in the bars of the mucky Midwest is which is worse-- the frigid, raw winters or the sweltering, steamy summers. On this day when one could drip perspiration by just standing outside, the boys played through their rounds in second gear. The sweat from the batters' hands made even gripping the bat a chore.

They were just about to wrap up the workout when a familiar sound came growling their way. The rattling of tappets from a worn engine was announcing the arrival of The Yellow Submarine. Stevie's poor excuse of a car took the corner and came into view. He squealed to a parking halt and got out of the car, and the boys all rushed to meet him. "Stevie, what the hell, man, how are you?" and questions of that nature bombard the pale and withdrawn teen. He didn't really respond too much at first, as it was apparent he was still living in the state of shock. None of the boys even brought up the suicide, as they wanted Stevie to know that their main concern was his well being. If the suicide was going to be discussed, he would have to be the one to bring it up.

"Man, good to see you guys. I needed to get out and see my friends again," he said in a shaken voice. The group made small talk avoiding the larger subject. Stevie looked very different to the boys. The pressure of his ordeal certainly had taken its toll. "So the Bummers are getting ready to kick some ass, huh?" joked Stevie as he lit up a Salem.

"Nah, we're preparing to get our asses kicked," spoke Wilbur.

"Well, you know what they say, it's not if you win or lose, it's the game that matters," replied Stevie being his usual philosophical self.

"Who the fuck came up with that sorry slogan?" shouted Punkwillie. "That's right up there with money can't buy happiness. Give me a grand and I can hire Lady Madonna for a month. Now we're talking happiness." This broke up some of the tension and things seemed to be OK cool, until Stevie reached into his pocket and pulled out another Salem to light. Nothing was said, but the boys looked in disbelief as the shattered teen tried lighting another cigarette with one in his hand already going. He was showing the signs of carbon monoxide poisoning.

"Hey, Stevie, how you feeling really? We won't talk about it if you don't want to, but if you want to get it off your head, we all know what it's like to live in bullshit and sometimes talking about it helps," said The Old Kid trying to comfort and straighten out his feelings.

Stevie bowed his head and dropped one of his lit cigs. "They wouldn't even let me attend her funeral, man. They blame me for everything and so do I," he softly spoke as tears filled his eyes. "I... I just don't know what got into us that night. It was hey let's do this and we charged out and did... and now she is gone."

"Look, Stevie, this was a mistake, a serious mistake, but you can't blame yourself. The world today makes people do crazy things. I'm telling you you're not to blame and to keep Evie's memory we must all carry on with a smile and stay strong. That's what she would want and that's what we must give her," remarked The Old Kid as the other boys all closed in around their damaged friend. Officer Davis, the most liked of all the Broadview police, drove slowly by. He saw the group of young male adults huddling as if to close the world out and make it go away. Officer Davis, like everyone else in Broadview, was upset at what happened, but in his wisdom he just continued on and went away.

The cheers went up as the senior class of 1968 graduated and now became alumni of the great school. Hugs and farewells were all about as these students turned an unforgettable page in their lives. The halls of Proviso fell silent, but the echo of incensed rage would echo for years to come. Hopefully, the school learned from the unrest. A much needed silence now kept vigil. The physical scars in the halls were repaired and, God willing, the emotional ones would soon heal as the students would understand one another a little better. Hopefully.

The Bummers were off and running in their prized softball season. They were severely overmatched by older guys who had played 16" softball since Eisenhower was President, but the boys did a nice job of not getting crushed. The summer was now in full swing as was the partying. The Old Kid and Michele were definitely a couple again and were together to the point where the boys complained to The Kid about being whipped. He brushed it off, as was his manner. The lad was smart enough to know that if he weren't with his lovely girl, he would be knee deep in some vice and trouble. The other Brothers were scoring more after the softball games than during. Hunnies came out to watch the local heroes and, of course, party with them after the game.

Being very normal was always very hard for the boys who were now looking for some new, cheap thrill to entertain them. Gambling was always a good vehicle for them, and in July Arlington Park held a rare match race between two up and coming three-year-old horses. The battle was going to be Gruzstark against Tornado. Both were unbeaten in nine races and the public demanded the match race. Cuno advised the boys to go heavy on Gruzstark, and they did. Mr. Excitement was correct as Gruzstark won by a neck and the gang cleaned up nicely. After the race the party was on as each lad had a good stash of moola. The celebrating went on all night as The Farms was raided twice. Steaks sizzled and the bull was shot as the boys kicked up their heels like young bucks should. Other areas of the country have scenic beauty and tons of outdoor fun, but flat-ass Broadview, with its drab industrial parks, has one great virtue, fun lovin' rowdies.

The summer with its mosquito bites and firefly nights had finally arrived, and The Brothers were going to soak it all up and puke it back out. Who says youth is wasted on the young? The following day came fast as the boys all had jobs to get to and, with little sleep, a softball game to play. Mister Mike and Wilbur felt like they had no energy in them for the game and made alternative plans. Somehow the idea of taking acid seemed to be the choice, as they knew the rush would wake them up. The game began at 6:00 PM at Schroeder Park. The Bummers were dressed in their red, white and blue uniforms with an obnoxious Tastie Freeze ad covering the back. No one really noticed that Mike and Will worked very little in the warm ups. The Bummers took the field to start the game. Mister Mike trotted out to his usual position, third base, and Will walked slowly to right field. He seemed to be really taken with the sunset, but again no one was paying much attention. Cuno warmed up and was ready to start the game with his special, high arched delight. The leadoff man for the opposing Rogues was a friend of the boys they called "Teets." The Rogues were a group of jocks that had a flair for the dramatics. One outstanding gimmick they employed was pink bats. Even with the Age of Aquarius exploding everywhere, pink bats were a little too much, but these were strange times. Cuno released the ball high into the sun-setting sky and Teets licked his chops. This pitch looked like a guy with a bad hangover threw it as it headed for the boy's wheelhouse. "BAM" was the resounding thud as the pretty, pink bat pounced on the huge globe with lizard tongue quickness. A brand new 16 inch softball is anything but soft. It takes at least four innings of pounding to mush it up a little. Time was not on Mister Mike's side as Teets crushed one like a rocket down the third baseline. Everyone saw the ball soaring right at Mike, everyone except Mister Mike. He was still in his before the pitch pose, bent over and hands at the ready. He wasn't ready and never saw it coming. There was a sickening splat when it hit him squarely between the eyes. If he wasn't in the twilight zone before, he was now. The ball seemed to stick in his face, then ricochet back to where it was launched. Mike dropped to the ground like a duck getting peppered with buckshot. A horrified gasp came from the onlookers and his teammates came running up to check on their third baseman. Everyone was deeply concerned except for the right fielder who was gazing at the western sky completely enthralled. Mister Mike lay on the ground reaching for trails of a ball that were no longer there.

"Wow, should we call an ambulance?" asked Musclehead. Mike was a tough nut and got back to his feet, but the blue rising bruises around his eyes signaled game time for him. He finished the game from the bench telling his teammates how cool pink bats really are. The only one agreeing was Will who somehow was having the game of his life going four for four, but he kept over running second base. Three times he was tagged out for this mistake, and on his final at bat refused to leave first even though he hit an easy triple. The Old Kid was the first base coach and screamed like a wildman, but Will just stood there, smiling. The Bummers lost again, but their loyal fans just loved the entertainment.

That night routine "A" was underway as they sat around their cars at Lindop and wondered what wondrous events would occur this weekend. The evening had a refreshing, cool mist that hung like halos around the streetlights. The lil foxes came out from their holes and joined the boys as they recalled and laughed about

Mister Mike getting smashed, as now the truth of his condition was known. The group of kids had become an extensional family of sorts. They had been with each other for almost a year and even though they bitched and teased each other, there was an underlying bond. Punkwillie was jotting down some jokes for a phone call to King B as the others drank and cranked the tunes. A Ford station wagon came into the lot at a rather fast speed and rolled up to the teens.

"It's Stevie's dad," said Wham Bam Pam who knew them well.

"You kids seen Stevie?" asked the man in the family car.

"No, sir, we haven't. We haven't seen him for days," answered Cuno. The car then sped off as fast as it arrived.

"What the hell was that?" asked the Sweetman.

"Oh, my god," spoke Michele as she covered her mouth as if being sickened. "Tonight is one month to the day." She did not need to finish as the shock came again to the kids.

"Holy shit. I called him yesterday and he said something about visiting her grave today, but his voice had a message to it," said Musclehead.

"Damn it! Let's go!" yelled The Old Kid as everyone filled the cars and sped off towards the cemetery on Des Plaines Avenue.

Not much time passed as the super fast cars caught up with the Ford wagon that was going to the same place. Once on Des Plaines, the kids had to let Stevie's dad take the lead because no one was sure where Evie was buried. The wagon darted into the second entrance of the graveyard and the escort followed. Bending through the twisted roadway the passengers remained quiet, trying to seek any recognition of Stevie's car through the night mist. The Ford kicked up stones and dirt as the other cars pursued.

"FUCK!" yelled Punkwillie, at the same time the station wagon violently skidded to a halt. Perched off the road, silhouetted against the moonlight, was the yellow, old Volkswagen. The group got out of their cars.

"You girls better stay here, please. If he's there, you may add to the hysteria. I don't think it would help his dad," requested The Old Kid. The girls knew this was not a time for debate and calmly agreed to stay in the cars.

The guys rushed into the curtain of fog towards the motionless Beetle. Their worst fears were soon realized as the sight of a green garden hose running from the exhaust to the driver's window came into view. The car was not running which gave hope they were in time. "STEVE! STEVE!" yelled his father as he reached the car. Stevie's dad ripped the door open and was sent back by the rush of the poisonous fumes. The group went into silent shock, a feeling they were definitely becoming accustomed to. Stevie was slumped over the driver's wheel with sickening, white foam dripping from his mouth. His dad reached in and pulled his son out, and cradled him in his arms as his tears fell on Stevie's limp body. The boys stood speechless and kneeled next to the grieving parent. Punkwillie looked inside the fumigated Beetle and noticed the gas tank was empty which explained the car not running. He turned off the tape player that eerily played "The End" by the Doors.

There was a note taped to a deflated beach ball, which Punk grabbed and unfolded. "It says 'Bury me next to Evie.' That's all it says," as he held the tattered paper in his shaky hand. There came a soft crying in the direction of the waiting girls as The Old Kid went down and told them of Stevie's fate.

"My boy... what did you do? Why again?" said the father choked with passion. He looked up at the boys standing near him. "He was always different, always stirring things up and even now after he promised me he wouldn't do this... " wept the grieving father. "And now, he even leaves a message that doesn't make sense. What was he thinking? He can't be buried next to her. She was Jewish and he's Catholic. It's not allowed... it's not allowed." The father buried his face into the lifeless body of his son and murmured words that maybe only Stevie understood. The Brothers stood there in quiet respect. They had nothing to offer but their presence. How can anyone comfort a parent holding what was once their dream? Somehow the boys all felt a sense of appreciation for each other. This needless, tragic death gave them a lesson in life that can't be explained, only felt. Stevie and Evie were now once again together, but in their final exploration they left a lot of people in pain and no beach ball was ever going to relieve that.

Yet again another ceremony was held at the big church. Father Hamer tried once more to summon the listeners with words of hope and understanding. The sunlight created a ghostly look as it glimmered through the stain glass windows. Stevie's silver casket was carried down the main aisle of St. Eulalia. As it passed Michele and The Old Kid, they squeezed each other's hands with a bonding firmness. The young couple was now well aware of the importance of a relationship and how it should be respected and cherished, not something to abuse with immature jealousies.

Stevie was laid to rest in a Catholic cemetery, miles from his requested burial ground. "A life unfulfilled will always end with empty wishes," spoke Stevie's dad at the gravesite.

The gathering left the cemetery and reentered life as the boys got together once again and toasted a friend gone by. They stood in a circle at their stomping ground parking lot and pledged to each other that no one would go down the road that Stevie and Evie chose. The right hands went up in the air and a loud, unanimous "SOLEMN" was shouted out.

Chapter 21
The Whole World is Watching

Chicagoans enjoyed the summer with its trips to the lakes and evening lawn chair gatherings. The word was spreading around town that the upcoming Democratic convention was going to be a real major display for the growing anti-war movement. The war in Viet Nam was becoming an issue that was causing major unrest at college campuses throughout the country. This new generation of young Americans were by far the best educated than any preceding it. The wealthiest nation in history was about to reap what it sowed. With the dream of parents to get their child the best education possible, other ramifications of this dream were materializing. The young, great thinkers were going to question their government and its motives. Rallies at campuses were becoming numerous and, to older Americans, seemed unpatriotic. "It's their turn. We bravely served in World War Two. Who are these spoiled brats that feel they don't have to serve?" was the sentiment among those of the "Great Depression Era."

The assassinations of the Kennedy's and Dr.King cast great suspicion and doubt about government that Americans never felt before. Talk of revolution peppered conversations, as the educated youth wanted their questions answered. The word was out across the country to make your voice heard at the convention in Chicago. Mayor Daley was a man that understood people and his popularity in Chicago was a politician's dream. He was experienced enough to know about the mistakes to over reacting in a stressful situation. However, his beloved city had just come out of tumultuous rioting, and he was receiving reports from the nice guys with ties that the communists were planning attacks on the convention. This proud man was not about to have the great city of Chicago become a platform for anarchists on the world's stage. He was calling in the troops and readying his police for clandestine action. Battle plans were being drawn and reactionary forces posted as banners hung welcoming one and all to "My Kind of Town... Chicago."

The Old Kid was pounding down the potato chips as if they possessed a life giving force. He sat alone in his family's den watching the TV news. The big story was about the citizens of Prague rebelling against their communist government. Soviet tanks were being sent in to squash these dissenters. The horrible images of people fleeing the monster killing machines made The Kid feel perturbed. How can a government be so malicious that it attacks the very people it supposedly represents? These citizens only wanted a voice in their life and leadership. "How paranoid must the Czech government be not to even let the people gather and vent their opposition? Is the military really needed? Can't there be a forum?" thought The Kid as he wiped his greasy fingers on his pant's leg.

Mister Mike and Punkwillie stopped over to check the daily sitch. The Punk plopped into a cozy lazyboy and heard a resounding crunch. "Oops, sorry, didn't see the bag," as he looked inside the now pulverized snack sack.

Mike pointed at the TV as the story was now about the convention being held just a few miles away. "I've heard some hippies got their heads cracked wide open last night in Grant Park. The Bogey's are out in force and shooting first, questions later."

The Old Kid sat straight up with a quizzical look on his face. "Say what? What are the hippies doing?" he asked.

"Just the usual protesting about the war and then, wham, out came the batons. The Mayor isn't fucking around. He doesn't want trouble," answered Mike.

"He keeps doing that and he'll get nothing but," shouted out The Kid. The Old Kid was watching the reports from the spacious city park-- films of hippies and other bystanders being smacked hard and kicked, as they lay motionless on the ground. "Didn't I just see this?" he thought as the images of Prague replayed in his memory. He questioned the difference between the all mighty United States and the suppressed communist block. Apparently, they both wanted to crush any opposing voice from their citizens. The spirit of freedom that lies in one's heart began to emerge from the young man. He felt compelled to witness first hand what the sitch was in Grant Park. "I'm nearing draft age and if I'm going to risk my life for this country, I want to know exactly why," he thought as he stood up. "Come on, boys, let's cruise downtown and see the sparring." Mister Mike, who was always ready for rough action, didn't hesitate for a second. Punkwillie followed his Bo-Shams out the door, but his thoughts were more about slamming it to Wham Bam Pam than yet another riot. The three climbed into the newly waxed GTO and shot down I-90 for the loop, where "His Honor, the Mayor" lay in waiting.

The boys made little chatter on the way there as a strong sense of foreboding took over. Their feelings became quickly justified as they had just entered downtown Chicago and spotted a long series of National

Guard jeeps. "Whoa, check 'em out," said Punkwillie. The Jeeps had metal fencing welded to them with barbed wire wrapped around. "I've heard of crowd control, but damn, what are they bracing for, Hannibal and his elephants?" joked Punk. The city looked more like an armed camp than a bustling city.

Several black Ford sedans zoomed by filled with nice guys with ties. "Hey, our fed friends are here. Gee, it's the G-men," joked Mister Mike. They found a nice parking spot near city hall, which indicated just how many people had the good sense to flee the area. The boys, however, were getting out and stretching as if warming up for the festivities.

The growing commotion was coming just across State Street and, of course, the lads ran to its calling. They came up to a group of semi-long haired men who wore shirts that had the word Yippies written on it. The Yippies had a pig on a leash as they paraded down State Street. Policemen started to surround them. One of the Yippies had a megaphone and started yelling into it. "Vote for Pigasus, a true pig for all the other pigs to follow." He started the slogan again, but the police would have none of it and jumped on the Yippies and wrestled the pig away.

The boys ran up shouting at the cops. "Hey, they're just talking. What the hell, they didn't do anything wrong," yelled The Old Kid.

Two cops turned around with billy clubs and raised them over their heads. "GET THE FUCK OUT OF HERE NOW," yelled the cops. The attention went back to the Yippies as they started to resist arrest. The over-excited police started pounding on the protesters as if they were armed convicts. The sickening sound of bone being split was heard as the once full of life Yippies were now bleeding from their heads with dazed and confused looks on their faces. The cops just wailed away even though it was obvious that there was no resistance from the unconscious men.

The Old Kid and gang took a look at that action and bolted for the huge clearing at Grant Park. "What the hell was that?" asked Mike.

"Freedom of speech is not free anymore," answered Punkwillie.

The boys were amazed at how fast the world had changed everywhere they looked. Throughout the vast park, arguments with authorities were taking place. Young and not so young adults in the thousands were gathering in the park under banners and flags proclaiming "The Whole World Is Watching-- Welcome to Czechago." Hippies were walking around with warnings that undercover cops were blending in. This was an overwhelming scene for the Broadview boys who just an hour ago were watching this on TV. It was as if they stepped inside the screen.

The Old Kid stood back to try to get a handle on the sitch. He saw the helicopters, police on rooftops with binoculars, National Guard troops with loaded weapons and fixed bayonets. "This is the land of the free?" he thought. "This is Prague western style. This is bullshit!" He wandered to a group really yelling up a storm and couldn't believe his eyes. He saw a mother in an Impala with two little kids in the back seat screaming. They must have been on an outing and somehow took a wrong turn and ended up here. Guardsmen blocked her from going forward with some actually pointing their rifles point blank at her. She was hysterical and trying to figure what to do as hundreds of protestor inadvertently blocked her from backing up. Loud, serious threats came out of the crowd to the bayoneted guardsmen standing in the path of the mother of two. "This is becoming a civil war, countrymen against countrymen," thought The Kid as nice guys with ties tried to restore order by ordering the nervous guardsmen to make way. No sooner did they part and the Impala slowly pull out when a bag filled with shit came flying at the soldiers. The boys pulled away from the scene as some of the guard began clicking their bolts loading a round into their M-14 rifles.

"Let's get over to the band shell," shouted Mike. "There is room there."

When the boys arrived to the safety of the band shell, civil rights leader Ralph Abernathy was on stage addressing people under a "Poor People's Campaign" banner. Julian Bond, another prominent civil rights leader, was in the crowd and Peter, Paul, and Mary were preparing to sing. Over by the huge, brown Hilton Hotel the familiar sound of commotion was rearing its ugly head. The boys stayed their distance, but curiously edged closer to see what was now breaking out. There were loud chants of "Tear it down. Tear it down" emanating from a group wearing "SDS" shirts. The main focus was around a flagpole as a young man began climbing up reaching for the stars and stripes flapping from a strong gust of the windy city. The young rebel had managed to rip the flag down and started to replace it with a blood spattered "Students for a Democratic Society" tee shirt. The jubilant cheers went up, soon followed by even louder, terrifying screams. The ever so patriotic Chicago police force had had enough, and was coming to beat the disobedience out of the young insurgents. A great rush of people came back towards the boys as canisters of mace shot into the air and landed into the unmasked crowd. City garbage trucks came rolling up Michigan Avenue with small cannon-like tear gas launchers attached to their tops. The events unfolding seemed unreal and nightmarish as America's angry youth was getting a good old ass whooping from the men sworn to "protect and serve" them. The out of control police were making animal-like sounds as they wielded their clubs on anyone within reach. Men, women, boys, girls, even news reporters were being brutally whacked and beaten down by the undiscriminating officers. The Old Kid noticed that some of the protestors were fighting back, and in some areas of the battlefront, they were beating back the beaters. This was just too good for the boys not to join in. The Brothers were not much for politics, but a chance to swing at the lawless lawmen was just too temping. The lads charged into the melee as clouds of choking gas and incensed, wild shouts filled the air.

The Old Kid looked down for a brief moment and saw the bloody faces of kids from his generation. This sent him off into a mad rush of anger and he immediately found himself face to face with a helmeted cop. The policeman had pure rage in his eyes and with both hands gave a back swing to The Kid's head. The Old Kid used his youthful reactions and ducked, leaving the patrolmen vulnerable for a fleeting moment. "Fuck'n pig bastard," shouted The Old Kid as he grabbed the off balance patrolman and starting wailing away. This all came to a screeching halt when a heavy, wooden baton cracked The Kid across the back. There was a tangled spaghetti mess of arms and legs in a real human cluster fuck. The Kid caught quick glimpses of his buddies flying through the air and landing into another crushing pile of rampage. Michigan Avenue was now filled with screaming confusion, muddled in a heap of hot dust, toxic gas, and violent mayhem. The convention delegates looked on in utter horror from their lofty windows in the Hilton as heads were cracked and bodies trampled.

The Old Kid laid with his face planted firmly in mother earth. The fighting had moved on and he slowly moved his body as his back shot with white heat spasms. Mucus ran from his nose like green lava. His eyes singed as if burnt by flamethrowers. His gasps for clean air were interspersed with raspy, spit coughing and shallow gagging. A small stream of blood ran down his face with bleeding scratches covering his entire body. He pulled himself up and realized he was near the magnificent Buckingham Fountain, a landmark attraction for families and countless marriage proposals. Now it more resembled Brandenburg Gate in Berlin after the Russian invasion. Beautiful and picturesque Grant Park looked more like Gettysburg with limping wounded helping the motionless. TV crews streamed in to catch the aftermath as both protestors and police licked their wounds and the injured were carted off to local hospitals.

The Kid looked for his pals and after a 30 minute search, he walked back to his GTO. The guard and police didn't bother him knowing the jails were already overflowing. If you were leaving, that was fine with the soldiers. He made it to the car, and to his happiness both Mister Mike and Punkwillie were lying on the orange Goat. The boys relived the battles and showed off their war wounds. They were certainly veterans in civil disorder. In fact, they joked how much weaker mace is outdoors than in. "Well, whether this will have an impact on the Viet Nam War I don't know, but the pigs in charge now know things are going to change," remarked the beaten up Kid as he bent down and picked up a peace symbol button with his bloody, raw hand. The boys packed into the GTO and drove out of town, under the watchful eye of a carload of nice guys with ties.

Chapter 22
Revelation

The boys drove into Broadview and knew that since it was nice out, Gino had to have the grill going. The long line of cars on his block signaled a major bash was ensuing. The Kid parked the Goat, and the weary warriors descended on the brown, brick home with the sweet smell of barbeque rising into the sky. The boys walked to the backyard and gave a rebel yell as their friends and friends of friends greeted them.

Michele stood in amazement as her crazy boyfriend walked up swollen and beaten once again. "Danny, what is with you?" she asked with hands going straight up.

"Hey, these are turbulent times," he answered with a smile that always seemed to melt her resistances.

There were many more kids at this blowout. Sweet Daddy had invited his cousin and she brought a nice collection of hunnies with her. Punkwillie, who was feeling a little sore and puffy himself, grabbed a beer and froze in mid chug. Across the yard with Sweet Daddy's cousin was the picture of health he saw at the Proviso West game, the cupid-firing cheerleader he almost fell off the bleachers for. Wham Bam Pam came up to him and quickly could see she was not registering with him at all. He only saw one person in the yard and knew he had to make his move soon. This girl wasn't going to stay unattended for long, and with the notorious playboy

Bobby-G on his way, seconds counted. The Punk slowly walked towards his conquest, as Wham Bam Pam stood snubbed like a dish of turnips at a kid's birthday party. Such is teenage love, here today, gone today. The voluptuous vixen noticed the skinny, tattered boy coming straight for her. The boy was calling all courage to his voice as he was flying through every line he knew and nothing fit. He was walking up, lineless, but bravely kept on.

Just as Punk was about to approach her, Billy Q came stumbling up drunk out of his gourd and fell on top of the girl sending them both down. "Perfect," thought the Punk as he lifted Billy up to his feet. Underneath, as if unwrapping a Christmas present, was the most beautiful girl ever known to man. "Are you OK?" said the Punk, paying no attention to his friend Billy's condition.

The lovely girl brushed back her soft, blonde hair and gave a look a fox gives its trapper. "Yes, I'm fine, thanks," she replied brushing cigarette ash off her blouse.

Now came the most important phase in this sexual ceremony: the next line. It had to hinge on cleverness without being too coy, show respect without being too mushy, plus a million other factors that must all fit neatly into place. "Do you like Jimi Hendrix?" asked the tense teen with a look of my god that's my line?

"No," came the one word answer from the babe of babes.

Alarms sounded in the poor boy's brain and he just thought, oh the hell with it, and just as straight forwardly tried again. "Do you like the Beatles?"

"Why, yes, I do," answered the cutie with a smile that sent the boy into a what-now pause. He had given her his litmus test. Anyone not liking the Beatles had no chance, no matter how cute and cuddly, but she answered correctly and was going to win the take home prize, him, whether she knew it or not. The Punk put the charm into overdrive as he saw the dreaded babe stealer, Bobby-G, enter the yard. The Brothers had a code of never hitting on another's girl, but Bobby wasn't one of The Brothers and the Punk had to lay it on thick and quick. All signs pointed to oops as Bobby made a beeline to the cutest girl at the bash, being the great hound that he was. Bobby-G cracked something about how the day just got nicer, but much to the Punk's great relief, his heart throb barely reacted and instead took a sip from the Punky boy's beer, a sure sign that this could be his lucky day. Bobby-G, a player's player, wasn't deterred and he brought out the full arsenal, but when his supreme scheme "A poet's dream" went unnoticed and uncared for, he threw in the towel. Game-- set-- match, Punkwillie!

The sizzling steaks courtesy of the Wisconsin Farms hissed on the grill to a medium rare tenderness, as the great laughter that only the young can produce filled the summer air. The Brothers were in their natural habitat-- beer, babes and brawling. After many hours of yippie yahooing and firing some healthy homelies, Punkwillie escorted his trophy catch to the awaiting chariot. They walked to the cool, super Nova where The Old Kid gave him a wink of approval from his GTO as Michele checked out the competition.

"Honestly, I don't mind driving you home. I have to go that way anyway," said the Punk as he powered up the Chevy.

"Oh, I'm glad you are," replied the hottie with a name he couldn't spell or pronounce. "Just don't go too fast. It would make me nervous," said the graceful girl.

"Oh, I'm a good driver. Don't you worry," answered the affected boy.

"I wasn't talking about your driving skills," answered the luscious little lady with a sly smile. Punkwillie smoothly reached for the 8-track tune player and gave his gypsy-eyed girl her first sugar kiss. With the opening xylophone vibrato from the Rolling Stones' "Under My Thumb" playing in the car, Punky boy backed up the Nova and sped out of the steamy lot and wheeled down the tree-rowed street, disappearing under a warm, humid, Midwestern sky.

Ride the Serpent